Lesbians at Midlife

Lesbians at Midlife:

The Creative Transition

**An Anthology Edited by Barbara Sang,
Joyce Warshow and Adrienne J. Smith**

spinsters book company
SAN FRANCISCO

First Edition
10-9-8-7-6-5-4-3-2-1

Spinsters Book Company
P.O. Box 410687
San Francisco, CA 94141

Of Essences from *Woman Plus Woman*. © 1989 by Dolores Klaich. By permission of the author and the publisher. (Naiad Press, PO Box 10543, Tallahassee, FL 32302)

Another View of Lesbians Choosing Children © 1988 by Angela Bowen. By permission of the author. (Complete version available as a pamphlet from Kitchen Table: Women of Color Press, PO Box 908, Latham, NY 12110.)

Two Excerpts from "A Burst of Light: Living With Cancer" from *A Burst of Light: Essays by Audre Lorde*. © 1988 by Audre Lorde. By permission of the publisher. (Firebrand Books, 141 The Commons, Ithaca, NY 14850, $7.95)

Cover and Text Design by Pam Wilson Design Studio
Copyediting by Camille Pronger
Production: Georgia Harris   Joan Meyers
                  Ann Morse   Kathleen Wilkenson
                  Lynn Witt   Meredith Wood
Typeset by Joan Meyers in ITC Galliard.

Printed in the U.S.A. on acid-free paper.

Library of Congress Cataloging-in-Publication Data
Lesbians at midlife: the creative transition / edited by Barbara Sang, Joyce
    Warshow, and Adrienne Smith
    p. cm.
    Includes bibliographical references.
    ISBN 0-933216-77-7 : $12.95
    1. Middle aged lesbians—United States. I. Sang, Barbara, 1937-   .
II. Warshow, Joyce, 1937-   . III. Smith, Adrienne, 1934-   .
HQ75.6.U5L394 1991
306.76'63—dc20
                                                      90-24743
                                                      CIP

ACKNOWLEDGEMENTS

First of all, in true feminist fashion we'd like to thank each other for the friendship that has lasted through the years and, now, through the production of this book. Our love for each other enabled us to celebrate agreements and resolve differences with care and support, so we are all three better for the experience.

Second, thanks to all the women who participated by responding to questionnaires, interacting in groups or consenting to be interviewed. We especially thank all the authors of contributions. Their eagerness for such an anthology and their concern enabled them to hang in there through delays and revisions.

We thank all the women who worked to publish this book, particularly Joan Meyers, who juggled input from our three different voices during the final editing stages.

Finally, and most meaningfully, our deepest appreciation to Sherry Thomas of Spinsters Book Company. It was her warmth, her patience and especially her skill that nurtured this book from an idea through a collection of disparate contributions to a finished product.

Contents

CONTRIBUTORS

Introduction

There we were, three women over 50, and none of us could find anything to tell us what to expect as lesbians who are aging. There are no "Passages," no developmental stages for lesbians, no indication that we exist at all, much less that we change and grow. There is little enough about women in general as we enter midlife and beyond; most of what there is tells us that the best we can do is live with the increasing losses we face, first of our youth, then our sex appeal, then our children, and finally our chances for love and companionship. This gloomy prediction is, of course, predicated upon the "normal" heterosexual course of life which includes the assumption that woman's main job, child rearing, ends in midlife, and her main source of approval is from men, who eventually seek younger women.

Our development didn't follow that pattern. Nor did that pattern have much to do with the lives of our friends or clients. We assumed that lesbians in general live very different lives from heterosexual wives in the traditional mold. But who was talking about the patterns of our lives? Where were the stories, the studies, the theories, the predictions about midlife lesbians? No one had done any extensive work on our growth and development. So we three friends who, not coincidentally, were midlife lesbians, decided to put on a panel about midlife lesbians at the 1987 meeting of the American Psychological Association. Although we were unlucky enough to be scheduled for a 9 A.M. Sunday presentation, 80 women showed up. Looking out into all those faces, we realized we three were not the only ones hungry for knowledge and affirmation about ourselves. From such small beginnings this book has evolved.

Ideas and contributions were solicited through personal friendship networks and connections which evolved from them, from notices placed in several women's publications and from flyers distributed at whatever meetings or gatherings each of us attended. Because all three of us are psychologists we tend to have a book somewhat top-heavy in articles by psychologists. Luckily, many women who were not psychologists also responded.

The process by which this book came to be is a vivid illustration of how women work together. At no point did the three of us assign tasks, yet by the time the work was completed, we had each contributed equally and each in the areas in which we were most competent and comfortable. No one has been in charge; each of us has delegated responsibility and accepted it. We have responded to each other with respect and caring, solving problems through discussions that left us all feeling empowered and using our interactions to energize and encourage each other. In fact, we have had such a good time producing this book that there is already another one on lesbian activists in the works.

This is a book of many voices. We wanted a book that would be by midlife lesbians, not about them as seen through the lens of some "objective" academic study. Submissions range from poems to first-person accounts to data based research articles. Sometimes trying to make sense of it all looked impossible, but we were not willing to sacrifice many of the wonderful pieces for the sake of an artificially imposed consistency.

This book is about choices. It is about making changes in your external and internal life, reconceptualizing who you are; about staying still and not changing, getting in touch with your inner core and with parts of yourself that have been dormant. It is about taking risks at midlife that you would never have dreamed of taking before and it is about deciding that you no longer want to spend your precious lifetime and energy doing what you don't want to do. In other words, it is about the midlife lesbian in all her aspects. And yet, try as we might to reflect the broadest spectrum of lesbians at midlife, we missed some, perhaps many, other aspects. We invite readers to add from their own experiences, to embellish what is written here and to fill in the blanks in what is not written here.

We rather arbitrarily divided this book into sections based on common themes. Each includes first-person accounts of lived experience and research papers which gather together the experience of many lesbians and attempt to develop some broad generalizations.

There are several sections you will not find here. There is no section specifically on sexuality although several pieces speak about bodily changes and their impact on sexuality. The decision not to have a section titled "sexuality" reflects our belief that sexuality/sensuality suffuses everyday lesbian life. We are sensual in sports, in caring for our mothers or our children, in contemplating our changing bodies or our lovers, and even in dealing with loss.

You will also not find a section on ethnic/racial diversity. Lesbians cross all ethnic lines; that diversity is who we are and we want it built into the fabric of this book. Contributions from lesbians of color and white lesbians are distributed throughout the book according to the content of each piece rather than the ethnicity of each author.

You will find in this book celebrations of growing older, celebrations of being lesbian, and a growing awareness that we are setting our own pattern of midlife. We do not follow the traditional woman's developmental line of turning, in our mid-forties, toward career and work fulfillment after having raised our children who have now left the nest. Even those lesbians who have raised children have been involved simultaneously in work. Nor do we follow the male line of development which leads men to seek deeper relationships and greater involvement with family after two decades of establishing themselves as workers. Because of this, you will not find a section on work. The patriarchal dichotomy between work and relations, or, for that matter, the rest of life, does not hold for lesbians.

Lesbians are a unique group who are self-determining; who have known from an early age that, like men, they would be self-supporting, and who, as women, value relationships highly. Learning more about our development will give all of us (and especially developmental psychologists and sociologists) the beginning glimpses of what people who are not confined to the rigid sex roles of this culture could become.

This book is also for the generations of lesbians who remain unknown to us, some perhaps even to themselves, and who may have had to temper the glory of their love with the fear of exposure and punishment for their life style. It is also for those visible old lesbians who offer an evolving vision of what it is to be old and powerful. Equally important, this book is for the subsequent generations of lesbians, born after the women's movement and Stonewall, who will encounter a world in which books such as this exist and who will grow up knowing that lesbianism is a healthy and strong way to live and that aging is a positive force in their lives.

The particular group of lesbians who are currently at midlife are a unique generation. Almost all the women who contributed to this book are lesbians: the editors, the publishers, the writers, the women who shared their lives by filling out questionnaires or participating in the various research studies. All these midlife lesbians are part of a generation which has never before existed and will never exist again. We are the only generation of lesbians whose adolescent and young adult years, the time when most of us became conscious of our lesbianism, were spent in the fearful, hidden and self-hating world before the women's movement and gay liberation and whose later adult years and midlife are being spent in an era totally revolutionized by these liberation movements. Suddenly, in the early 1970s, when we were anywhere from 19 to 35, all the definitions changed. No longer were we sick, developmentally retarded, sinful or crazy. The secret belief that we had harbored deep within us, that we were just as normal and okay as the rest of the world and that the kinds of women we were and the way we lived deserved to be honored, suddenly was a secret no longer. After years of being vilified we were now validated.

The journey that is this book begins in a poem by Shirley Glubka and ends in one by Angela Van Patten, marking the voyage from growing child to role model. The first section, "Embracing Changes," establishes our uniqueness and reminds us of our herstory with several first-person accounts of living before and after the women's movement. JoAnn Loulan launches us by sharing her amazement at finding herself using the words we have all heard and all promised ourselves we would never say: "now when I was your age." She vividly reconstructs the atmosphere and ideology of the early years of the lesbian movement and then offers some suggestions for "taking advantage of what is available to us" at midlife. Next, Ayofemi Folayan contrasts her experience as a black lesbian before and after coming out in Los Angeles. Adrienne Smith shares with us how her increasing comfort with her lesbian activist identity led to a revaluing of her Jewish roots. Lauren Crux echoes and reinforces the theme of increasing self-acceptance, recognizing this as a time of "both danger and opportunity," celebrating her lesbian existence as her body shows the effects of aging. To conclude this section, Claudette Charbonneau and Patricia Slade Lander report on their research on women who have made the major change from hetero-sexual to lesbian at midlife. The commonalities they found and the questions they raise about sexual identity being "set" early in life, set the stage for questioning all the "accepted" definitions of midlife.

Our journey through changes continues with "Transforming Loss." Each of the selections in this section tells of women changing the experience of loss into one of growth and love. The funeral of Jane Chambers, whose death at 45 was a great loss to the entire lesbian community, is movingly described by Dolores Klaich. As a disabled woman, Susan Turner has always dealt with body changes. Now the loss of a lover forces her to confront her difference while valuing her uniqueness. Finally, Joyce Warshow shares with us her personal experience of her mother's aging and death and then discusses an issue many of us may be faced with, caregiving of aging parents.

"Relating as Daughters, Relating as Mothers" (or not) is where we go next. Jewelle Gomez contemplates four generations of women in her family, asking herself how her life as a "non-traditional lesbian, Afro-American writer" can honor both her heritage and her individuality as she deals with middle age. Joyce Warshow interviewed midlife lesbians about their relations with their mothers, finding some intriguing connections to a lesbian's self-acceptance. Next, Ronnie Lesser, in response to the lesbian baby boom, reports on women who do not want children. In common with many other writers throughout this book, Lesser found that how we feel about ourselves as women at this time in our lives affects our comfort with decisions about children. A woman who decided to have children within what appeared to be a "regular heterosexual" marriage, Matile Rothschild, chose to divorce her gay husband and come out as a lesbian while her children were adolescents. She writes about her experiences within the straight and the lesbian communities as an "older" mother with teenage

children. Our last selection within this section is by Angela Bowen, "a Black
woman who had children the old-fashioned way," that is, within a heterosexual marriage. She explores the entire concept of lesbians choosing
children and what that may mean for lesbians of all ages and for their
children.

From relationships with children we move to relationships with each
other in "Maintaining our Equilibrium in Couples—Or Not," at the heart
of our voyage through midlife changes. First Jean Greggs and Elfrieda
Munz, each in her own voice, describe how they've pursued creativity
through their twenty year interracial "marriage." A poem by Angela Van
Patten tells of two women trying to maintain a balance as lovers, a theme
that is explored in depth in the following study by Marny Hall (with Ann
Gregory) writing about how couples maintain their balance between work
and intimacy. Finally, Clare Coss reminds us that many of us are not in
couples. She writes of her interviews with several single midlife lesbians.

The next section, "Our Changing Bodies," is introduced by Robyn
Posin's moving first-person story of her growing love for her maturing
body, which more and more reminds her of her beloved grandmothers and
aunts. Next, the present-day health concerns of midlife lesbians have been
compiled by Judith Bradford and Caitlin Ryan from the National Lesbian
Health Survey. Hysterectomy is the subject of the next two selections, first
in a powerful personal account by Adalaide Morris of her own experience
with surgery. This is followed by Susanne Morgan's lucid explanation of
the changes to be expected in our sexuality after menopause or hysterectomy and what we can do to enhance our lovemaking. Joan Nestle then
tells us how "gray hair and textured hands are now erotic emblems" and
that lesbian sex after 40 is desire perfected." Our final selection in this
section provides the research evidence which verifies and generalizes what
Nestle, Posin and all of us are becoming aware of. Based on interviews with
41 women, Ellen Cole and Esther Rothblum confirm that "lesbian sex after
menopause" is "as good as or better than ever."

Just as lesbians welcome and embrace the bodily changes that come
with age, so too do we welcome spiritual growth as described in the
next section, "Rediscovering our Creativity and Spirituality." Carmen
de Monteflores calls these changes "time's gifts" and, in prose that is close
to poetry, shows us a panorama of her personal awarenesses. Muriel Miguel
describes the effects of her Native American heritage on her experience of
midlife and on her creativity. Next, Barbara Sang shares with us the
conclusions she draws from the responses of over 100 midlife lesbians to
questions about their current life concerns. As lesbians look toward our own
forms of spirituality, we are reclaiming and reinterpreting goddesses, finding female strength and power in old forms. Madonna Gauding, meditating

on the goddess Kali, shows us these new visions. Then, in two poems, Miriam Carroll talks of her pleasure in becoming a crone. This leads us directly to Jacquelyn Gentry and Faye Seifert's description of the croning ceremony and experiences of several women who have become modern day crones.

The final section, the end of our journey through midlife changes, offers us resources we can use in "Preparing for Our Future." Mary Lorenz tells us that fitness and fun after 40 is not for jocks only, suggesting an incredibly varied list of sports in which we may participate. To help us prepare for a financially secure future, S. Lisa Hayes discusses financial planning, including several charts which will help us develop retirement plans, even on limited income. Next, Paula Ettelbrick details legal documents we need to prepare so that we and our lovers are as protected as possible. Finally, Audre Lorde, in two brief pieces, shares with us her awareness of living fully in the present, acknowledging her privilege, her mortality and her joy. We end our journey as we began it, in a poem, recognizing our inevitable growth into role models for younger lesbians.

We hope your journey reading this book will be as joyous and rewarding as ours has been in gathering the writings of this remarkable group of midlife lesbians. The biographical statements of each of our contributors appear at the end of the book. The rich variety of women who contributed represents only a small sample of this entire unique generation of midlife lesbians. We hope the women of our generation will see in this book a true reflection of their lives. This book articulates the fact of our existence. Through silence we have been ignored. By remaining silent, we cooperate with our oppressors and collude with those who would deny our existence. By speaking out, by proclaiming to the world that we, as midlife lesbians, have a strong and solid being, we challenge the world to deal with us as the self-determining women we are. Whatever our differences, we are women who celebrate our aging.

Adrienne J. Smith
Chicago

Joyce Warshow
Barbara Sang
New York

June, 1990

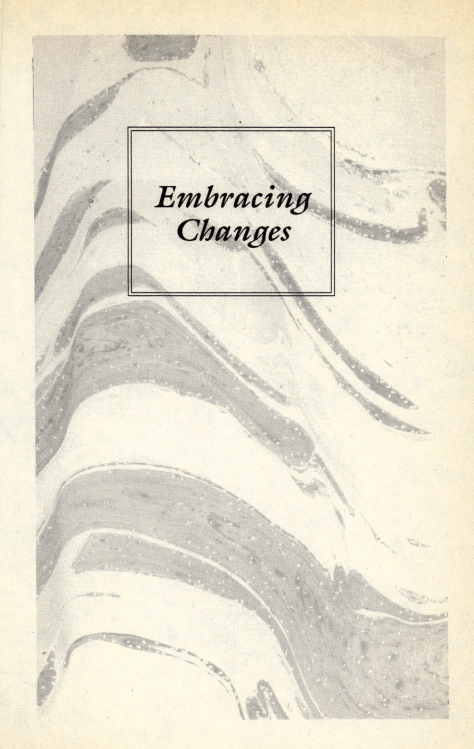

Embracing Changes

Unfinished

SHIRLEY GLUBKA

I was a child contained and careful,
cautiously enshelled. But I believed
my world was roomy. For did not Truth
stand large with classic lines against one wall?
And was not Love just soft enough for sitting
near the window as I read? What could be
more spacious than the ancient house of Faith?
Containment not yet named remained invisible.

I grew up and, growing, cracked the shell
I had not known was there. All form fell from me.
I traded Truth for existential risk, stood on bare air.
I breathed excitement for my breakfast every day.
I was thin and sure and freer than before.
I did not notice how abstraction
had replaced abstraction in my life,
how all was white on white,
how some connection still to reality
had simply not been made.

Nor did I notice this:
that evil never thins to absolute abstraction.
Even weakened it is substantive, embodied.
Even ghostly it is cold and can be touched.
More to the point, it could touch me.

"Now When I Was Your Age": One Perspective on How Lesbian Culture Has Influenced Our Sexuality

JOANN LOULAN

There is something funny about watching a women's professional tennis match and finding your hormones chasing after a woman on the screen who is both an adult and also 22 years younger than you are. We used to be the ones who were in our twenties. We used to be the ones who thought we had the pick of the crowd because of our age. Our pure sexual energy kept us moving all the time. We used to have fewer qualms about waking up in the morning and finding ourselves single. The thought of dating didn't send us into a month-long depression; it was the only reward available after the break up with a lover. We were titillated by dating. There were lots of us out there in the bars. After 1970, we could always find each other if we lived in a city with any population at all.

Well, have you been in a bar lately? They're still full of women—women who are 20 to 30 years old at the outside. They are picking each other up. They are standing in groups meeting each others' friends. They are dancing to unintelligible music, doing dance steps I'm sure I can't learn. They are wearing leather and what I call neurosurgery haircuts (you know, buzzed at the side, colored various shades, strips cut in various directions—like they have just been prepared for brain work). I swore in high school I would never act like my out-of-it mother. She hated the Beatles ("You can't understand their lyrics, their hair is disgusting."); couldn't learn our dance steps ("I don't understand how you kids make your bodies move like that."); she didn't like our clothes ("Those skirts are too short and make you look cheap."); and she couldn't set her hair (What a dork!). How could I be repeating her pattern? After all those years of therapy—and such superior credentials to begin with (not the least of which is being an ex-hippie turned lesbian)—how could I be like she was? Easy. It's called midlife.

What is happening here is that we really do have a different culture from lesbians in their twenties. I always thought the generation gap would never be a problem for me. When I turned 40, my first thought was, "I'm 40 now and I never have to go on a ride at an amusement park again in my life. I am now a bona fide grown-up and don't have to do anything I don't want to do." What a relief. Yeah...and then there's sex.

It seems like in the past few years, the rules have been changing. At least when *I* first came out in the mid-'70s in San Francisco, men were responsible for everything bad. Women only did good. Lesbians who were being sexually and physically abused by women in their lives were quiet about it. There was too much pressure to toe the party line. It was a thrill to finally have a forum to talk about the pain inflicted by men. The years of keeping silent about male oppression were finally ended and we were reveling in a community of women. The brutality we inflicted on each other in the name of political correctness was only meant to "cleanse" the community of "male" standards. One of the areas in which this purging showed up involved sex.

I'm not sure how it started, but somehow any expressed interest in sex was seen as male-identified. We prided ourselves on never objectifying women and the definition of objectification became more elaborate as time went on. There were silent and not so silent votes on dress, behavior and political work. Anything that was seen as part of female objectification or oppression was eschewed. By the mid-'70s any woman wearing clothing that showed breasts or hips, or wearing traditional symbols of adornment (make up, high heels, jewelry, etc.) was up for judgment. If you wanted to be in the visible lesbian club, there was an androgynous imperative. We began neutering our appearance.

In my town, the clothes a "good" lesbian was expected to wear were t-shirts, jeans (occasionally regulation sports shorts), flannel shirts, Frye boots and down jackets for cold weather, Birkenstocks and baseball-type jackets for warm weather. If you diverged from this uniform, you were suspected of problems with your lesbian identity (gee, maybe you were straight or, dare I say, bisexual?), or perhaps even worse, were guilty of serious infractions of class consciousness. The latter was evidenced mostly in the wearing of silk or good wool suits, which was seen as hiding in your class privilege in order to pass for straight.

This concentration on dress has historical significance. Creating a low visibility for ourselves through our choice of clothes, including dressing like men, certainly has served a significant function in women's history. It has protected some of us over the centuries from being sexually exploited and abused by male cultural mandates. We as women have been expected to merchandise ourselves in largely sexual ways and conventional expectations of our dress and appearance have reinforced that. Lesbian feminists in the '70s demonstrated their refusal to go along with the expectations of female dress in a culture that exploits females because of their dress. As a result of this refusal, the lesbian nation became stronger, more defined and more visible. At the same time, because we became so preoccupied with lesbian cultural correctness, we became more rigid.

We were so busy being concerned about political correctness, that sex got lost in the shuffle. It is important to acknowledge the internalized homophobia this suggests. At least in public, any sexual expression was thought to be in bad taste. In our struggle to create a new vision of lesbianism, which included a political analysis and a unique arts-centered culture, the transitional generation of lesbians appeared to the world to be asexual. Our appearance, our discussions, our political agendas, our activities often completely ignored the sexual component of our lives. To talk about what attracted us to one another, to dress in a seductive manner, to tell each other what we did sexually was seen as male-identified. We believed sex and sexuality was not a subject we should be processing as a community. This was such a confusing message. While we were celebrating each other, women's bodies and not being subjected to heterosexual sex any longer, at the same time the experience of being with our own or another's genitals was not a topic for discussion.

When talk of sex began to surface in the community, it was framed in a political context. Monogamy and non-monogamy alternated as the acceptable models from year to year, community to community, always with political analysis attached. One year, it was male and heterosexual to be monogamous. The next year, non-monogamy was the worst form of male oppression.

In most major cities the "S/M Wars" began in the early '80s. There were what seemed like endless discussions in every conceivable form of lesbian communication (newspapers, books, poetry, debates, political forums, individual gossip, therapy sessions, etc.) about sadomasochism. Was it just fun sex between consenting adults, or was it a replay of female oppression? The "good" lesbians and the "bad" lesbians were divided now according to the kind of sex in which they engaged. When it came to sex, the dominant opinion was that in order to be in a "good" lesbian relationship, you had to follow the rules. There must be no hint of sadomasochism. Equal opportunity orgasms and equal initiation on the part of both partners were the order of the day, along with monogamy or non-monogamy depending on the time and community.

We teeter-tottered back and forth with both internal and external homophobia and misogyny keeping us off balance. There seemed to be no acceptable lesbian cultural sex history that we were willing to draw from or embrace. We got rid of the butch/femme concept on the grounds that it mimicked heterosexual role models and had nothing to do with lesbian relationships. We made rules about discussing sex, what kind of sex we could have and who we could have sex with. Any lesbian who had sex with a man was out of the club without a second consideration by "the committee." Sex with men was the ultimate transgression against the "lesbian national bylaws." There were many rules with less dire but still negative consequences.

What was so painful about those times was that important aspects of our lives were subject to judgment in ways that divided us. From a sexual perspective, we had so little information and what we did have was mistrusted. Anyone creating new information was thought to be breaking rank. Even talking about it in small groups was seen as objectification. There was no need for straight men to bring informers into our groups (although the FBI in 1989 admitted doing so since 1953)—we were quite willing to purge our ranks frequently. The movement lost a lot of good lesbians along the way, simply because it got to be no fun being judged all the time for the slightest infraction. Often we seemed like eighth-graders at their worst. Here we were, desperate to fit into society somehow, trying to gain insight from our pain. We were willing to dialogue until our lips fell off just to get to the truth. At the same time, how you wore your hair was often given as much weight as the *real* issues such as female oppression, lesbian oppression, racism, classism, ageism and able-bodyism.

Inevitably, however, through this new strength and visibility, a community emerged which is increasingly diverse. As we enter the '90s, lesbians seem more willing to accept variety. The younger lesbians that I talk to don't find the rules we made so useful anymore. They seem much more able to accept diversity than we were at their age. It seems perfectly okay to discuss sex. Some younger women dress seductively. Some wear make up. Some are quite comfortable embracing butch/femme, while others are androgynous in appearance. They seem perfectly willing to accept that bisexuals exist—after all the time we spent making everyone see that bisexuals were worse than heterosexuals; they wanted to have their cake and eat it too. In the under-35 crowd, it seems perfectly acceptable that some lesbians engage in S/M; though some young women are upset by S/M, they seem much more willing to live and let live than many middle-aged women are.

With all these differences quite visible in the younger lesbian community, I assume they don't put each other down the way we did. Maybe this is a middle-aged woman looking wistfully back at youth wishing we had had it so good. Maybe this isn't how it is at all. I just remember that we were much more uniform in our day. We were much more uptight. In fact, the word "tight" doesn't even mean what it once did!

So here we are, ready to go on with the second half of our lives. We have a unique opportunity. We can do what our parents never seemed to be able to do. We can have what we want. We can use what we have learned, instead of being bitter about how we worked our fingers to the bone so the young ones could reap all the benefits, or how the new generation is going to the dogs. We can take advantage of what is available to us. I'm not suggesting we all go out and learn how to do S/M. I'm simply suggesting that we take advantage of the changes in the lesbian community. Instead of reaching backwards for old solutions, how about creating new ones? Let's use what the younger lesbians seem to take for granted. Instead of using the excuse, "Oh, I'm too old for that," let's start thinking about what we really want and how we can get it.

I think this time in our lives is a perfect time to ask ourselves: "Is there something I want to change?" All that we have done in the past is important, but there may be something we feel we have missed. There may be something we want to learn to do. Now is the time.

"Coming out" is a perfect example. A friend said recently, "Well, I haven't been out all this time, why start now? My parents are in their eighties. If I lost my job, I'm too old to get another. My neighbors would flip if they knew my real identity."

Actually, middle age is a unique position. We can tell the truth in a way we may never have before. At this point, our age is an advantage. If we aren't married to a man and haven't dated men for many years, what do we think co-workers, family members, neighbors think? Now that we are no longer in our twenties, many people have long ago stopped asking us if we are getting married. Young women are much less likely to be taken seriously. When we get older, people actually start listening to our opinions. We advance at work so that we become the experts. We are now the ones that have been at "x" job for ten to twenty years. We are truly the grown-ups. Along with this status we are given a certain kind of respect. Our parents may have momentary slips, but except for the seriously intrusive ones, we are not told what to do anymore. This is a perfect opportunity to "come out."

At midlife, our lovers are also granted a particular status. Sometimes this is just because she too is older and people take her seriously. Sometimes it's because the relationship has been going on for years and the family sees her as one of its own. Sometimes it's because we have been alone for so long that when we start seeing someone, our families are happy that we are connected again. Perhaps it's also because most people stop thinking of middle-aged people as sexual objects. Sex isn't the first thing that straight people think of when they see us as a couple.

In the area of sex, getting what we want seems hard. It is difficult to change old habits, but it is possible. If we are single or in a couple, we may have fallen into patterns that are safe, but don't necessarily make us happy. Now is an opportunity to ask ourselves: in the whole realm of sex and sexuality, are we feeling fulfilled? If the answer is "no," it doesn't mean we have wasted our lives, or that we must change everything about our lives, including our lovers, to make sex what we want it to be. In fact, it may simply mean finally taking the matter into our own hands (and perhaps mouth) and creating the sex life we want right where we are.

Single women may have the greatest difficulty seeking sexual fulfillment in middle age. This is not our fault. We look around. It really does seem that our peers are all coupled. It's a cultural phenomenon; being coupled is seen as superior to being single. Even if we are lonely in a couple, the fear of being alone is even more frightening. Dating is difficult. Where is it we meet single women over 40? It is not easy. They aren't just floating around the bars. Get-togethers sometimes seem contrived. Meeting older women is not impossible, however. I think the biggest part of the problem is that many of us never learned how to date in the first place and we are self-conscious.

Let us not forget our own rich past. Some of us *have* dated. We have done it successfully and we have done it unsuccessfully. We have met wonderful women. We have made fools out of ourselves. We have spent hours working on the dating process with our friends and in therapy. We have lived through it. It is difficult sitting in our living rooms waiting for the perfect women to come along. If we are single and we have not been going out because we're "too old," or we haven't been asking anyone because they might reject us, or we have been sitting home alone when we don't want to because we don't know anyone to ask, I say, like Judy Grahn in *Edward the Dyke:* "Lost your lover? Comb hair, get dressed, go out, find another."

Let's stop acting out around dating and just do it. Make a list of 50 women. Put the ones on the top of the list that we know will likely reject us. Ask them first so we can get it out of the way. The most amazing women have been rejected. Why not us? After the "Most Likely to Say 'No' List" (like Tina Turner, k.d. lang, our ex-lover's lover), how about the "Most Likely to say 'Yes' List" (the new woman who moved to town and doesn't know all our ex-lovers; the woman who has spoken to us every time we have seen her with her friends in the last month; the woman who awkwardly smiles as we walk by her at a party). Believe it or not, there are women who want to go out with us. We seem to always be waiting for them to ask us out. Why do we think it will be easier for them? Do it just for practice, like jumping into cold water. Just hold our noses and call. We may be pleasantly surprised. We may be totally bummed out. Call the next woman on the list. No, we are not objectifying women by having a list of them we would like to go out with. We are honoring these select women.

Despite what single women think, the coupled women are not better off in terms of our sex lives. In fact for many, changing our sex lives without leaving our lovers seems impossible. I believe we can change our sex lives, but we have to be willing to do whatever it takes. Most of us have a difficult time with the idea, much less the action. How do we tell our lovers that we want something more? That we have faked orgasms all this time? That masturbating to fantasies is often more fun than sex with them? That we are attracted to that new woman who moved into town and want to ask her out although we know we have finished with our non-monogamous stage and settled into this mature, committed relationship? That we are still envious every time we see a single lesbian who has this complete freedom to ask other women out, even though we know when we were single we didn't really ask anyone out anyway—but at least it keeps our minds occupied because we are terrified to tell each other how bored we are. Whew!

Bored with sex with your lover? How about introducing new activities into your routine? What have you got to lose? At this point, she must have seen you in your most embarrassing positions. She must have known you to be outrageous from time to time. How about being outrageous in sex? We often look towards a new relationship, girl friend, or job to give us courage to change. How about making that change ourselves? Here is an opportunity for us to create what we want in our own bedrooms. That sexual self that we have dreamed of being: now is the time to create her.

I believe that our partners know when we are bored with sex. In most instances, they're bored too and are just waiting for us to make the move. Here's your opportunity. Make her day, or night or afternoon. We don't have to start with what is wrong, we can start with how we would like to make things right. Let's bring home a sex toy that we have always wondered about. Ask our partner if she is willing to experiment with sex. There is no reason to wait. We aren't going to have an easier time doing this if we wait until next month.

Midlife is the time in our lives when many of us come to believe the idea that our life is not a dress rehearsal and if we don't get on with it, one day it may be too late. This is the time in our life when we have had friends —or ourselves—diagnosed with serious illnesses. We have had friends die. We are looking at our own mortality. In sex, even though we were raised differently (both by our parents and in the lesbian community), there are unique ways to nurture ourselves and the lovers of our choice. Sex and sexuality can be changed. It's simple. You don't have to move, change jobs, lose weight. You just have to work with your attitude. What a sweet reward, too. There you are having your dear body stroked, loved and excited by your favorite lesbian. There you are, changing your sex life in ways that fulfill you. What a sense of accomplishment, what a boost to your self-esteem.

This process is not always easy. It is not always easy to work at healing ourselves. It isn't clear why that is, but many of us have a difficult time changing behavior in order to heal ourselves. The suggestion that I find most helpful is to do it today. Do something small so you don't scare yourself. Make your list of women *today*. Then tomorrow make a strategy of who you will call. Then the next day rearrange the list. Then the next day make a new strategy. Then the next day make the priority different. Then the next day, just call someone.

Coupled women can do things in equally small increments. Tell her you are going to make a surprise for her. Make a plan to stay overnight somewhere other than your home. Take your lover camping, or to a motel, or stay overnight in a friend's empty house. Staying away from home does wonders for many women's sex lives. The most important part is to just simply make the moves, say the words, bring in the toy that is going to start the process to change the sex between the two of you. It doesn't have to mean you change your whole life. Maybe the change is just one part. Why wait?

Taking control of sex in a way that makes us feel better and more fulfilled will help to heal us. It will heal the heart. This individual healing can work in many ways to heal the community. As middle-aged lesbians, we have seen a lot. We have lived through many times of hurting one another. This is part of why it is so hard for us to heal ourselves and each other now, but we have an opportunity to change ourselves and to have a part of that change spill over into our community.

I think the challenge for the lesbian community as a whole in the '90s is connected to the healing being described in various literature concerning the dysfunctional family. I am talking about creating dialogue, not demands. I am talking about being willing to listen to one another, instead of lecturing one another. I am talking about one lesbian being open to another lesbian's experience. And I am talking about asking women to educate themselves instead of following the politically correct line. There has to be room for all of us to be a part of the community. As the times get harder and lesbians are under more pressure from straight society, it is essential that we create a place that is truly safe. There needs to be a forum for lesbians to talk about their erotic nature, to talk about their sexual needs, to be able to let other lesbians know what is important to them.

As we move towards the exalted position of the crones in our community, as we move out of middle age into old age, we must be ready to accept the responsibility. In our middle years we can practice making ourselves worthy of the description "wise." We must earn this title. I suggest we do it differently from other generations. I suggest we learn from our mistakes and those of others in our community. Let us be willing to see that there are no enemies here, only women trying their best to do their best. Women working sincerely at being lesbians. Women who want to be accepted by one another in a way that we never were in the past. Here is our chance to make that happen.

It Is a
Very Good Year

AYOFEMI STOWE FOLAYAN

I have had an incredibly hard time writing this piece. In some ways that doesn't make any sense because I am an out and proud lesbian, excited to have reached the age of 40. Yet there is some internal wall that stops the words and feelings from emerging onto paper. The process of acknowledging where I am in my life as a lesbian has forced me to look back over where I have been and to deal again with the old pain. Coming out for me was more than stepping out of the closet and declaring myself a lesbian. First I had to figure out that I *was* a lesbian.

Today there is a visible lesbian community. Here in Los Angeles, there is a monthly Lesbian Writer Series and four bookstores which carry a range of lesbian titles. *The Lesbian News,* published now for fifteen years, advertises therapists, chiropractors and real estate agents, all of whom provide services as and for lesbians. There are several women's bars and even recovery programs where lesbians are welcomed.

It wasn't always so. The word "lesbian" didn't exist publicly when I was first coming out. There was no affirmation that other women shared the emotions that churned inside. The community was underground, seeking each other out through codes and signals, meeting in bars and private parties. *Everyone* was closeted at work or school. Black women, in particular, didn't use the word lesbian to describe themselves. It was a word I associated with characters in books, not real people.

There is a Frank Sinatra song that goes, "When I was seventeen, it was a very good year...." Well, when I was seventeen, I had no clue that it could be a very good year. I had just been released from a psychiatric facility after eight weeks of intensive psychotherapy and drug therapy. I had been admitted to this hospital by my parents after they discovered me making love with my best girl friend from high school.

I didn't even know the word "lesbian" yet. I didn't hear that label for another eleven years. I didn't understand what I was feeling or experiencing as a lesbian. Like most adolescents, I was propelled to sexual activity by confusing emotional and physiological signals I could neither define nor explain.

Back then it would have been impossible for me to imagine my life today, living openly as a lesbian. It was 1967, well before Stonewall, before women's music festivals or women's liberation became visible. The assumption was that a female would finish high school, get married and settle down as a happy homemaker. There were even essay contests, sponsored by the Betty Crocker Company, about becoming "A Better Homemaker of Tomorrow."

I grew up in the strict fundamentalist Pentecostal Church. My grandmother, grandfather, two uncles and a cousin were all ordained ministers. My social life was defined by the limits of a full calendar of church activities, including choir, bible study and youth group. Then, at fourteen, I saw my first movie, an action forbidden by the tenets of my church. I was so enthralled by the film *Dr. Zhivago* I returned to see it thirteen times! I kept waiting for the lightning to strike, but all I experienced was the joy of a really romantic love story. I reasoned that if the church could be so wrong about something like movies, I could begin to question other rules.

Sex as a concept was a "black hole" to me: highly charged and totally incomprehensible. While I had crushes on my girl friends, it never occurred to me that there could be any sexual content to those feelings. When I was around boys I was mostly bored, unless we were intellectually matched. By the time I found myself "practicing for dates with boys" with my girl friends, it was still not clear to me that those feelings could exist in a context of their own.

As our rehearsals progressed beyond kissing to other sexual activities, such as petting, I became less and less interested in the "real" performance. I was thoroughly inebriated by the heady wine of my increasing passion. Yet, I would not have defined any of our activity as sexual, because I did not have the context of lesbian to define it.

I was crushed by the indictment of my family, my church and the community around me, which called me a pervert. I submitted to their external pressures to conform, to be "normal." After my psychiatric imprisonment, I hid in a disguise of heterosexuality to avoid the punishment that had been so swiftly dispensed. While I proceeded to get married and have children, there was a part of me that resisted, that struggled to stay alive.

While married, I continued to have affairs with women who were as confused as I. We each thought we were "the only one" and that somehow we had been fortunate to stumble upon each other. Even after I had been involved with four or five women, it still did not occur to me that I was a lesbian or that these feelings I had for women had any validity.

I often say that it is surprising to me when I meet a lesbian from some small town in Iowa. "How did she know that she was a lesbian?" I ask myself. I struggled so hard to come to terms with who I was, partially because I had no community to reflect and validate me. After two marriages and two children failed to convince me that I could fit into the heterosexual mold, I moved to Los Angeles at the age of 23.

There I came into contact with a lesbian community. Women who called themselves lesbians, who wore jeans and Birkenstocks and carried backpacks, who congregated at women's bars. Over the next few years, just being around these women who were lesbians produced a major transformation in me. I went to concerts and dances, sang in the Los Angeles Women's Community Chorus (which welcomed all women of whatever sexual orientation) and gorged myself on a mental diet of lesbian books.

I didn't "come out" until the Briggs Initiative, a referendum on the California ballot in 1978 that threatened to attack homosexual teachers and anyone who supported their right to teach. I was so personally outraged by the homophobia explicit in this potential law, that I worked actively on the campaign which successfully defeated the initiative. In a sense, I leapt out of the closet, never to return.

Since then, my individual evolution has drawn on that core assumption that I am a lesbian. Politically, that has meant a commitment to ending all forms of oppression and to improving the quality of life on our planet. It is important at this point in my life for me to continue to encourage women who are struggling with coming out issues today, in the continuing context of homophobic oppression. Personally, that has meant taking my full identity with me wherever I am. Sometimes that has made members of the various other communities I am part of, such as the black community, the disabled community and the politically progressive community, uncomfortable.

The journey I took to reach a clear and calm acceptance of myself means never looking back with some sentimental confusion about the past, never apologizing, never again suffocating in the cloud of confusion and ignorance that surrounded me as a young lesbian. In the words of the Judy Small song, "I'm going to keep on walking forward, never turning back, never turning back!"

The Ripening of Our Bodies, The Deepening of Our Spirit

LAUREN CRUX

I am 42, a lesbian in early midlife. These are the middle years, middle passage. Time has changed. It passes both more quickly and more slowly.

I realize that I want to write a lovely narrative of how I have reached some kind of inner peace as, in midlife, I turn inward. I would like to say that this is not a time of crisis for me, but a time of re-orienting, engaging life more deeply, the spiritual flowing through me, sustaining, nurturing. But much to my dismay, because I said it would never happen to me, I am in crisis. It is a time of both danger and opportunity.

On days when I feel particularly lost, I remember that poem where Adrienne Rich asks,

> Dear Adrienne:
> I'm calling you up tonight
> as I might call up a friend
> to ask what you intend to do
> with the rest of your life...[1]

The existential possibilities threaten to overwhelm me.

I know I should feel grateful that I have choices in life at all, but mostly I fall into dismay, because I have, over the years, lost all clear sense of what I want. Yet, I feel the pressure to choose something. I no longer count my life from my year of birth, but rather count forward to when I will die.

I am grieving the loss of love. It has been over two years since my lover and I parted. A recent affair I hoped would develop, ended in hurt and confusion. I am left shaken, insecure, lonely. There have always been lovers, why now, in midlife, does it seem so hard? The doubting voices ask, "Is it because I am no longer attractive; am I 'over the hill?' Will I be alone, without a lover the rest of my life?" Even though I know better, the voices chisel away at me.

I stand naked in front of a small mirror. At another moment I would recognize as lovely the lines which form a large "V" crossing from clavicle to breastbone. Would see the beauty of the creases, soft and deep from sleep, the quick strokes of an artist's brush depicting birds in flight. Today I see only my body's aging and I am frightened, shocked by this reminder that there will be an end. I feel a desire to clutch my body, hold, preserve it. Stop the birds in mid-flight.

In three weeks I am scheduled for knee surgery. "Not bad," I am told. I have a 50-50 chance the surgery will alleviate the pain of patella femoral disease. If this surgery does not work, I will need a second, major surgery, otherwise my knee will continue to deteriorate. I cringe inside, remembering the pain from the surgery on my other knee when I was a teenager. I feel shaky, not sure I could bear another more serious surgery, the pain of it, the months of physical therapy that follow. Old body memories surface.

I become aware of the sound of the waves as they pound against the cliffs near my home. I am reminded of a wild blustery day, bodysurfing with a lesbian friend. The tides are high and the currents so strong that a swimmer could be swept hundreds of yards down the coast in a matter of minutes. The waves climb chaotically, their tops blown frothy by the wind.

My friend and I are strong swimmers, we have both been competitive bodysurfers. We know the beach and the currents well, and although the surf is rough and there is some risk, we feel certain we can manage. Between swells, laughing and gossiping, telling stories of our sexuality, our longings, cheering each other on, we applaud each wave well ridden and watch to make sure we each surface safely.

After one long ride into shore, I swim vigorously to get back out to the high surf. Strong currents pull, choppy surface waves bounce against me. I am working hard, content and reveling in the challenge. A board surfer comes near, asks pointedly in a clipped British accent, "What are you doing out here?" I think of a retort, but respond openly with what is clearly apparent. "Bodysurfing." He clucks, grimaces and snaps as he powers past—a little too close to my head—"You must be mad as a hatter."

That was five years ago. My knees hurt less then and I could stand the cold water more easily. I still surf strong waters, but I compensate for the cold by wearing a warmer wetsuit and not staying out as long. I tire more easily. To reach one of my favorite beaches I have to walk down a steep hillside. This has become increasingly painful, difficult. As I step slowly, guardedly, down the slippery path, I am conscious of my aging, weakening knees. Once in the water I will become ageless, timeless again, feeling myself return to that sense of inner peace I am so often missing on land. The painful walk to the beach only increases my desire to enter the waters.

It is true that my body is deteriorating, though not necessarily as a function of aging. There are many people who are infirm in early childhood, others who are vibrantly healthy and agile into old age. I have had knee trouble and have been in increasing pain since age fourteen. I have already given up many of the sports I love—basketball, softball, running. A few remain—surfing, hiking, bicycling, but at the moment, even these are impossible for me.

A friend attempts to console me. "You can turn to other interests, you have your mind." She is right, of course, I have always made my way, adapted, and know I will continue to do so, but her suggestion does not address the horror I feel lurking. It sits around the edges of my life, waiting. When I feel its presence I look at my life and ask, is this it? Lonely, afraid, muddling about with no particular goal or direction in mind. My body announcing that change is inevitable and that I am only mortal. On a good day, to be mortal, to be ordinary, is very satisfying. But on a bad day, all my residual grandiosity tears away at me—all the shoulds and oughts of a lifetime. I understand that at this point in my middle years I have an opportunity to dismantle the remaining childhood obligations of who I was supposed to be, rather than who I am. I can assure you, I was never supposed to be a lesbian.

One day recently, when I was feeling miserable, a good friend said to me, "But your life is so rich." And indeed it is. I have worked hard to make it so and had my share of good fortune. I have wonderful friends who sustain and nurture me. I love to meander outdoors by the ocean, in the mountains, and always feel renewed. I write poetry, take photographs. enjoy hanging out, gossiping, making music. I have work that most days is meaningful and challenging. I feel passionately about living. But so too I struggle sometimes with an inner sense of emptiness—the residual torment from childhood, thinking I will never be enough. This despair can and does erode the passion. As I swing from one to the other I feel like a self torn open.

I return to the waters, to a time three years ago: the sun is out, skies are clear and a huge swell has rolled in. A perfect surfing day. The waves are faultlessly shaped, glassy and inviting. I am recovering from a hysterectomy so I only stand on the cliff edge and observe. Soon I lose myself in the poetry of the day. I can feel the ride as I imagine gliding swiftly down the face of each wave; note how high I ride, turn, when and where I cut out, how I dive down deeply and surface again behind the wave. Imagine heading out once more for open waters, for the next swell.

In the midst of this deep sensual reverie, a man's voice interrupts, asks, "Hi, how ya doin'?" He is a board surfer I know from this area, who has seen me in the water many times. I explain why I am watching and not surfing. He is sympathetic and upon leaving wishes me well. He says with sincerity, "I hope you recover soon and get in the waves. You know, you don't see many middle-aged women doing this sort of thing."

Whereas once I was called "Mad as a Hatter," I am now called "Middle-Aged." I come of age into *their* world, understand viscerally its effects. I feel stunned to be pulled out of my world, where I am a happy, erotic, lesbian surfing fool, who happens to be in midlife, to be dragged into the current of a *socially constructed* obsolescence.

I return home, enter the house and find anxiety waiting for me like an intruder. This happens often now. I don't know what is happening in my life anymore. I know that I am unhappy. Even though my life is richer and more full than ever before. It doesn't make sense. And it is the not knowing, the non-sense, that seems the most distracting to me. I come to understand that I have held my life together with knowing and understanding. Trying to be good and do things right. "Squeaky clean," a friend described me. Staying in control. But now, an aching heart, a body that feels broken down, no clear career direction, or any direction for that matter, leave me feeling helpless, fearful.

I feel my world tearing apart. My sore and aching knees frighten me and remind me that I cannot know what the future holds. Meridel Le Sueur invites us to dismantle the patriarchy's language of aging, suggests we use the word "ripening" instead. I like that—I am ripening. For a moment, peacefulness. And then it fades. Thoughts of my mother:

My mother is dying of Alzheimer's disease. She is blind and no longer lucid; she recognizes no one. Her body has lost its boundaries, incontinent, flaccid. My mother, once strong, proud in body, is relentlessly deteriorating. Her dying is slow and ugly and although we were not close, I feel a wrenching. I hear her crying out in a moment of lucidity that she wants to end her misery. I would like her dying to have dignity. I cannot know if this will be my future, but I worry. I realize it is time to update my living will, think, perhaps, I should join the Hemlock Society.

My father is old and looks tired. When I have dinner with him, I have a strong feeling that he will die soon. He is loving to me, respectful, for the first time in my life. His gentleness disarms me, the old resentments, the grief rise to the surface. Once home, alone, I lie on my floor sobbing. All the old structures are being dismantled.

One evening after working out in preparation for my knee surgery, I walk from the gym to the pavilion across the street. This is post-earthquake Santa Cruz, December, 1989. We have tents where once there were buildings. Five different eateries are now housed in the pavilion I visit, five separate businesses working cooperatively to survive. I am inspired by the resilience and creativity of the people of this city. But I also feel sad as I remember my favorite buildings now destroyed, as I think of hundreds of people still homeless. Such loss. And yet, our town survives, because the people here rise up to rebuild and to re-create. Out of destruction, vision, commitment. What is the source of this spirit?

What helps me rise up and keep on? At this point in my life, I have survived enough crises, hard times, that I know I do get through. When I was younger I was never sure. But now, I am more able, willing to reach out for help.

I seek the soul of the ocean in my landed life. Where do I find it now?

To answer I keep returning to the things that I love, to what helps me get through. A close friend, my surfing pal, drops by to tell me that the waves are huge. Knows I am laid up with my knee, but asks if I would like to drive out to Steamer Lane and stare at the ocean. "Of course," I say as I put aside my work and off we go. There, while standing admiring the huge swells, we tell our stories, how our lives have moved since our last visit.

This is a deepening friendship and I feel myself soothed inside her caring for me. She cries about trouble with her lover, afraid to be alone. I talk about wanting a lover, tired of being alone. We discuss intimate details. We laugh about the intricacies of lesbian love life and the banalities. She tells me how relieved she is that her young nieces, who learned this Christmas that she is a lesbian, remain loving and unafraid. They still tumble and climb all over her.

There is a kind of spiritedness in lesbian life that I cherish. We have a lively, ongoing interest in our woman/lesbian lives—an interest that is firsthand, not filtered through someone else. That interest changes and shifts as we deal with our aging, but it does not diminish, for we are not obsolete to one another.

To borrow from a friend, "I am wiser now and more reckless." And in my world I am not an exception. I am used to lesbians of all ages, young, middle, old, being active in various ways in mind, spirit and body. There is an intention, a focus given to me by the definition of our lives as lesbians. To quote Nicole Brossard, "Amazons and lesbians are the only women not invented by Man. In this sense, they are figures both utopian and damned..." and, "The lesbian is a mental energy which gives breath and meaning to the most positive of images a woman can have of herself."[2]

I find myself thinking of my encounter with the surfer who named me middle-aged. A poem begins to form. It is a way I can complete an experience interrupted. I turn a mirror on my life and write what is mine, leave out the rest. This is another way I get through, to turn my pain and my joy back into the world as one turns the earth over to prepare for planting.

"There is no sacred reflection of the lesbian." I find these words in my notes and cannot remember if they are mine or borrowed from someone else. But I like them. What do they mean? I am only just now beginning to understand. I will try to explain, but first the poem, which is my attempt to create a sacred reflection.

Love Story (Steamer Lane, Santa Cruz, 1987)

I stand on the cliff watching.
Waves gather
momentum,
rise full and ripe, one
after the other.
Glass-clear,
the form holds, perfectly.

It is a day
that comes only rarely.
Longing bursts in my chest.
To dive, plunge, into
this other life.

I have known
the icy chill,
as the first water slickers
inside my wet suit—
"seal skin"
they call it.
Black and sleek,
each arm lifting up, reaching forward
finned feet kicking
against current, over
reef, rocks, tangled kelp,
intent on that place
far out where the
swell builds
slowly, so slowly at first.

There are no edges here.

I want the center peak.
Swim until I ache.

Now the wave towers
huge and bold.
This is not vanilla love.
This is rough stuff.
It holds, lingers.
This is the invitation, a moment's
generosity.

I have only my body.
Ride a high line along the
translucent shoulder.

The huge peak spills over.
The water tears at my suit,
pounds my belly,
thunders.

I laugh out loud.

Yes, yes!
Yes, to it all!

When I join some friends at the beach, it is an easy, unhurried day. We have the water to ourselves. There is a lull in the waves and we gather near. I watch the light reflect off the early evening fog onto their faces, faces with laugh lines, deeply creased. And I see women who love their lives, who are conscious of the struggle we all live through, but who are still able to play. Still able to rejoice, to celebrate life. I see strong women, not necessarily of body, but of spirit. Women, not invented by men, who allow me to re-invent myself. I see something that opens me to the sacred. I am reflected back into wholeness. Breath and meaning infuse my life.

To my knowledge I have no lesbian mother, nor grandmother. I cannot make lesbian children. In time marked by biology and procreation I exist, as a lesbian, only in the present. There is no written history of aging as a lesbian. This is the first time in history as we know it, that so many of us are "out," known to one another and passing through midlife. Ahead of us, there are only a few old lesbians who have recorded their stories, or write them now. As we age, we pass through with a hunger to know and speak with each other. To learn each other's history.

As we write these histories, place our own images in our own texts with our own words, we create our own sacred reflections. As we look into each other's eyes, and hold our gaze just that extra second, we give witness to our existence and to delight in each other's lives. In our friendships, in the families we create, our children, our work, our politics, art, letters, we create time, reinvent history. We reclaim our past, our future. I no longer exist only in present tense. Time takes on new meaning.

ENDNOTES

1. Adrienne Rich, "Contradictions: Tracking Poems, #6," *Your Native Land, Your Life,* (New York, London: W.W. Norton & Company, 1986), p. 88.

2. Nicole Brossard, *The Aerial Letter,* (Toronto: The Women's Press, 1988), p. 141 and 121.

The Example of the Sea Birds

MARGARET CRUIKSHANK

Walking at Baker Beach in San Francisco one day, I realized that I had never before looked closely at the flight pattern of the local birds. As I watched for a long time, I saw them flap their wings and then coast, flap again and coast again. This pattern signifies midlife for me, a time to work hard and then coast before exerting myself again. Effort balanced by rest. This was never my pattern as a young woman, when I was driven by emotional deprivation to scholastic overachievements. When my college psychology professor, a kindly old nun, told me that my IQ was too low for my high grades and recommended a rest, I replaced hard study with golf and murder mysteries but soon grew bored and returned to hard study. When I stopped working, then and for many years afterwards, I experienced not true rest, just a slight lessening of pressure. As a middle-aged woman, I am beginning to learn how to rest. I follow the example of the sea birds.

I like being 48. I've grown beyond mere survival as a way of being, to feel secure, expansive, hopeful and healed from childhood and adolescent wounds. Middle age is not the cause of these improvements, only the time of them, but experiencing them now makes me associate this period of life with self-renewal. At 48 my mother, trapped by depression, alcoholism and loathsome family duties, was trying to maintain the facade of the successful *Better Homes and Gardens* wife and mother. My midlife fate is gentler and results from good luck, class privilege, therapy, feminism and freedom from the daily responsibility for others.

One sign of change is that in my late forties comfort is very important to me. As a young woman and even until recently, I believed I liked austerity for its own sake, not from any character-building motives or from fear of bourgeois excess, just to be simple. I didn't own a car until I was 30. I produced several books without a real desk. A comfortable apartment did not matter to me. I couldn't change until I experienced physical comfort as good and saw that emotional deprivation can be projected onto one's surroundings. From my perspective at midlife, my earlier austerity was a sign that I didn't value myself highly. I now have a few more creature comforts, including a lumbar roll for my back and a futon bed. As midlife unfolds, I will acquire a desk and perhaps even a couch. I laugh at myself for not owning a coat—jackets have been good enough. But surely a middle-aged woman deserves a coat.

At 48 I also choose psychological comfort, to the extent I can identify it. Physical comfort certainly fosters psychological comfort. When I feel uneasy or troubled I try not to stuff down those feelings as if scrunching my sleeping bag into its small stuff bag. I welcome tears. I try not to fall in love with alcoholic women. They are charming, brainy, seductive, but I need more steady attention than I can get from them—a midlife discovery that may not save me from future entanglements but should at least become a check on my behavior.

I've begun to question my old assumption that psychological comfort for a lesbian feminist means being totally out of the closet. Recently I completed a gerontology internship at a senior center where I was not out. Because I now have a strong bond with the members, whose ages range from 60 to 90, I am still doing a monthly program for and with them. I doubt that my rapport could have been established if I had introduced myself as a lesbian. "But now their respect for you is based on a lie," I can hear myself saying in my more militant lesbian period. "But I am not *only* a lesbian," I protest today; "I have many other selves." My earlier self sneers, "Coward, hypocrite—you can't go *back* into the closet any more than you can put toothpaste back into the tube." But apparently I can choose, in or out, a luxury I would not have if I lived in a small town or if my books were better known. Rethinking that choice, I wonder if I assumed that the old are more homophobic than others, or was it just their obvious difference from me that made me wary?

Controlling the way I was perceived during my internship certainly created psychological comfort for me. Coming out would have obscured my other selves. Expecting to be liked at the senior center, I became much warmer than I would have been earlier in my life. What a relief not to have to make a political statement by my mere presence. Taking on a stigmatized identity requires more bravery and stamina than I imagined fifteen years ago. I expect to do it again, but I feel healed by the peaceful experience of not having to do it all the time.

A third way I am more comfortable in midlife is spiritually. In my early thirties when I became a feminist I was already moving away from spiritual or religious influences. Zealous feminism, which felt like a religion of its own, contributed to this shift. Fifteen years later I had figured out that a political movement could not satisfy all my emotional and spiritual needs and that it was all right to be spiritual. Now I'd go one more step and say it is absolutely essential if I am to be well emotionally and psychologically. What does this mean exactly? I go to no church and profess no creed. I have no guru (the very idea seems a little silly, a sign no doubt of my Midwestern origins). All it really means is that I acknowledge a spiritual side which needs some expression. Meditation, for example, yoga, an occasional retreat, hikes in the woods or along the ocean, breathing music, a period of quiet sitting by a lighted candle—anything to remind me that rational life is not the only realm I can move in. When my yoga teacher sounds gongs and I feel a comforting peace from the vibrations, I know that my experience at that moment is rooted in the material world. I have no desire to transcend matter, only to feel my feelings and be aware of the life force in and around me.

I have been especially conscious of my spiritual self since an experience two years ago. After a long period of therapy and because of a serious illness, I went to a homeopathic clinic in the high desert where "guests" (not patients) see doctors and nurses, get massage, explore their dreams, hike, swim, sit in a hot tub next to a statue of Buddha and fast. Biofeedback, drawing, work with clay, yoga, meditation and dance all helped me uncover the psychological roots of my physical illness (precipitated by my father's death) in a completely non-coercive atmosphere. Quaker influences were strong there. I did not mention to my Midwestern relatives that the staff included a psychic.

For two weeks I was completely unskeptical. Free from the numbing distractions of normal life (simply not driving for two weeks can improve anyone), I let myself feel, as never before, the pain of being a child in my family, especially pain of neglect and psychological abuse but also the pain of being suppressed and controlled. I felt compassion for my parents for the first time in my life, but only after repeatedly feeling rage so intense it frightened me. Both feelings probably came only because I was in a totally safe environment, where emotions were freed in many ways, through swimming, painting, dream analysis and journal writing. Opening to long-repressed anguish allowed me to know that my parents had had their own pain that prevented them from keeping their needs separate from mine. I felt a deadness, a hollowness deep inside me. Gradually, surrounded by gentle, loving people who gave me a glimpse of what a normal family would have been like, I began to feel as if I had a core self after all, and by the end of a second two weeks at the center, four months after my first visit, I knew I would never be ill again, at least in the old, despairing way. The positive spirit of that time has never left me. How healing works remains a mystery to me (although I believe sessions with a very skilled therapist laid the groundwork for this experience); I only know that I was touched by a power I had no access to in ordinary, busy life, a power transmitted by the vital and spiritually developed people at the Center (mostly older women) but dependent on my receptivity.

At this time in my life, when I feel lucky to have gone through such a transformation from sick to well and when making myself comfortable is a priority, I find that certain things cease to matter. Apparently this happens in old age; maybe a lesser experience of it occurs also at midlife. I have unexpected flashes of patience at times when earlier my response would have been impatience or contentiousness; for example, when impeded by bad drivers in San Francisco, kept waiting in long lines, or put on hold (a terrible irritation to a woman with no core self). Now I practice breathing. I see if my neck needs a little workout. Disputes within the lesbian community don't interest me much anymore. I enjoy the gossip as much as ever. In my youth, denouncing stupidity was part of my professional identity. Error had no rights. Now I am sorry to see stupidity flourish, but I am more likely to smile at it than to rage.

At midlife, I am more patient with myself, too. If I act badly, miss a deadline, or forget to do something, I try to observe what happened in a detached way, without condemning myself. The next level of patience will be to remind myself of all I do well, which is hard for me as the survivor of an emotionally disturbed family, or perhaps for any woman raised in a sexist culture.

These changes have accompanied a shift in my lesbian feminist identity. Although I am still very staunch, I have changed from being chiefly a lesbian to someone who values many facets of herself, some of which were suppressed by chronic illness and depression. The decade 1975-85 was my lesbian supremacist period, and it was a wonderful period. Then over the next two years came softening influences, the breakdown that led me to the healing center, recovery and a return to graduate school. Lesbianism is still central to who I am but it seems muted now, and I am not as much a public lesbian figure as before. School has made me feel more a part of mainstream life.

In my lesbian supremacist period I was influenced by separatists, especially when teaching women's studies and gay/lesbian literature. Their bold ideas stimulated and sometimes shocked me. In the 1980s I notice that separatism is hostile to traditional therapy and for good reason; therapy offers an explanation of suffering that runs counter to the explanation of separatists, who locate the source of suffering in the evils of patriarchy. It's not quite as simple as that, although I can understand why separatists would feel distant from lesbians who have found private solutions to their dis-ease in therapy, in spiritual explorations, in holistic healing. but not in feminist politics. Private solutions are not enough but at least they alleviate pain and help steady us for political action. The hurt and anger coursing through some separatist writing seems not to have changed much over the years.

Paradoxically, my lesbian identity is more secure now than when I was more militant and more focused on lesbianism because I am surer of who I am. Anger at patriarchy was invigorating, but an equally appropriate target for my wrath could have been my alcoholic family. It's a question of balance. If psychologically healed at an early age, I still would have been drawn to lesbian feminism but my anger would not have been disabling. The great and small injustices of male domination still anger me: the difference is that now I express anger more selectively. It is one of many stances I can take toward the external world. When I accepted lesbian feminist ideology uncritically, I overlooked the torments particular to my own situation; I had a demonology that permitted me to denounce much of the world around me. While living in a state of psychological discomfort I needed to strike out at others. Now I see that although many problems are external and political solutions are necessary, and although heterosexism certainly oppresses me, I am responsible for creating the emotional equilibrium to cope with this life. I must heal myself. How? Partly by kindness to others: women, children, men. By believing that a great reservoir of goodwill and kindness is available to me and that I can tap into it. A similar idea was presented to me in my Catholicism and by the Girl Scouts, but it was too abstract to take root, and it directly contradicted my family experience.

I strive for emotional harmony in other ways, too, for example, by living in the present. That's hard. I can barely do it. But in midlife, I see the splendid possibilities of a life lived that way. I feel whole when I focus on the present moment. Although the Zen spirit in me is rather faint, it helps me breathe deeply and observe, each day, some unexpected beauty or pleasure—a visual image, a gesture, colors, shapes, the intricately lined face of an old woman I like at the senior center. I stop and look. As a young woman I was oblivious to nearly all of what I saw in an ordinary day. I rushed past. To prove my importance, I had to. Now I keenly observe others, myself and my physical surroundings because I want to know what is happening in the present.

It may be that the shift in my lesbian identity is an unconscious reaction to my perception that, as I age, I will probably have to rely, perhaps to a great extent, on mainstream institutions for help and support. I do not foresee that the lesbian feminist or the gay movement will have either the cohesiveness or the resources to give its members the benefits that are offered, for example, to the Jewish old of San Francisco. Admittedly, the comparison is a poor one in that our groups are newer and our roots less deep. Maybe some day lesbian culture will be as developed as Jewish culture is now. But it may be that gay or lesbian is not as sustaining an identity as Black, Jewish, or female. Until recently, I looked forward to an old-dykes home. Hard-working women may indeed create such a place, but now I am not sure I'd be comfortable there unless I had many other things besides lesbianism in common with the other residents.

From my vantage point of middle age, I see that the theme of my early years was struggle. Even in my thirties I saw myself as embattled, for example when creating a women's studies program in the rural Midwest, a view that now seems grandiose. Nevertheless, until I had lived long enough to begin to heal ancient wounds, I could not see that battling obstacles around me was a replay of my early struggles against my controlling father. Struggle was familiar; I knew no alternative. In midlife, I have peaceful times. When I walk on the beach, my thoughts aren't constantly spinning; I actually see the birds flying overhead. Valuing myself, I needn't perform any feats to prove I am worthy. Although increased physical and psychological comfort would be welcome, I am content with what I have. My lesbianism is securely established. I needn't measure myself by the standards or expectations of others. Finally, I feel free.

Redefining Sexuality: Women Becoming Lesbian in Midlife

CLAUDETTE CHARBONNEAU
& PATRICIA SLADE LANDER

That a woman can spend half her adult life seeing herself as a heterosexual, marrying and bearing children, and then, in midlife, become a lesbian puzzles most observers and quite often the woman herself. Yet from rural Idaho to metropolitan New York, women are redefining their sexuality and becoming lesbians in midlife.

What are the social dynamics involved in this process of change? We will discuss this question in light of a survey of over 30 American women who had recently changed their sexual identity. Their experiences challenge the common assumption that sexuality is "set" at an early stage of the life cycle. They also illuminate the social context which was supportive to their redefinition of the lesbian stereotype and their own sexuality.

We interviewed women who ranged in age from mid-thirties to mid-fifties and were of varied ethnic, religious and class backgrounds. A third had grown up in working-class families; the rest had come from middle- and upper middle-class homes. Twenty percent were African-American or Caribbean-American. The remainder described themselves as coming from mostly European ancestry. Each woman gave her own version of her transition from heterosexuality to lesbianism in a lengthy first interview and then responded in a second, and sometimes third, interview to a series of questions dealing with her former images of lesbians and shifts in those images, her political and social activities, her support groups and sources of conflict in her married and lesbian life.

All the women we interviewed had accepted the traditional definitions of woman's "proper" role as that of marriage and motherhood. All except one (and she had six children and had been engaged three times) had been married for periods ranging from 1 to 32 years. Over half (seventeen) had remained in long marriages of ten years or more. All have since left their husbands. All but six were mothers; several had large families of four, five and six children, but most had two or three children. Of the six who had no children, four had tried unsuccessfully to conceive.

Until a series of events led them to ask themselves why they were heterosexual, these women, with few exceptions, had never even considered the possibility that they could be lesbians—they had never questioned the assumption of heterosexuality. Our informants, then, are not those who considered themselves bisexual or lesbian and who chose to marry either to try to change or hide their sexual preference. Many were initially quite surprised to find that they had fallen in love with a woman or were sexually drawn to other women, and even more surprised that they were willing to embrace the label "lesbian."

Our informants' most consistent history of any willingness to challenge the status quo was political. Many had had active commitments to social change in the past. Twenty of the 30 women had participated in political work, running the gamut from mainstream organizations like the local PTA or League of Women Voters, to electoral campaigns and voter registration drives, to membership in more radical groups like Women Strike for Peace and participation in anti-war demonstrations. Only two of the 30 informants had no experience in politics.

Because they had a history of protest behind them, some of the women were accustomed to seeing themselves, and to being seen, as outsiders. As one put it: "In terms of can I live with the social sanctions and all that stuff included in the word 'lesbian,' that was not an issue for me. I have been a political pariah for a long time."

This history of political activism, however, must be seen in light of the fact that in the past most of our informants had been primarily absorbed in their roles as wives and mothers. For some, the demonstrations had to be squeezed in between dressing three kids for school and getting the car fixed. One woman, whose involvement in civil rights was expressed by her being a foster mother for two teenagers from the South, reminded us that the first years of her marriage were "like getting the ring on the merry-go-round." Another woman's commitment to racial equality was demonstrated in the fact that she (like seven others) had married a man of a different racial background from her own. She told us: "I used to sit in the park in the morning. My main thrust was to get the breakfast out of the way and think about what I was going to have for dinner, and to get the kids dressed and out in the park to be with other women, to sit there and see what it was like talking to adults. And all we ever talked about was our children! I didn't care what was going on in the larger world, only whether my child was even thinking about going to the toilet."

When she changed her sexual identity, each woman was confronted by a social situation in which she was the "new lesbian" and, to many "old gays," not necessarily an "authentic" one. For all, the change was enormous. Having lived their lives as heterosexuals, they all underwent a radical reorientation and redirection. Whether the major catalyst was the sudden enlightenment of a political analysis or a special encounter with a particular woman, the reversal of years of habit was momentous.

Almost all the women remembered—often with precise dates and much detail—specific events that framed the change. The shift in sexual self-identity was so dramatic that the steps stood out in their minds. For each of the women, there was a confluence of events, none of which were causative but all of which provided a supportive context for change. The most important turning points the women mentioned include: serious illness; leaving a marriage and reevaluating expectations of relationships with men; periods of celibacy; the impact of the women's movement through reading specific books, attending consciousness-raising groups and/or specific conferences and cultural events; rethinking the lesbian stereotype.

Whether it was a conscious context or not, all of the women were in midlife, in a society whose popular culture was stressing this as a time for reassessment, a time to think about changing careers or changing partners (always assumed to be heterosexual, however) as the children grew up.

Like their midlife status, the women's movement provided a broad context for change by creating a climate in which women could ask questions and look at themselves from a different perspective. Half of the women did not specifically refer to the women's movement in their discussion of their transition from a heterosexual to a lesbian identity, nor did they have a history of involvement with feminism in their pre-lesbian days. But the other half had been actively involved in the women's movement in a variety of ways: seven had joined consciousness-raising groups; they and others had worked on particular issues like health, abortion, careers for women or violence toward women. For several, particular moments in a feminist environment served as a catalyst. One woman, who began a lesbian relationship in the fall of 1980, spoke of having been "totally exhilarated" by a Meg Christian concert attended mostly by women. One mentioned the impact of a feminist theater troupe; another, of participating in a Women's Studies meeting at her college.

Several of the women experienced an even more profound awareness of their place in the life cycle when they confronted the senility or death of a parent or a grave illness of their own. The realization that death and the transience of life are not vague philosophical abstractions, but concrete realities brought about a change in perspective. As one woman said after she had to "close up my mother's life": "I think any time you see a person of that time, whose life is coming to an end, who's been a vital person, you begin to look at your own life pretty carefully and decide what it is you feel you want to do with the remaining years you've got." At the time of her mother's illness, she was living with her husband of nineteen years and her two teenage children. Five years later she was living with a lesbian lover and the children were on their own.

In the United States, divorce has become an important rite of passage. Half of the women who volunteered to be interviewed had been divorced for several or even many years before their lesbian awakening and many cited this break—or the moment at which they thought of leaving the marriage—as a turning point. In two cases, the husband left the woman, but usually the wife had initiated the separation. The marriages of the fifteen divorced women ranged from 1 to 23 years (average 12.3 years). The two shortest marriages involved violent husbands, as did one marriage of 21 years. For the majority, their marital relationships had been nonviolent.

Leaving the marriage was rarely a casual turning point. The decision meant letting go of an important piece of ideology; these were women who had grown up believing in the sanctity of marriage and who had derived a strong sense of identity in fulfilling the traditional heterosexual role of wife and mother. As one woman stressed: "I mean, I considered myself married. I believed when you said 'I do,' it was forever. I was absolutely serious about that." Her friends and acquaintances had also thought of her and her husband as the ideal couple and she remembered their saying: "My God, if your marriage doesn't work, nobody's marriage is going to work."

For these women, separation and divorce were major turning points that allowed them to feel more independent and make various plans, though sometimes still with the thought of remarriage. "There was no question I took my first apartment after I was divorced with the notion that it would be big enough for somebody to move in, and certain expenses and jobs and everything were designed along the lines that within two or three years I would be married again—absolutely no question in my mind."

Most of the women, though, felt they had had enough of heterosexual marriage, but that did not mean they were ready to question heterosexuality. The period after divorce was usually a time for many affairs, sometimes combined with going to school. Eleven of the fifteen women who were divorced had a series of affairs or a second long-term relationship with a man. In most cases these affairs reaffirmed or even improved the woman's heterosexual self-image. One woman remembered that her sex life with her husband had been poor. "I just never experienced orgasm and I didn't know what was wrong." She assumed that any difficulties stemmed from her, since she had been a virgin at marriage and she had thought her husband was far more knowledgeable than he actually was. In her affairs after her divorce, she discovered that she could be sexual: "Each succeeding relationship was a little better. So I felt I was making some headway, things were getting better...."

Another woman described the period after her divorce as one which included sexual experimentation. The occasional presence of another woman in these situations did not lead to thoughts of lesbian alliances, however. In fact, she had walked into a consciousness-raising group a few years later "very clear that I was not a lesbian. It was okay, I knew all about it, I'd been through it...."

But she, and many of the other women, did, at some point, begin to worry about whether they could have meaningful relationships with men in the future. One woman told us that during her second major heterosexual commitment: "Maybe two years into that relationship, I told the man I lived with, I told my mother, I told my closest friends, 'Well, if this doesn't work, I'll never be involved with a man again.' But I never said that meant I would be a lesbian."

As they reached midlife, some of the women were forced to question what it was they had or still expected to have from a relationship with a man. One remembered consciously cutting back on her social life after a few years of actively relating to men because she was juggling three major commitments: work, mothering three children and going to school. Moreover, she noted that relationships with men seemed to have become problematic. Her situation as a single mother increased the distance between her and most men. "Our lives were just very far apart, we had nothing in common, it was creepy. And the older I got, the worse it got. I mean, basically they were okay. It was just like they were from another planet. Here I was, a single mother with three children, and no matter who they were, their lives were nowhere near where mine was."

Another woman spoke of how after an eleven year marriage, followed by six years of short- and long-term affairs, she settled down to an acceptance that her life, in some ways, would not be fulfilled: "I thought, well, maybe there is just no romance out here. Maybe I'm looking for something that really isn't there. I realized that there had never been a man in my life who had satisfied me, in any way, to the extent or depth that I wanted." Her readiness to acknowledge to herself that she no longer expected to find a fully satisfying relationship with a man and, in fact, had "stopped looking" was an important step. She went through a short period of celibacy, which was followed by her first lesbian involvement.

For at least half of the women, a period of detachment from men seems to have been a necessary prelude to their becoming lesbians. Although they did not always consciously define the period as a time of celibacy, many of the women who had been divorced had not been involved in sexual relationships for two months to several years before their first lesbian experience. Among the women who were still married and sharing the household with their husbands at the time they became lesbians, three had stopped conjugal relations for a short period before. The time apart was not necessarily a catalyst in itself; but it seems to have provided a space in which, consciously or not, the women reassessed their lives.

One woman cited this period of celibacy—which she had never experienced before—as a watershed: "For eight months I had no relationships. I was involved in going back to school and was really all turned on by life and was just having a dynamite time. Everything was good and I was like, 'Wow! There's no man in my life and I'm having a ball!' " The realization that she could be happy and productive without a man undid years of socialization; she was then in her mid-forties.

A third of the group mentioned the intellectual process of reading, and feminist texts in particular, as important turning points. Often they recalled specific books and details from those books with great clarity. One woman, for example, remembered having been disturbed by the isolation of the heterosexual heroine at the end of Marilyn French's *The Women's Room* and wishing for a better solution to women's lives. Another remembered discussing Betty Friedan while watching her children at a neighborhood playground in the 1960s and feeling, "What a revelation this is!"

Another woman cited as a major turning point going to her first all-women's weekend. She went with a neighbor, a housewife like herself, and realized "I guess we were two of about twenty straight women who were there—if there were that many—and the rest were lesbians. I'd never knowingly been with a lesbian before." Her reactions were not mixed with fear or ambivalence; they were totally positive. "I didn't say, 'Oh my God, what am I doing here or what have I done?' Everybody I talked with was wonderful and friendly and warm." She left the weekend telling herself, "I know I have to have more of this."

While there were unique configurations of events for each woman, one turning point was essential for each and every woman: the rewriting of the lesbian stereotype, whether this occurred as a slow process or as the result of one particular encounter. A theme that emerged from the interviews concerns the distorted view of lesbians with which all the women had grown up. Most of the women assumed that lesbians were so foreign that there could be no possible connection. The moment, then, at which each woman recognized a lesbian as less alien was significant. One woman recalled seeing a television program on homosexuality about six years before she became a lesbian and of being struck, at the time, with the parallels to her situation. As a young African-American, she had gone against the advice of her peers and married a white man. The kinds of things that were said about homosexuals rang a familiar bell. The outcries—What will the neighbors say? What will happen to the children?—had been said to her and she felt a sense of kinship.

Another woman was startled when her older sister, whom she had always admired and who was married like herself, became a lesbian. She went for a visit and found that she liked what she saw: she liked her sister's lover and she liked the living arrangements (both women had children and they were all residing together in a large apartment). Three years later, at age 43, after a 22 year marriage, she too became a lesbian.

One woman attended a reunion of former nuns and learned that several were lesbians; another heard of an acquaintance's college-age daughter being a gay rights activist and was intrigued; another knew that a co-worker she liked was beginning a lesbian relationship and this caused her to reexamine her own feelings.

One of the women, who was trying to recover from the breakup of her 23 year marriage, asked to be taken along by friends on a holiday weekend. On the drive up, her acquaintances seemed tense and ill at ease. Finally, they blurted out that there might be some lesbians at the resort and would she mind? Rather wryly, now, she remembers answering, "Oh, live and let live." She had never, as far as she knew, been near a lesbian. The friends then confided that they had become lesbians. She was amazed at this news and realized that her vision of reality had been extremely limited.

Another woman said that upon first meeting her lover she never thought the woman was a lesbian: "She didn't look gay to me. She was small and attractive. She was very feminine. And I discovered you don't have to dress up like a man. I didn't have to change; I could be myself."

Several women followed what we might call a "feminist path" to lesbianism, a pattern for "coming out" that has been known since the early days of the women's movement. For these women, becoming a lesbian was a direct and conscious outgrowth of their commitment to feminism. For them, lesbianism was a deliberate choice, the logical last step in the process of political analysis. As one said: "The arrival at being a lesbian was such an intellectual position for me. It was politically impeccable. It made sense." She was terrified, actually, before her first lesbian experience: "What if I go to bed with this woman and find it really terrible, then what am I going to do?" She felt there were no other options left. "Lesbianism seemed to be the only reasonable place for a woman who thought and felt the way I did. I had spent seventeen years dealing with men. It was enough."

For all the women, the change in self-identity and life style was profound, and all of them felt a need to explain the shift in some broad context. Some presented the shift as a process of self-discovery, which included feeling "for the first time I am me" or "the fog has lifted." Others talked of their shift as a choice, where there were other options: to be celibate, to be bisexual, or to remain heterosexual.

Those who felt they had always been lesbians but had not known it found their sexual experiences as lesbians immediately satisfying: "It was like being a balloon and just flying loose." "It was so natural." On the other hand, some who felt they had chosen lesbianism had more difficulty adjusting sexually: "I was very nervous and there was a time when I wasn't really sure that my sexuality wasn't more connected to men than to women, even though I loved her more."

There were also differences in their past heterosexual adaptations. To a great extent, the women who now look at the process as one of self-discovery had not been deeply involved in the sexual aspects of hetero-sexuality. They had longer marriages to one husband and very few or no affairs during their marriages. Nine of the sixteen who see themselves as having "discovered the lesbian within" were still married at the time they decided they might be lesbians. In contrast, only three who saw their process as one of "choice" were still married.

While married, the women who stressed self-discovery may have had complaints—about sexual, emotional, or financial relations with their husbands—but so did all of their friends. They had been committed to the idea of the nuclear family and motherhood and had put their energies into volunteer work, party politics and part-time jobs. One woman who felt that becoming a lesbian was like her "ship coming into harbor," told us how one day she had made a survey of her neighbors to see if their husbands were better lovers than hers and decided that in comparison with their stories she had no complaints. In contrast, when one of the women who spoke of choosing to become a lesbian found herself in a similar situation, she didn't survey her neighbors; she went out and had two heterosexual affairs for comparison.

On average, the women who spoke of choice had had more varied sexual experiences: they had had more affairs, with more men, before, during and after their marriages. While only one woman stated, "I became a lesbian because I hate men—period," it was clear that many of the "choice" women had been consciously looking for more egalitarian relationships in midlife or for new commitments to women's politics and women's culture.

The women who spoke of choosing to become lesbians have also tended to be more vocal about their new identity—to their former husbands, their children, parents and colleagues. One co-founded a large feminist enterprise; one is a feminist editor for a major publisher; one is a lesbian speaker on college campuses; one became a lesbian health expert and lesbian therapist; one has built a radical health practice stressing the healing power of women.

Those who feel they have "discovered" their lesbianism, which was always there, are not exactly in hiding. But with one or two exceptions they have been quieter and more cautious in their ongoing relations with the "straight" world of family and work.

This contrast in degree of openness between the women who have described their change from heterosexuality to lesbianism as a choice and those who see it as a process of self-discovery offers a sad commentary on the degree of homophobia in our social systems and cultural values. The power of choice has, to some extent, overcome the stigma of deviance, which still seems to cling in some subtle ways to those who see their core as always having been lesbian. But despite the differences in their presentation of self, both groups are startling confirmations of the potential for radical change in later stages of the life cycle.

(The data is based on interviews with volunteers recruited through major mailings, notices in newspapers and distribution of flyers in the metropolitan New York area between 1981-84. We would like to thank the women who volunteered to speak with us about such personal and important moments in their lives and who recognized the urgency of documenting the fact that women can change their sexual identity well into their maturity and after years of functioning successfully as heterosexuals. This project was supported by a grant from the City University of New York PSC-CUNY Research Award Program.)

First of All I'm Jewish, The Rest Is Commentary

ADRIENNE J. SMITH

So it is better to speak
remembering
we were never meant to survive.
—Audre Lorde, 1978

This is a personal story of a lifelong voyage toward lesbian and Jewish consciousness. My upbringing as a Jew was casual, to say the least. We did or did not go to a Reform Temple, depending on the weather, other commitments or sometimes just mood. We did or did not observe various holidays. In December we celebrated both Hanukkah and Christmas. I remember one year when there was a tree (an annual event) in the living room, a menorah in the dining room and a ham being prepared in the kitchen. At thirteen I was confirmed, not bat mitzvahed.

But the Jewishness seeped through. Not in rituals and religion; to this day I know almost no Hebrew and follow the prayers by mimicking others. It seeped through with German relatives who drifted through our house, refugees from Hitler (I realized later); with the unquestioned charity to those in need of a home, a meal or a job; with my father's hatred of Joe McCarthy combined with his pride that we lived in a country that allowed him to speak; with our support of the NAACP as well as the UJA.

The product of a German mother and a Russian father, both Jews, I also learned prejudice at home. My mother and her family never saw my father, an uneducated immigrant, as the equal of my American-born and college-educated mother. In attempting to identify with both, I learned how to be both oppressed and oppressor. Later that expanded to an awareness of myself as a member of a persecuted minority—Jewish—with a pride in special ability and sensitivity, also Jewish. The messages about my safety as a Jew were also mixed. I grew up in a Jewish family in a Jewish neighborhood and so was protected. At the same time, Hitler was rampaging through Europe and Israel did not yet exist. Thus, while I was comfortable and accepted locally, in the wider world we were everywhere in danger. I learned about the "we" as a Jew, not only internationally but historically. We were persecuted everywhere and had been for all time.

I learned early about being an invisible member of a minority. My name, together with my blonde hair and blue eyes, led to frequent assumptions that I was not Jewish. As an undergraduate in downstate Illinois, I was challenged to prove I was Jewish by a farm girl who had never seen a Jew before. Even when I worked for a rabbi, a surprised temple member who met me exclaimed, "I didn't know the temple hired non-Jewish workers." Despite the Mogen David I now wear, this assumption is still made.

My ability to "pass" allowed me to pursue graduate school and the subsequent building of a therapy career with little or no consciousness. Not only did I not concern myself with being Jewish and what that meant in a white, Christian and, frequently, anti-Semitic world, I did not deal with being lesbian. After fifteen years of living a closeted lesbian life I began, at age 38, to feel confined. Suddenly (although I think midlife changes only seem to be sudden) I needed to be known as an individual and as a lesbian. When I discovered feminism I came out—burst out is more accurate—as a feminist and shortly thereafter as a lesbian.

As I reached 40 and beyond, I sought out more understanding of my roots and greater identification as a Jew. I visited Israel, read books such as *World of Our Fathers* (sic!) and *Life is with People* and talked incessantly about being Jewish. As a middle-aged woman, my life focus has increasingly turned from career development to a desire to be part of a community and a tradition. Feminism, lesbianism and Jewishness, each in its own way, provides such community.

Not until I came out publicly as a lesbian did I become aware of just how much my Jewishness meant to me and for me. By acknowledging membership in a persecuted minority and by publicly espousing radical (feminist) ideas within my profession of psychology, the unspoken values and the world view I had absorbed as a Jew became increasingly salient.

The Jewish foundation of my activism comes from my sense of identity as a Jew and the emotional understandings and responses I have acquired as part of a cultural and ethnic group. The consciousness I developed as a member of one minority group has translated almost directly as I have recognized my membership in other minority groups.

One of my most basic identities as a Jew is a sense of sharing with an entire people, of being part of a community made up of millions of others no matter how scattered geographically. I have a deep sense of a tradition which includes all my ancestors and descendants. For Jews, this sense of connection is reinforced continually, perhaps most dramatically in the yearly Passover story which states "We were slaves in Egypt" (not "they," as part of the story explains). In less formal but no less pervasive a fashion, many Jews, in one way or another, respond to major news items with the fearful thought, "Is this good or bad for the Jews?"

While as a Jew, I always felt myself to be part of a community, my first consciousness of being a lesbian was of being different in a very negative and a very isolated manner. Since I became aware of my lesbianism quite a few years before the Stonewall "riot"—the event which sparked the current gay rights movement—the search for others like myself was furtive and frustrating. Where were my contemporaries? Who in history had been lesbian or homosexual? I read medical texts, sleazy novels and homophobic biographies. Aside from my lover, I knew only a handful of other lesbians and gay men. All of us lived in fear that the "wrong" people would find out. It was not until the birth of the gay rights movement that the "we" took shape and I had others with whom to interact openly.

Almost immediately I began to assess the costs and privileges of being visible. For me, the cost of continuing to hide my lesbianism after many years in the closet had simply become more than I could bear. The need to pass, to use cover stories or twist pronouns, to pretend to live a life I did not live and to not acknowledge the life I did live had begun to subvert my sense of identity as a human being and to undermine my worth as a person. I left my establishment job, came out publicly and almost instantly became involved in activist organizations.

After years of feeling isolated, the joy of again being part of a community propelled me into activism. As a Jew, the certain knowledge that I am part of a larger whole, that I am not alone even at my most lonely, that I can travel anywhere in the world and establish connection with other Jews has come to parallel the identical sense I now have that I am part of the larger lesbian and gay community.

After the major midlife change of coming out publicly I became increasingly active in various feminist and lesbian organizations. During the past several years and especially since turning 50, my activism has been focussed almost entirely within my profession of psychology, specifically in the lesbian/gay movement within the American Psychological Association. It is through my work with this group that I have become aware of the similarities between the lesbian/gay activist community and the Jewish community.

There are three elements that are part of what I call "the Jewish character" that are for me the same as elements of the "lesbian/gay activist character." The first of these is the one I have been emphasizing and which ꞏꞏꞏter to activism, that is, a deep sense of community, even of family, ꞏꞏꞏmbers of a group to see themselves as part of a larger ꞏntinuity of tradition and history. My Jewish sense that we ꞏle for each other and for the survival of our culture is reflected in the activist's awareness that we are working for each other and for the young people who will follow us. As lesbian activists we are very conscious that we must build our own "family" since frequently our families of origin have shut us out. This is much the same as the Jewish response of building our own communities after various nations denied us participation in their communal life.

The second similar element is a knowledge that we are working/fighting for our lives. To be a Jew or a lesbian/gay activist is to be aware that our freedom, our rights, our very existence is threatened constantly by enemies who see us as less than human. For any reason or for no reason whatever we can be deprived of our homes or our jobs. Our reputations can be attacked; indeed our very bodies can be subject to violent physical attack. Since our survival depends on the success of our work as activists, we work with incredible intensity and dedication. And, again like Jews, we monitor our world continually for indications of homophobia and respond immediately with as much strength as we can muster.

The third element, and the one without which none of us could continue to function, is the sheer joy, exuberance and sensuality of working within the lesbian/gay activist community in psychology. Eastern European Jews, with whose cultural tradition I identify, are frequently depicted as celebrating life and their ability to survive, as taking pleasure in whatever life offers and in finding the absurd even in difficult circumstances. Perhaps the most easily available expression of this approach to life is *Fiddler on the Roof* but any of Sholem Alecheim's stories or Marc Chagall's paintings also demonstrate it. In my experience of lesbian/gay activism there have been, from the beginning, marvelous combinations of seriousness and humor. The underlying structure of gay/lesbian life styles, and therefore activism, is the same as that of feminism, that is, the questioning of "standard" gender roles. In activism this translates into an ability to act playfully, to deal with sex, gender and social norms humorously. No one is expected to "act like a lady" or to be "a real man." Much of this humor is of the type known as "gender-bending": some of it is designed to unsettle the assumptions of masculine and feminine behavior of our more "establishment" colleagues.

Within our lesbian/gay activist group, both women and men are free to hug, to share feelings, to cry together and laugh together, to act assertively or empathetically and, not least, (with thanks to Emma Goldman) to dance together.

As I look back on this journey of self-discovery I realize that coming out as a lesbian, one of my major midlife changes, was in large part the stimulus to coming out as a Jew. Gay pride, the result of reclaiming a stigmatized identity and redefining oneself, has led to Jewish pride so that over time I have embraced all my identities. As I became aware of the almost universal heterosexual assumptions of our society, I also became aware of its equally pervasive "Christian" assumptions. This assumption of commonality with the dominant culture not only denies identity to the individual but denies uniqueness to the group and culture as well. Redefining this uniqueness as an enriching heritage rather than a despised difference, celebrating my identity as a member of an outsider culture, means celebrating the survival of a group that was, as Audre Lorde said, "never meant to survive."

(This paper was excerpted from an article originally published in *Women and Therapy*.)

Coming Out as a Native American

LEOTA LONE DOG
as interviewed by BARBARA SANG

The thing that is unique to my midlife experience is I feel like I've come out as a Native American. By that I mean that when I came out into the gay community, I worked in that community on issues for lesbians— fighting for our rights, lesbian mothering, custody issues. But in the back was also being Indian. That took a back seat.

I grew up in Manhattan and Brooklyn, except for about five years in California when I was very young. I'm 42 now.

I was raised in mostly white communities. The racism was intense. I even felt racism for the other races who weren't present. I was it in that community.

My mother was fairly traditional in her spiritual beliefs and my grandmother reinforced a lot about being Indian. We listened to Native American music; my mother wore braids and a band. I didn't, I hated it. I didn't want to be noticed. I didn't want to be attacked. But I can't run anymore. I have to deal with this aspect of my life.

There's a lot of fear about coming out in our Native American community. It just wasn't politically correct to be gay or lesbian when Wounded Knee or Alcatraz were going on. It was bad enough to be Indian in New York—that was lonely enough. But to be gay and Indian, I asked myself "Where would I ever find another one?"

But you have to deal with yourself and the forces of nature and acknowledge that. Once I came out, I haven't backed down. Either accept me on those terms or don't accept me. I had known I was a lesbian since I was eight and had lived in the closet. By the time I was 25, I had had enough. I had to come out and there was no way I was going back. But I'm still afraid each time I have to come out. If we ever march as a group in the Gay Pride Parade, I know they'll be taking pictures because there's a group of Indians and I'm afraid for my job. I don't want to have to address that at my job.

My job is with the phone company. It's all male; I'm the only woman manager in my department. It's really a totally different world. I have to stop the people who work for me every time I hear something racist coming out of their mouths. I can't be afraid that they might be offended. I'm offended! I've gotten more assertive as I've gotten older and I don't let people slide. If I feel that I'm the butt of a joke, I'm not laughing anymore. I guess it's also because I don't feel so alone in my identity.

When I found Salsa Soul, a Third World organization, I thought maybe I'd found company. But it was more a Black women's thing; the other ethnic groups came and they went, they came and they went.

In the lesbian and women's groups I've worked on in New York City—Kitchen Table Press, Salsa Soul, Third World Women, other organizations—I've almost always been the only Indian. But while working at Kitchen Table Press I met Chrystos and Beth Brant and we started to communicate. That's the first communication I had with any Native American lesbians.

For so long I just wanted to assimilate somewhere. But there was always something deeper inside that and once I started meeting Native American lesbians I felt like I was in a glass cage and I had to get out. At some point I realized that more than my being a lesbian, I had to deal with being Indian, with my internalized self-hatred of being a Native American and my stereotypes of being a Native American. I wanted to find the pride, but I didn't quite know how I was to get that.

In the gay community, they wanted it in the background. "Oh, we feel you're one of us," they'd say. But I wasn't. Because even though I wanted to be able to be "one of them," I kept wanting to be acknowledged for who I *really* was.

In '87 at the March for AIDS in Washington, there was a group of us gay Native Americans who got together and talked about having a gathering which then took place in '88 in Minneapolis. It's important just to know there's a support system, especially for a lot of brothers and sisters who are on the reserves and very isolated, who are afraid to come out. If they do come out, now they'll have some place to go.

I feel like a minority within a minority in the gay community. You're in a subculture. In the Indian community you feel like you're in a sub-subculture. And the paths of the gay community and the Indian community don't even cross. I don't want that separation, I want all of it together.

Here in New York City at the Community House, homophobia is rampant among the Indians. But I find that although someone may be very homophobic, we're still very close as Indians. So there's a duality there. If you don't talk about being gay or lesbian and you're being Indian, it's another thing. A couple of us have been trying to have gay meetings at the Community House, but I think people will be too afraid to come.

I have not had a lover for two years and it's good because I haven't learned how to live my life and have a lover at the same time. So this is my choice, though I never thought I would choose it and be happy with it. A relationship doesn't have to be confining, but I haven't found a way *not* to have it confining. I tend to take a back seat or make a lot of concessions and compromises. I'm learning that I don't have to do all those things. Not that compromise isn't needed to make a relationship work.

Right now I don't want to process anything with anybody in a relationship. I'm on the other end of the spectrum and I'm sure I'll swing back to the middle, but right now I'm very happy to just do whatever it is I want to do.

That freedom is probably the biggest thing that has happened in my life. I've never been secure enough before to want to be on my own, but it's been wonderful. I have women that I see, there are people that I see, so I'm not totally alone or isolated. At the same time, another part of me is thinking about whether or not I want to spend the rest of my life without a partner. I don't know if I have to make that decision for the rest of my life. I know for the fun that I'm having, I don't know if I want to.

I'm having resistance to midlife. I'm not ready for it yet. I was okay when I reached 40. I was fine. Forty and a half, I freaked out.

I was in the mirror looking for the gray hairs, looking for the wrinkles, looking at my body. I guess I expected this deterioration to be instantaneous. It was vanity, because really I wasn't worried about anything else because the rest of my life is exciting. I don't feel the constraints. Now I'm 40 I can do whatever I want to do. I'm not worried about what this one says, or that one; it's breaking me out of my shell.

On the other hand I'm worried about the physical limitations, like not being able to walk as fast as I wanted to walk, or run like I used to run, or my eyesight going. I can't see so well the things that are up close anymore. But I wouldn't ever want to go through the trauma of being 20 or 30 again. That was horrible and depressing. Now I feel much more sure of myself.

Another midlife change—a pretty big one—is my daughter growing up. I felt very alone. I was excited about not having the responsibility, but I had been a mother for so long.... And being a single mother, we were definitely a family unit—just her and I, always. Now to see her going off and having to make her own mistakes.... I guess any mother feels this. There's nothing you can do about them making their own mistakes.

My husband was Black, so my daughter is Black and Native American. She identified a lot more strongly with her Black identity. I think the reason is there are a lot more Blacks. Even now, at her school (University of Massachusetts) there's a Native American community, but it's very, very small. The Black community at school is the one that she identifies with. But not totally, because I think she's now in the process of investigating her Native American self. On campus they do have an association and they do have an annual powwow in Amherst. And she's a part of that.

The stereotypes about Indian people are very strong and very negative. It's what you see whenever there are depictions of Native Americans: the savagery, the poverty, the drinking, the drugs. Nothing about Indians gets depicted as formidable. If anybody says, "Indian," the immediate response is "woo-woo-woo-woo," and somebody starts jumping around. It's blatant, like the commercials you see on television all the time, or Morton Downey coming on this show with an arrow in his head, one of those gag things. If the same type of things were done to depict Blacks or Jews, forget it. But it's not the same way with Indians. There are things happening now, like the Native American Dance Theater, that are beautiful. But in general, the racism is constant and you have to be ready to fight it on all levels.

I'm real excited that my niece, who is eleven now, is so excited about going to powwows and that she has decided she wants to dance. Last year we went to one, where there was a woman with beautiful regalias, beaded regalias. She was just gorgeous. My niece said, "I have to meet this woman, I have to know who she is," So she got introduced. And now my niece wants to dance. That's so exciting for her. She's so strong in her identity; she's right out there with it. Kids make fun of her in school, call her all kinds of names, and she says, "I don't care, I'm Indian and if you don't like it, it's too bad." Such strength! I hope it's because of me and my mother and that support system.

I see myself as having been the opposite of her. Sad as I am to say it, I was hiding. I didn't want to really be Indian. Yet much as I wanted to reject my culture and ignore it, it has always been there in the teachings of my mother and my grandmother. My mother's mother. (My mother doesn't like me to say "grandmother.") It's always been there for me, so I have been rediscovering it.

My mother's extremely excited about all this. She had not been to a powwow for many years. When she came to live with me, I started taking her to the powwows again. She says, "I feel like I'm in another land when I go to these powwows," and it's true. It's not like going to a street fair or something like that. There's so much more going on. It makes me feel good to see this happening with her and I can see she's very happy about what's happening with me.

I sundanced, year before last out in South Dakota, and I plan to do it this year. It's a four-day ritual of prayers and learning—a way of life. I had been to a couple of sundances as a spectator and you're always a part of it, even if you're in the arbor and not dancing. But to be one of the dancers is a very humbling, moving, sad experience.

I was also trying to deal with some issues that were coming up around my father who I hadn't seen since I was eight. He lived in South Dakota and just passed away last year. When I was first dancing out there, one of my wishes was that he would come there to see me. He didn't come there, but each time you dance, you dance to a certain direction and there are lessons to be taught in each of those directions. The direction that I dance in, I learned a lot, but I also realized I had a lot to learn. There's not a limit on how many times you can dance. I could dance for years and years and I would be learning more and more.

Transforming Loss

Of Essences

DOLORES KLAICH

Jane Chambers, dead at forty-five of brain cancer.

The *New York Times* headline, February 17, 1983, read: "Jane Chambers Dead; Won Awards for Plays."

In the text of the obituary, the fact that much of Jane's playwriting had been concerned with lesbian issues was nowhere mentioned and the fact that she was survived by Beth Allen, her lover of fourteen years, was nowhere cited. Both of these fundamental truths about Jane had been edited out of the press release sent to the *Times*. For the record, Jane Chambers's essence never existed.

It was damp and cold that February day, a funeral day. Two hours east of New York City we approached the village of Southold, New York, a conservative Suffolk County settlement on Long Island's North Shore. This was farm country. Potato fields stretched, frozen, and vineyards, the grapevines looking fragile against the rough winter landscape, came into view. Traveling as we were toward a recognition of death, the vineyards, a new enterprise planted to save the farmland from developers, to make the land pay so as not to be destroyed, loomed symbolically.

I had tasted the fruit of the first of the vineyards at a wine-tasting benefit party held to raise monies for the library in the South Shore village of Bridgehampton. We, the East End Gay Organization for Human Rights (EEGO), had donated to the library a specially bound edition of one of Jane's plays. It was given in memory of Linda Leibman, who had lived in Bridgehampton and had been active in local politics. Linda, a founder of EEGO, and one of my closest friends, died at the age of thirty-nine. She too had cancer. Jane had come to the South Shore to Linda's funeral. Now I was going North to hers. Thirty-nine, forty-five. Such early deaths.

As we entered Southold, the church was unmistakable—tiny, plain, beautifully wooden white, a little lopsided with age—with a parking lot three times its size where already, early, cars were arriving. For the most part the cars were full of women. There were some men, some nuclear male-female families, but mostly women, carload after carload. Inside, I found close friends with whom to sit.

I had heard the news of Jane's death while in New York and had driven out from the city with a young woman, a stranger. She had been a recent acquaintance of Jane's; she had interviewed Jane and the cast of one of her plays for a radio show she hosts on a local New York station. The young woman had talked non-stop during our two-hour trip, her life story tumbling out in an amphetamine-like rush. It had been good, the way she had filled my silences. She was so alive at twenty-five. She was so openly lesbian: "Yes," she had said, "everyone at the radio station knows. I feel no need to hide. What do they think? I think they're curious."

We who were gathered in the church were mostly of a certain age. We had been through the closeted family wars: weddings where our lovers came disguised as best friends; graduations, bar mitzvahs, christenings, holidays. Funerals. Through the years these social verities had offered no honest place for most of us. At the best of times it had been awkward, at the worst, tragic. We had learned to play society's closeted game; we had endured and we had survived. So many of our friends had not. Excited, direct, my young passenger came with no such dissembling baggage.

Then, there were Lucille Field and Patsy Rogers at the piano, Lucille singing one of Patsy's songs. In the front pew sat Beth Allen, Jane's lover. Next to Beth was Jane's mother, Clarice, a deep Georgia woman with the accent of many of Jane's plays. Clear-eyed, erect, salt of the American earth, Clarice sat with her arm around Beth, a strong presence. Next to Clarice were a row of caretakers, the women friends who had seen Jane through her dying. In front of me sat Dolores Alexander and Jill Ward who, in the heady feminist '70s, had opened Mother Courage, the first women's movement restaurant in New York. Dolores had been one of the women who, in Betty Friedan's kitchen, had helped to establish the National Organization for Women. A few years later she had been purged from NOW for being lesbian, which she wasn't, at that time. To my left sat a friend, a psychiatrist, long a force in the American Psychiatric Association, and, in recent years, a spokesperson for that organization's Committee on Gay, Lesbian, and Bisexual Issues. Next to me sat Irene Gould, a survivor of Nazi Germany, now an officer of the East End Gay Organization for Human Rights. Next to Irene sat Chuck Hitchcock, a professor at a local college, disowned by his family because he is gay. David Wilt, his lover of many years, was down front, a pallbearer. And on. Survivors, all of us.

Then, the faces I did not recognize—parishioners. Jane was a member of this Unitarian church. During the service, the parishioners would join in sharing spoken memories of her. Three of them would play, scratchily but movingly, a Bach violin concerto.

The minister rose, a young woman with an Afro-like hairdo. She spoke of parishioner Jane, she who had sung the hymns too loudly—slightly off-key. The Reverend Sara Campbell stressed the devotion and caring of Beth, whom she called Jane's life companion; she saluted the core of women who had helped Jane through her dying; she honored Jane's social consciousness work on behalf of women, blacks, lesbians, pausing after she said lesbians, the word causing a terrific silence in the church. In a church, at a funeral, in a conservative Suffolk County, New York small town. Granted, the church *was* Unitarian. Nonetheless, tears came. This was not a lesbians and gays-only memorial service held in some closeted environment which, until recently, had been the only way we could mourn honestly.

There were hymns, John Denver's "Country Roads," an eerily beautiful a cappella chant called "Simple Ceremonies" about a Native American woman who was a healer. Prayers, meditation. During the sharing of memories a young woman, an actress from one of Jane's plays, rose and said Jane had introduced her to her lover, who sat next to her and stood to read a poem she had written for Jane. Others rose—lesbians, gays, straights: mourners. Then, near the close, another actress, a close friend of Jane's, read Lil's goodbye speech from Jane's play *Last Summer at Bluefish Cove*—Lil, who was dying of cancer. Last came the ringing of the church bell, led by survivor Beth, followed by Clarice, and rung by all of us as we exited the church.

Later, at a small cemetery we stood stunned. It had been an extraordinarily moving service, a service of grace. In awe we said to one another: Ten years ago this never could have been. Jane's was an honest funeral. There had not been one hypocritical word or gesture. Good God, I thought, a real lesbian funeral, a funeral of a woman who was, among many things, lesbian, and so acknowledged. The normalcy of that.

Jane, knowing she was to die, had planned her exit. The honesty with which she had lived her lesbianism in her last productive years continued with her death. So many of us remembered the isolated dying and deaths of friends and lovers through the years—those years when most of us hid our loving, required to be dishonest for the sake of...of what, decorum? Good God! We thought of how those friends and lovers had been shipped off without us to family burial grounds for ritualistic burials and eulogies that had little to do with the essence of their lives, how we had endured the pain of that, suffered the humiliation, internalized our grief and mourning. The toll of that.

Jane Chambers, New York City playwright, daughter of the deep South, with her lover Beth Allen, had set down roots in a small town on the North Shore of eastern Long Island. There, she practiced her art, living a full, honest life, integrated into the community, nudging it when prejudices reared. As I threw my handful of dirt onto Jane's casket, words of Adrienne Rich, which I had read at my friend Linda's funeral the year before, came to mind: "When a woman tells the truth, she is creating the possibility for more truth around her."

Crisis of Loss

SUSAN S. TURNER

My lover of eleven years left last month; suddenly I have an acute case of midlife. I expected a midlife confrontation to be chronic in its symptoms. You know, to sort of creep up on me. Chronic would be the unexpected telltale signs that remind you of the passage of time: the twenty-year-old lesbian next door just discovers Chris Williamson at album number twelve when you remember buying *The Changer & The Changed;* or your lesbian support group that started with ten women in a dark, old room above a broken-down theater now holds dances for a hundred at the local YWCA.

But an acute case is the crashing-in knowledge that you are no longer young; that you are halfway through your life and it is moving along steadily. It is the sudden and painful awareness of your own mortality: a friend is diagnosed with cancer; your child leaves home; or for me, a lover with whom you expected to grow old and live with forever, only lose to death, leaves.

I had inklings of impending midlife before my lover left. As a woman with a disability, the result of childhood polio with all of its ongoing medical considerations, I have always been aware of my own mortality. And as a disabled woman I have always dealt with issues about my body—physical limitations, physical changes, body image. For disabled women the aging process is felt sooner than for non-disabled women, since the non-paralyzed parts do double work for the paralyzed parts. Because the remaining senses work overtime to compensate for a lost sense, as in blindness; or the body requires triple-time energy to battle the regular fatigue of multiple sclerosis, we are more aware of and sensitive to the slightest changes that come with the passing years. Maybe the daily double load taxing our disabled bodies actually accelerates our aging process. But because of this, aging may be more familiar for me than for an able-bodied woman who first encounters those changes. Since body changes for us are expected and usual phenomena, disabled women are sometimes less tolerant of able-bodied women's concerns about those changes, forgetting how new it is for them.

Before I was 40, probably at 35, I was already aware that I was not as physically strong as I was at 30. At the 1978 march on Washington for the ERA, I walked the one and a half miles with my usual crutches and braces. In the 1989 march on Washington for women's right to choose safe and legal abortion, I rolled in my new sport wheelchair. Dealing with my decreased strength and increasingly aching joints stirred up old issues about disability. I dealt again with feelings of loss but these seemed connected to disability. I did not connect them with midlife or aging. Yes, I need to go to bed earlier now at age 43. It frustrated my lover, but she understood—or did she? She left. I began to question the changes in my body that brought changes in my life style.

I realized how I hadn't really had to think about it because she knew me "when." She knew me when I could walk in civil rights marches and still stay up all night making love. She knew me when I worked two jobs, mothered my son, led a lesbian support group of 500 and did my own housework. She knew me when I was a "super crip." She knew me when I was my version of an Amazon.

To be disabled and discover (finally!) at age 30 that I was lesbian was wonderful. For the first time my huge biceps from crutch-walking since the age of six, that I had always hidden because they were "unfeminine," were now admired. The strength and ruggedness of my hands were commented upon positively now. For the first time in my life, the fact that my body didn't fit the patriarchal stereotype of beautiful didn't matter. What a liberating feeling! Being a lesbian helped me to come to love my own body.

Yet could I truly be an Amazon? The Amazon model of a lesbian is athletically strong, active and fiercely independent. Dykes go hiking. Dykes play softball. Dykes are tough. Dykes make it on their own. Dykes don't need to be carried to the bathroom in the middle of the night, as I do when I don't have my braces on.

The inkling of midlife was there before my lover left, as I noticed the changes in my body. But her leaving made it acute. It made me single again, alone again in the lesbian community, aware more of my differentness in the very midst of a maturity that lets me value my uniqueness. Being in a couple in the lesbian community defined me as sexual and made me less "different." As a 30-year-old lesbian, I had the strength and energy to compensate by being outrageously seductive.

And so I am single again and the women I meet won't have known me when…. Yes, I feel comfortable generally as a disabled woman in the lesbian community because my sisters have reached out with loving arms— at least emotionally, if not always physically. For lesbians too, just like the rest of society, often don't enter into intimate physical relationships with disabled women because of their own discomfort. Actually, it is probably a lack of knowledge that breeds a lack of understanding and misconceptions. And those misconceptions and uncomfortable feelings often come from able-bodied people's own fears of dependency and powerlessness—which their fantasies link with disability. For a midlife woman, a disabled woman may stir up even more of the able-bodied woman's fears about the changes in her own body, changes that don't fit that woman's own version of Amazon for herself.

So now I notice the blond hairs that have turned white and the lines around my smile and the crinkles around my eyes.

Years ago I remember saying that it was easy to be an "out" lesbian. I had already had lots of practice being different, growing up disabled. You can't be a "closet" cripple, I'd laugh. And yet, in reality, to be either disabled or lesbian is to be one step from the "norm"; to be both, puts you two steps away. At times it is wonderful to not have to conform to the mainstream. At other times, it is downright problematic. And so I begin to realize that being old in addition to being disabled and lesbian will put me three steps further away from the "norm," whatever that is.

I also feel midlife now when I look at my eighteen-year-old son. The breakup brought a reorganizing of our family and our household. It is a natural time developmentally and logistically for my son to contemplate venturing out on his own—and time for us to let go of him. I feel the loss as women often do in midlife when their mother role changes significantly as their children become adults. But I really don't want to let go. I have begun to realize how often I have sprinkled my conversations with anecdotes of my son this, my son that, of his everyday doings. I always let people know that I am a mother, that he was my son, not my lover's. Oh dear, I begin to question what this says about me psychologically as a disabled woman, and politically as a lesbian. Because if the truth be told, I have a special investment, I suspect, in my son making me "normal." He is what gives me validation in the heterosexual able-bodied world as a sexual being.

Moving out from my lover's and my shared home brought some midlife financial realities. Aren't Amazons self- sufficient? But the concrete realities of being a disabled midlife lesbian shout out to me as I think of future financial security—the lack thereof, I mean.

Women in their forties and fifties, especially middle-class women, often begin to question if they have been successful in their work: is it what they expected, what have they accomplished? Compared to our mothers and grandmothers, my generation had the world opened up to us. That is, my generation of able-bodied women. Women at this age also may ask themselves what have they produced/created that will follow after them? Women with children, lesbian and straight, may find that children satisfy this question. But for me, as a disabled woman, I am not questioning. I am still rejoicing on some level at being in a career at all. It is a known fact that disabled people, especially women, are not encouraged to pursue higher education and careers. Many state vocational rehabilitation programs still consider "homemaker" a career goal for far too many disabled women (and never for disabled men!). As disabled women we come to work or career success later, if at all, compared to non-disabled women.

There's an attorney whose path I have crossed both in the disabled community and the lesbian community over the years. Once I began to think of midlife issues I was eager to track her down and talk to her as one of the few midlife disabled lesbians I had met. She had been a successful attorney heading a civil rights organization ten years ago. I did track her down and was shocked to find out that not only was she not my age but was not yet 35! It is so rare for disabled women to be so far along in their careers so early, I just couldn't believe it. She agreed she was the exception to the rule. Disabled women are unemployed and underemployed. Studies show that able-bodied white women earn 74 cents for every dollar earned by able-bodied white males, while disabled white women earn 33 cents for every dollar. Disabled black women earn thirteen cents. To be lesbian risks further discrimination. To be old, even more employment insecurity.

On top of that is the dilemma of health care. Lesbians do not have the heterosexual privilege of being covered by a partner's health insurance. Being underemployed limits your ability to afford health care and having a previous disability sometimes makes it impossible to get health care coverage at all. Too often disabled women face a painful decision whether or not to pursue a career or job when the income means they will lose the Medicaid that pays for the orthopedist's next office visit or buys the new $1,500 wheelchair.

Losing my lover was felt acutely in another way. I am afraid of ending up in a nursing home. That is not entirely unique to being disabled or lesbian, except that already being disabled I am at greater risk of needing total care sooner in my life than other people. Being single, as the majority of disabled women are—lesbian or straight—I have less family to take care of me. Another scary part is the denial of disabled people's sexuality in general. I fear losing a piece of who I am, isolated in an institution.

I have a dream and a belief: the wonderful part about being a disabled lesbian of 43 years is that by the time I need it maybe my lesbian sisters and I will have created feminist environments in which to live collectively and cooperatively as we grow old together, sharing our abilities and disabilities.

So, yes, now I notice my wrinkles and beginning gray hair and have debates in my head again for the first time since I was an adolescent about what it is to be "normal." I have flashes of fear about being alone. But mostly, I am just sad that my lover who helped me grow so well to midlife has left. I am not sad that I am disabled. This body is who I am. I'd be someone different if it weren't for this disability and I like who I am. Being disabled is the part of who I am, I believe, that understands and relishes difference. It is the part of me that has also taught me what are the important things in life.

And I am not sad that I am lesbian—loving women is the part of my life that brings me the greatest joy. And I am not sad to be 43. Sitting squarely in the middle of my life, I can see from where I've come and what I have survived that all those parts of me are integrated into the whole of who I am, physically, emotionally, spiritually.

Maybe that's an Amazon.

Eldercare as a Feminist Issue

JOYCE WARSHOW

My relationship with my mother became authentic when she was 78 years old and I was 38. Before that I was too afraid to be close, or to express too much affection, for fear of being taken over by her emotional draw on me or my need of her. It had been hard to differentiate who needed what from whom.

The pattern that evolved was as follows; she made it known, usually indirectly, that she needed something from me. Because she didn't feel she had the right to ask, her message was never clear. It could be a hurt look when, at twenty, soon after my father's death, I was about to go out with my friends. Or it could be some implicit request embedded in the denial of wanting or needing anything.

I was never sure what was being asked, but I responded to the implicit demand with explicit anger. "Tell me what you want? Nothing I do seems to be enough." My expression of anger led to feelings of guilt. Why had I been so adamant in my rejection of her wishes? I would compensate by doing too much, which in turn made me feel resentful, and so the cycle continued.

After working in therapy on this issue, I learned to ask my mother exactly what she was requesting so that I could then ask myself if I could meet the request without feeling pulled out of myself. I no longer felt that her wish was my command, as though there were no difference between us. Because I was no longer so overly identified with her that her condition felt like mine, I could be more supportive. She no longer "made me sick."

Things really turned around when my psychotherapy group challenged me to "come out" to my mother. I said that she was getting a little senile and couldn't possibly deal with it. Soon after, she was invited to a family affair in San Francisco. Because she was starting to be a little forgetful and disorganized, she couldn't make the trip on her own. I rearranged my schedule so that I could accompany her. In some ways this journey was like a spiritual pilgrimage. We looked at ancient trees in the redwood forest which seemed to give assurance of continuity; at the Asian Art Museum in Golden Gate Park we looked at the bodhisattvas with their infinite smiles.

Somehow I felt encouraged to take the risk and really talk to her rather than continue to maintain a stance I had developed of being remote but benign.

I told her that if she wanted to be close that she would have to know who I am. I told her about my life and my lover. Her response was a great gift. She said "If you're going to live with a woman there might as well be sex." I couldn't believe it. My own ageism and feelings of superiority for being American-born made me think this could not have come from her because she was 78 years old and an immigrant. I asked her if she was disappointed that I hadn't given her a grandchild. She said that she had been disappointed when my marriage didn't work out but that she thought I had a wonderful life, and that I did good work and she liked my friends.

From then on my connection with her was authentic rather than perfunctory. It was less obligatory and more pleasurable to be with her. In fact, the neurotic interchanges were ended on that trip as well. In the past, my mother's denial of her needs and her rejection of anything given to her evoked annoyance in me. At the end of this trip we needed to buy a tube of toothpaste. When it was time to leave I suggested she take it home. Her response was, "What am I going to do with a whole tube of toothpaste?" Instead of getting annoyed, I said, "Okay, I'll squeeze half of it out and then you can take it home." We both laughed and that was the end of that style of interchange.

After this trip my mother began to fail. She started visiting a nearby senior citizen's hotel to "try it out." She was losing interest in cooking even though my brothers and I shopped for her weekly. After several attempts at home health care failed, she finally chose to give up her apartment and move into the hotel.

The hotel was a cheerful place with lots of activities in which she participated and which she seemed to enjoy. Her only complaint was that she wanted to do more for herself, "like wash a floor." When she came to my home for Chanukah, she was so happy to peel potatoes for latkes that I was afraid I would run out of them before she had her fill.

Her sense of humor remained intact even when her short-term memory failed. Once when I helped her dress for a family occasion I told her, imitating an uncle of mine, that she looked like a million dollars. Her response was "I think I owe you some change." The day after her joyous special 80th birthday party with 50 relatives and friends, dinner and dancing, she forgot that it had taken place. When I showed her pictures of the event, she didn't recognize the "old woman."

A year later, the hotel told us that she needed more supervision than they could provide. A hospital stay and a problem with incontinence made her eligible for a nursing home. She was admitted to the Jewish Home and Hospital for the Aged, which we had decided on after much searching to find a placement where the food and customs would be familiar and where the staff was committed to advocacy for the aged.

During the nursing home interview, she was asked many questions most of which she could not answer. When she was asked where she had spent the previous night (she had spent it at my home) she replied, "Do I have to tell you everything?" Her "cloak of competence" seemed to protect her from the shame of not knowing, but afterwards she asked me, "What has become of me? Is this why I went to school for all those years, just to become stupid?"

At the home she made friends, got involved in activities and seemed genuinely happy to see us during visits. Gradually she needed more and more assistance in getting to activities. She didn't remember what she had done during the day. As her memory loss worsened, a major way we had of communicating was to sing together. She sang Russian songs as well as the Yiddish and Hebrew songs she had taught me. People would gather in her room and sing with us.

When my mother forgot how to hold the telephone, her 96-year-old roommate helped her, but asked her if it was because she was a "greenhorn" that she was having difficulty. Although my mother didn't remember such details, she continued to relate to me with her usual intuition and wisdom. She remained one of the people with whom I most enjoyed speaking.

During this time I was considering having a child through alternative insemination. When I spoke to my mother about it she was surprised that I had not done it before but said, "If that's what you've decided, you should do it fast, because it's not always possible just when you want it." She then proceeded to tell me that having children was a wonderful experience for her and she hoped that it would be possible for me, if that's what I wanted.

During one of my visits she told me that she was very disappointed in herself because she had wanted to do something with her life. Although I tried to assure her that she had by having children and working for something she believed in, she felt it wasn't enough and that it was difficult when you "always have to be home to feed the family."

Soon after, she broke her hip and had to be hospitalized. Subsequently she was had to use a wheelchair. Her incontinence worsened when she was given "Attends" (large diapers for adults) and told to eliminate in them between scheduled "evacuations" (trips to the bathroom). While this was not the official policy of the Home, it was a frequent practice when there was a shortage of staff. She was highly distressed with these restrictions. While she had always been quiet about her woes, she started to complain bitterly and loudly. She was given Haldol (an antihallucinogen given in cases of severe mental disorder) which put her into a stupor.

When I discovered through my own investigation that the research done on this drug did not include the elderly, I was appalled. Also, I thought that this drug was being administered to make the staff 's job easier rather than to help my mother. I asked the psychiatrist if he didn't think that more might be done to get residents into activities so that they could feel more alive and connected instead of drugged. He told me he would take it up with my mother's doctor and social worker. It wasn't until I brought this matter to the attention of the Friends and Relatives, a support group, that anything seemed to change.

I had shown the group an article about a study done with reputable nursing homes in New England. Even there the practice of using psychotropic drugs for maintenance rather than for medical reasons seemed to be prevalent. We invited the psychiatrist to address the group. The result was that family members began to educate themselves about the individual needs of their relatives and the administration knew that there was an active, concerned group which would hold them accountable if the best interest of the residents was not being served.

One afternoon we were in the music room. I was playing some tunes on the piano and we were singing together. She said to me, putting her hand over her heart, "I have such a wonderful feeling for you in here and I know you feel that way too." I said, "Yes, there's a special relationship between mothers and daughters." She responded, "I'm so glad you think of me as your mother." What a strange mixture of emotions that evoked! She could feel my love, but she no longer knew I was her daughter. She remembered her daughter as a little girl and she started to call me "lady." Sometimes she would ask, "Lady, has my mother been here yet?"

As she became more confined, she was more distant and less responsive. The singing stopped and she no longer enjoyed the garden or any of the programs. I had to allow several hours after each visit with her to deal with my own sadness, helplessness and residual guilt before I went to work. My family no longer lived in daily contact and could not share caretaking. I was a lesbian who had chosen to be self-supporting through a career which held great meaning for me. I had consciously chosen not to care for my mother full-time and yet at times still felt the guilt of having not followed the socially approved role for an "unmarried" daughter.

It was difficult to talk about what was going on. My previous lover would get depressed and I'd end up having to console her. My current lover was very supportive, but being a realist, didn't see what was tragic about an old woman about to die. It was very sad to see my mother this way, but I couldn't mourn her because she was still alive.

I felt powerless to help my mother. Because I needed support and wanted to offer support to people who were going through similar experiences, I started a group for friends and relatives. My two year participation in this group was an important factor in my ability to deal with my mother's deterioration and death.

A friend who was close to me during this period said that my dreams were evidence that I was having difficulty letting go. When it came time to make a decision not to take heroic measures to sustain my mother's life during a serious illness, members of the group were very helpful to me. One of the members was a lawyer who talked to us about living wills. Another woman was a hospital administrator who told us a story encouraging us to allow the elderly to die in peace. A doctor told my brothers and me that it was usually those who had a good relationship with their parents who were the ones most likely to let go, whereas those who had unfinished business panicked at the thought that it might remain unfinished when the parent died.

When the home called to tell me of her passing at 3 A.M., I immediately wrote the following letter to her which my brothers asked me to read at her funeral, and so it became her eulogy.

May 3, 1984

Dear Mom,

You wanted to do important things in life. You worked in the library in Russia, educating the peasants about the revolution until that dream was shattered.

You came to America and your relatives tried to find a husband to take care of you so you wouldn't have to work in the sweatshop belt factory on the Lower East Side. You were only twenty and shy and bewildered by your new life. The complete works of Tolstoy in Russian, which you brought with you to America, didn't help you much then.

Charlie was a good man. He was kind and caring. He tried to understand your woman soul, your spirit and your passion. He loved you and he fathered your children.

You loved giving birth, you told me that. Later you wanted your American children to help you to understand the ways of the new world. We talked to you and you listened patiently as we tried out new ideas. We filled you with our adventures, which you relished as though they were your own. You encouraged us to be active and involved. You taught us to roller skate, horseback ride, swim, dance. You yourself sang in a chorus and loved to take long walks around the Camp Boiberik Lake. You were a long distance swimmer in more ways than one, steady and sure.

You encouraged me to live out my fondest dreams, especially because you were thwarted in some of yours because you were a woman. You taught us respect for the dignity of all especially as expressed in the creative spirit. You valued education and you enriched our lives by providing those experiences which would help us to value our rich cultural and spiritual heritage. We experienced a positive Jewish identity at Camp Boiberik, or in Habonim, the labor Zionist youth group which shared the values of your organization, Pioneer Women. You worked for Pioneer Women for many years out of your own need for community and social commitment.

You helped me to value the ways in which I was different or unique instead of being ashamed of them. I thank you for my values and my ethics, my joy and my capacity for deep connections to people. I thank you for inspiring love and friendship among your children, Martin, Dottie, Eddie and myself.

You have had the most profound influence on my life. I love you and I will try to pass on the legacy that you have left me in my work and in my personal relationships.

Love always,

Joyce

In order to further deal with the feelings aroused in me through experiencing my mother's final years, I sought further information about how caregiving affects other midlife women. I discovered that seven million people, 75 percent of them women, provide care to a parent in this country every day. The National Institute on Aging projects that by the year 2040 the over-65 age group will have grown from 2.2 million to 13 million, with many more of this group over the age of 85. This means that elderly as well as middle-aged women will increasingly be expected to provide care.

Although eldercare now rivals childcare as an issue for legislators to address, the federal government has actually reduced funding for such programs as nursing homes, home health care, day care and respite care (part-time help for full-time caregivers so that they are able to attend to their own essential needs). Medicare does not cover chronic long term nursing care and there is little in the way of private insurance. Programs meant to help maintain the elderly in the community are inadequate, sporadic, or nonexistent. A recent study by the American Association of Retired Persons (AARP) found that emotional rather than financial support was most crucial to elderly parents. However, they frequently chose not to ask for help for fear that they would overburden their middle-aged daughters whose support they needed.

Congresswoman Pat Schroeder articulated three goals for the proposed national family policy: to acknowledge the rich diversity of American families, to protect families' economic well-being and to provide families with flexible ways to meet their economic and social needs. "Government policy cannot be based," she comments, "on a static definition of the family, but must take into account that Americans live in a variety of family structures.... Understanding this diversity is essential if we are to avoid creating government policy that penalizes families that do not fit a particular mold."

Certainly lesbians are among this "diversity" of families and, at present, we have little representation and are rarely included in the policies which affect our lives. As women in "the sandwich generation" (sandwiched between elderly parents and children and work) we have been told that caregiving is our central role whether we've chosen it or not. Women have always been asked to provide care as an alternative to costly professional home care or institutionalization. This is especially true now with soaring health care costs. It is assumed that women, will have the resources, willingness and commitment to take on the care of a dependent parent.

The "unmarried" daughter has historically been considered the best candidate for caregiving. Her career, friendship network or intimates were considered expendable. However, it is no longer viable for us to bear the brunt of our society's need for eldercare. Midlife and older women are in double jeopardy, experiencing both the effects of sexism and ageism, and in triple jeopardy if we are of an ethnic or racial minority, lesbian or disabled. According to Tish Sommers and Laurie Shields in *Women Take Care,* older members of minority groups "are more likely to have held physically debilitating jobs, to have lived in housing that was less than adequate and therefore to have more chronic diseases and disabilities which they have developed at younger ages than their white counterparts."[1] A smaller percentage of elderly blacks and Hispanics than whites live in nursing homes and a disproportionate percentage of minority women are providing the day-to-day care in these homes.

Caregiving produces a great deal of psychological, physical and financial strain on midlife women who are trying to meet their parents' needs, other family needs and their own needs for career and personal development when there is little or no assistance, according to Elaine Brody's research on caregiving.[2] Caregivers of all ethnic groups have reported feelings of helplessness, depression, anxiety and emotional exhaustion. As I learned from my own experience, workshops I conducted on caregiving between 1985 and 1988 and my reading, many factors contribute to the degree of stress in caregiving. For parental care, these include the severity of the problem, the kind of care needed and whether the parent needs to share the daughter's home.

Important relationship factors can also contribute to stress: whether the parent is pessimistic or cooperative, if she is interested in the daughter's life or totally self-absorbed and the previous and current relationship between them. For the caregiver, whether one has support from one's partner and siblings, availability of resources for emotional, physical and financial support and the degree and nature of competing responsibilities are important factors as well.

For a lesbian, having her parent accept her life style and her partner makes a tremendous difference in whether the caregiving is obligatory or part of an ongoing positive relationship. Whether the partner accepts the need for caregiving is also of major importance.

We must accept that we can't make it all better and that we need to go beyond the tragedy of our parent's ill health or dementia to find new ways of relating. So too, over identification with the parent may be detrimental to both parent and caregiving daughter because the daughter may be drawn into the parent's reality as though it were her own. It is possible to be empathetic with the parent and still not neglect our own needs and other aspects of our lives.

If we feel unfulfilled and unfinished in our own lives, it is all too easy for us, having been socialized as women to care for others, to use caregiving as an excuse to avoid dealing with an overwhelming world. When we have little sense of our own self, we have little to give to others and we end up resenting the depletion of our limited resources. This is particularly significant for lesbians because it takes time for us first to know who we are and that we're okay before we can develop enough self-affirmation to pursue and enjoy our work and relationships. Through caregiving we come to recognize that our parents' aging is part of an inevitable process that we in time will experience and that the same dignity and care we want for our mothers, we will want for ourselves and our lovers when we have similar needs.

This chapter, stemming from my own experience, describes the dilemma of the white, middle-class, American woman who no longer has the possibility of a large and caring extended family with whom to share care of aging parents. Many of my observations and generalizations may not apply to women within extended families, or women who have chosen to focus on caring for others, whether children or elders.

ENDNOTES

1. *Women Take Care: The Consequences of Caregiving in Today's Society* (Gainsville, FL: Triad Publishing Co., 1987).

2. "Parent Care As A Normative Family Stress," *The Gerontologist*, 1985, 25.

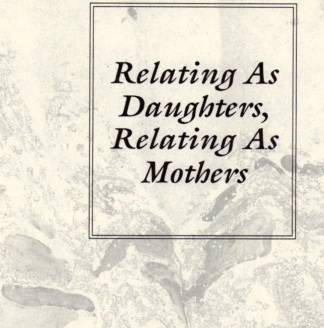

Relating As Daughters, Relating As Mothers

In The Heat of Shadow

JEWELLE GOMEZ

A gallery of photographs has adorned the walls of my various apartments since I left the Boston home of my great-grandmother in 1971 to live in New York City. Each of the faces—my mother, Dolores; her mother, Lydia; her mother Grace; and yet another, Sarah, before her; alongside my father, brother, step-mother—has each in its own turn been a focal point for me. Most often though it has been the face of my great-grandmother Grace, the woman who raised me, that most fascinated me. She, who was always most reticent to have her soul captured on a piece of shining paper. Her square Iowa tribal face was often shielded by wire spectacles that concealed her impish humor but not her unyielding resolve. From my childhood perspective (one I've clung to until most recently), she embodied the security of my youth, the impressive influence of our past and the endurance of African/Native American women.

Her daughter, Lydia, with whom I've been most close in the past ten years represented the possibilities of beauty. In the pictures her face shines with charm, intelligence and sensuality. I never dress, sing, kiss, teach or sew without seeing that face, for she was the one who taught me those things. But she died this summer and I cannot touch that loss yet. It is the face of my mother, Dolores, which holds my eye now as I feel the chilly departure of my youth. Hers is a face of uncertainty, the unknown. Although it is clear we are all descendants of Sarah, whom I never knew, Dolores and I grow ever closer in resemblance each year. Her portrait among the others is arch, sophisticated, distant, like many done of glamour-ous women in the early 1950s. I can see the painted line of her eyebrow, the deliberate softness of her jawline, the romanticized wave of her hair. In the corner her inscription to me in 1952 is still faintly visible in the dramatic script I was so used to deciphering in her letters to me when I was a child. What shocks me is that I am now older than my mother was when she gave up custody of me and inscribed this photo as a remembrance. I don't know why this makes me suddenly afraid except perhaps that she was clearly a "woman" in this picture. She represented adulthood, something children can never really reach. Instead we shed our skins and one day awaken to be another person—the adult. The continuity is indiscernible to me. The continuum seems tentative, as if we hopscotched through our lives landing solidly in certain ages and less so in others. Who was I at 11 or at 26, the age my mother is in the picture?

She always seemed as solid as Grace or Lydia in her self-knowledge and self-determination. It is only later that I come to realize this was not true. Her life was a mass of contradictions, missteps, childish judgments not so different from the ones I made at 26. But I have no child to judge my photograph.

It is her face which confuses me, worries me as I step into what they call middle age. My misunderstanding of who my mother was as an adult and my clear understanding of how our culture's definition of middle-aged life has changed for women, combine to leave me unsatisfied about my future—even terrified of it. I know some women who cannot allow their lives to be changed by the redefinitions of middle age that have been wrought by the Black Power movement and the women's movement. There is always a certain investment in the traditional even when it is despairing and oppressive. Many women still cling to the comforting stereotypes as if they can transform themselves into Pearl Bailey or Donna Reed—either good-natured complaints or sweet contentment. I have cousins now, only 30 years old, who, burdened with children and missing boyfriends take easy refuge in the myth of middle-aged behavior. They in their youth know the speech patterns, the behavioral patterns, the attitude so well, it is haunting in its familiarity. One aspect of traditional Afro-American culture has provided us with a couple of solid pictures of who we grow up to be. The long-suffering matriarch who gathers her extended family to her bosom and regales them with stories of her exciting yet simple girlhood, the things they are missing because they don't exist anymore. She is revered much like my stepmother, Henrietta, who at 71 has spent her life raising other people's children with a wit and graciousness unmatched by anyone I've ever met. Her life settled down into middle age, then old age, with a pointed purpose—children. Her role as caretaker almost required her to be middle-aged in order to be acceptable, so she may have started becoming middle-aged at age 30 like my cousins.

On the other side of the myth stand Dolores and Lydia, women who had little contact with the idea of middle age. Their lives moved ahead as if there were only eternity, and the road map had been given directly into their hands. At family gatherings I did not hear the discussions of middle-aged discontent, the things undone, the anxiety, confinement or unfulfillment. They seemed to take advancing age as only one other element to be included in their daily calculations, like rain or a high wind. None of their lives were bound up in the lives of their children, so the crises attendant to that link and its dissolution were barely visible. My great-grandmother took the news of my decision to move away from home after college with amazing equanimity. I'm sure she didn't disclose the sadness it brought her because she thought that inappropriate to the natural order. When I did move I called her on the telephone every day, unafraid to declare my love and my missing her because she did not represent a trap laid to ensnare me, luring me back to the nest. She seemed a woman going on with her life. The few months that remained for her at age 85 included a visit to me in Manhattan as if she wanted to really give me her blessing.

Now for me at 40, having no children, no property, living the non-traditional roles of lesbian, Afro-American writer under the enigmatic gaze of my mother, I am frightened by the prospect of middle age. If I, as lesbian/feminist poet, reject the traditional perception of who I am, what do I replace it with? I've no idea. My mind says there's really no limit. I write; I work as an activist; I'm continually building friendships. What is there to be afraid of? Most of it seems to be physical, my body doesn't move for me as it used to. While the exercise craze has hit the lesbian community with equal if not larger force than the general society, I've managed to evade the compunction to rise at dawn and run through city streets or submit to the rack masquerading as a Nautilus device. So I may be in worse shape than some but I refuse to feel guilty about it. My body aches and is stiff. It does not heal. It mocks me with its readiness to become old. And there is a certain amount of comfort in that too. My body has relieved me of the obligation to pursue daring physical feats. Will I ever learn to ski? Do I care?

But it really isn't the body—it is the replacement image. There is none. I'm not washed-up, at the end of my rope, over the hill, on the decline, or any of the other euphemisms, at least not overtly. But what am I? I keep looking at Dolores' picture—the quizzical line of her brow, the direct confrontation of her gaze. There is something there, I think, which might tell me of a new opening, even if it is one she might have missed. She cannot be dismissed because she had a penchant for falling in love with braggarts with unrealistic visions of life. The issues I had, still have, with my mother (about politics and hair care mostly) sometimes overwhelm the practical love I feel for her. As powerful as these issues are they cannot overshadow that look. Are there answers there? I am as uncertain as the future her look promises. What do I have that will allow me to look back at others with such self-possession?

I take some comfort in my "professional status"—that is, the publication of my work and my audience's appreciation of it. That is a gift not available to many women, even in the liberated '80s. But to identify myself only as what I do is a mistake that men have made too often throughout history. But what do I make of myself, embarking on a new and serious relationship at 40, with a little of the romanticism of the previous twenty years' debacles, but more of the practicality of a diplomatic negotiator?

It may simply be the fear that all feminists must face: how to balance the power of control over my own life with a need for support and encouragement. The women in my family seemed to be able to handle only one of these things at a time. My mother let her life be subsumed under those of her partners. She chose gregarious, charming men who controlled the shapes of both their lives, while her prime function was to maintain a full-time job and still look pampered. My grandmother, Lydia, landed at the other extreme. She allowed men to enter her life for prescribed periods of time for her own enjoyment. When they became too intrusive they were banished back to their own apartments, their own lives. She repeated this process through her middle years with a sort of stable of men who never seemed to tire of her attentions and rejections. She was extraordinarily clear about her independence and managed to forsake most expressions of need, as if the two could not cohabit within her any more than she could with a man for more than six months.

The ache in my knees and hands make me certain I don't want to give up that right to supportive companionship, any more than I'd consider becoming anyone's appendage. And it is entering the middle years—the aches and the uncertainty—that make the questions more pointed. I want my answer to be somewhere in my mother's face but more likely it is in the faces of both Dolores and Lydia. The balancing act is what I'm afraid of. My body and my ego feel particularly fragile now while they are in transition from a solid past to an unknown future. Taking to the high wire to figure out where I'm strong and where I'm needy feels like stretching my resources too far. And I've always been afraid of heights.

Taken all together, the portraits of the women in my family have been a great sustainer over the years of my adulthood. Each in its own turn has meant something specific, has conveyed some particular lesson that I've needed to learn in order to move on to the next phase of my development. The part that I'd not really reckoned with is the reverse side of that coin. Taken all together, the lineage and triumph they represent is also a burden. They did not express themselves in the same womanly way that I do. They were less likely to articulate who they were and what they saw as the definition of their lives. As heterosexual women coming of age in the 1920s, '30s and '40s this was not required of them, in fact, was discouraged because they were women and because they were not white. That silence, even as I take courage from their examples, is a curtain between me and what my life after 40 can be. And because they survived so magnificently, with such style and humor, they have become legend to me. Their pictures have become icons enshrined in the nave of my apartments lending inspiration but also casting a shadow.

I begin to see that my life cannot be fully patterned on theirs, if simply because it's 30 or 40 or 50 years later, socially, politically, economically, if simply because I am a lesbian and they were not lesbians. But the shadow that their lives projects still hangs there and it is not cool. It is hot with expectation. It makes me sweat as I climb onto the wire and learn what happens when I try to see what a black lesbian looks like when she lives longer than the statistics say she should. And I'm still afraid of heights.

How Lesbian Identity Affects the Mother/Daughter Relationship

JOYCE WARSHOW

This is a preliminary study to explore how a midlife lesbian's identity and participation in the lesbian/gay community impacts on her relationship with her mother. I undertook this study after experiencing changes in how I perceived my lesbian identity. After noting the profound effects on my relationship with my mother (see *Eldercare as a Feminist Issue*), I wondered if this was true of other midlife lesbians.

Twenty-four lesbians between the ages of 40 and 57 participated in two three-hour discussion groups held in New York City and in a nearby beach community. The participants were middle-class white women, two-thirds of whom had completed graduate degrees.

Participants responded to open-ended questions such as "What are some of the changes you have experienced in midlife?" "Are you 'out' to your family and friends?" "In what way, if any, has your lesbian identity influenced your relationship with your mother or with your partner?"

Based on these discussions, I developed a questionnaire and sent it to 30 lesbians from the same area who were in the friendship network of the original participants. Twenty women responded, seventeen of whom had previously participated in the discussion groups. Only two of the final respondents were women of color.

Lesbian Identity

When asked about feelings about lesbian identity, responses fell into four categories: non-accepting, defensively accepting, accepting (private) and accepting (political). Two women who expressed negative feelings about being lesbians were assigned to the first category (non-accepting). These women felt that it wasn't their choice and they would have preferred to be "like everyone else." One wasn't quite sure she was lesbian, although she preferred to relate to women sexually.

Eight women identified themselves as lesbians, but felt that it "wasn't exactly something to be proud of." I placed these women in the category "defensively accepting (defensive)."

Six others felt "comfortable" or "good" about being lesbians and had disclosed their identity to family and friends. Some had also been open with those associates at work with whom they felt close. I categorized these as "accepting (private)." These women joined lesbian and gay organizations primarily for the social contact. One woman said, "This is who I am and I'm fine with it."

Four women were politically active in the lesbian/gay community, participating in a variety of social service organizations, or as lesbian/gay civil rights advocates. I placed them in the "accepting (political)" category. One woman who typified this category said, "It's not enough to be a lesbian. It's important to be visible to make it safer for all of us."

Mother/Daughter Relationships

Eight women described their relationships with their mothers as unchangingly negative. Some of the descriptions were, "I have nothing to do with her," or "I feel very distant from her.... She doesn't know who I am. I don't enjoy spending time with her, but it makes me feel guilty when I don't."

Seven respondents reported that their early negative relationships with their mothers had changed over time: "She extended total control, was always negative, didn't acknowledge what I did that was good. Now she's more positive in showing affection and gratitude, giving positive feedback...she accepts me as I am."

Three other women had unchanged positive relationships, characterized by these comments: "I love to spend time with my parents. They encouraged me to be independent. I 'came out' at sixteen. They love my lover. They think I'm a wonderful human being."

Two women idealized their mothers and had never had any conscious negative feelings about them. One said, "My mother died when I was seven. I tried to do things the way I remember her doing them. That helped me to keep her alive within me."

Lesbian Identity and the Mother/Daughter Relationship

Seven of the ten women who had the most positive feelings about their lesbian identities had relationships with their mothers that had changed over time from negative to positive. Of the ten women who had the most negative feelings about their lesbian identities (non-accepting, or defensively accepting), eight had negative relationships with their mothers which had not changed over time. I also found that while these women participated in the lesbian/gay community in varying degrees, over half spent more than 90 percent of their social time with other gays and lesbians. However, those who were comfortable about being lesbians were less likely to segregate themselves. These women participated in lesbian and gay organizations as well as in mixed groups as openly gay individuals.

My main finding, that the women with the most positive lesbian identities were those whose relationships with their mothers had changed over time from negative to positive, suggests that these daughters had engaged in the psychological work necessary to accept their lesbian identities. They were then able to change their previously negative relationships with their mothers.

According to developmental theory, certain life events can create a crisis at one time in life, but can be more acceptable at another. It would seem that lesbians must deal first with their internalized homophobia before they can have satisfactory relationships, feel in control and participate more fully in the world. A woman I know came out to her mother at 21 and was told by her that she would rather see her dead. The daughter proceeded to develop ulcerative colitis and almost died.

My own experience was that I came out to my mother at a point when I was not only clear about my lesbian identity but also happy in my relationship and in my work as a psychotherapist. My mother's response was "I like your life. You do good work and you have wonderful friends."

Several variations of the mother/daughter relationship emerged from the present study. In a relationship where the mother had been physically and/or emotionally abusive the daughter had first to deal with how that abusiveness affected her, apart from how her mother's homophobia affected her. As one woman said of her mother, "Her nonacceptance of me as a desirable person affected my well-being, but she was so off about homosexuality, it never really affected me."

Still other relationships were characterized by mothers who had learned to put other people's needs ahead of their own in the way many women have been socialized to do. The task of going out on one's own (differentiating) may be particularly difficult for the daughter in this relationship. In one instance a woman's lesbian identity actually helped that process: "Sometimes I think this is the only area where I have acted in my own behalf without considering her reaction, without needing to expose my choice to her scrutiny."

A third pattern that emerged was one in which mothers took pleasure in the daughter's development without demanding agreement with her ideas about what is "right" or "good." An example of this was given by a woman who had come out at the age of sixteen. "My mother says I'm a wonderful human being and she loves my lover." This woman has been in a 30 year relationship, is successful in her career and is a director on the boards of mixed as well as lesbian/gay organizations.

My second major finding was that more than half of the women spent more than 90 percent of their time with other gays and lesbians, but those with clear-cut lesbian identities were less likely to segregate themselves.

This may indicate that lesbians need to have a period of separatism while forming their identity as part of a minority. As has been the case with women, blacks and the differently abled, the establishment of a strong identity helps us to integrate into the larger community and to counteract the negative effect of the mainstream tendency to view those who are not average as abnormal.

Those women who had gone through such a period of separatism, which often included celebrating their lives as lesbians, had a positive lesbian identity and had integrated other interests and people into their lives. It was usually after such a period that women re-evaluated their relationships with their mothers.

This is vividly stated in the letter of a lesbian daughter to her mother in which the daughter writes, "I'm now no longer a divided person, alienated from myself and from the world." She attributes this change to the realization that the hurt comes not from being a lesbian, or a woman, but from "having our human rights, power and intelligence denied us." The writer concludes that part of taking charge of her life means a re-evaluation of her relationship with her mother.

Deciding Not to Become a Mother

RONNIE C. LESSER

We are in the midst of a baby boom. When I go to work in New York City the streets teem with mothers, both young and middle-aged, wheeling baby carriages. My friends and acquaintances, lesbian and heterosexual, single or in couples, are preoccupied with deciding whether or not to have children. This phenomenon is not limited to New York City or to my circle of friends: movies, television programs and newspaper and magazine articles appear to herald a national obsession with motherhood.

For myself and other women who are now middle-aged, this focus on motherhood represents the second change in *zeitgeist* that we have lived through: brought up to believe that mothering was an inherent part of feminine identity, the women's movement in the '70s taught us to question this belief. We recognized that the biological necessity for women to bear children could be separated from the subsequent arrangements for how they would be cared for and by whom. We came to see motherhood as an institution that is socially constructed and which society justifies and maintains through social ideology. It was not until the Industrial Revolution and the advent of capitalism that the ideal of mother and child enclosed together in the home, separate from man's world of wage earning, aggression and power became a fundamental social prescription. At the same time it became internalized as a basic category of feminine identity. Women came to see themselves as feminine because they like children, want to bear them and raise them, want to eschew satisfactions in the outside world for the pleasures inside the home. Women who dare to stray outside of these boundaries have to contend with the dual furies of societal rejection and intrapsychic feelings of being worthless, unfeminine, selfish, unnatural and alienated from other women.

Traditional theories in psychology reflect and reproduce these ideological beliefs by viewing a woman's desire to bear and raise a child as a biological imperative. Even today, female development is viewed by many as being impelled through a unilinear, universal progression towards motherhood and heterosexuality. Women who vary from this theme are dismissed as deviant; as something to explain away. By viewing motherhood as a woman's destiny, theories in psychology have overlooked the extent to which it is constructed in a nexus of economic, social and political structures.

Under the influence of the second wave of the women's movement, we learned to recognize the social and economic underpinnings of the institution of motherhood. This led many of us to derogate mothers and to idealize women who worked in the public sphere, ironically mirroring patriarchy's contempt for "women's work" and idealization of "men's work." Whereas prior to the women's movement being married and having children was the essence of what seemed "natural" and "meaningful" and was not questioned, after the women's movement, for many women, not having children seemed "natural" and "meaningful" and was not questioned. We seem to have come full circle into a world which once again idealizes motherhood. Nowadays it is almost politically incorrect to question why so many women are having children and anything short of affirmation is looked upon with suspicion. Ideology about motherhood infuses the ways we define what is feminine, our freedom to question whether we want to mother, our conceptions of what is natural and meaningful for a woman to do, what we see as selfish, as well as our thoughts and feelings about the experience of being a mother. Unreflective acceptance of ideology, whether traditional or feminist, is dangerous. Thought is then captive to style.

Today, the ability of lesbians to have children through artificial insemination or adoption marks a fundamental change in the possibilities within a lesbian identity. A lesbian who comes of age with the knowledge that she has the option to have children without a man is living in a world which is very different from the one inhabited by a lesbian in the past, who knew that coming out entailed giving up the option to mother. Today, lesbians who don't want to have children face the need to make this decision in a world that reveres women who mother and disapproves of those who don't.

As midlife lesbians who are now deciding whether or not to become mothers, we are in a unique position. We now have choices about mothering which we never had before. Further, we have experienced a shift in ideology from a view of mothering as a natural aspect of feminine identity, to a derogation of mothering, and back again to a romanticization of motherhood. Choosing whether to become a mother today is an often grueling process of sifting through contradictory personal feelings and cultural beliefs in an effort to identify one's own true preferences and desires.

My study was an attempt to explore the experiences of lesbians who decided not to have children. Fifteen professional women between the ages of 36 and 47, a majority of whom were white, were contacted through notices in gay newsletters and through my own connections in the lesbian community. These midlife lesbians agreed to be interviewed either by phone or in person. The interview consisted of three general questions: 1) When did you first start to think about whether or not to have children? 2) How did your thinking and feelings change between then and now?

3) Did gay-related issues influence your decision not to have children (e.g., concerns about the child having to deal with homophobia)? The answers to each question determined the different probe questions which followed. Generally, probe questions were used to obtain a more articulated view of respondents' thoughts and feelings about not having a child.

The fifteen participants fell into one of three categories: 1) no regrets, 2) unresolved ambivalence, often without awareness, and 3) varying degrees of regret and feelings of loss.

Group I consists of five women who had a clear, non-ambivalent sense that having children was not something they wanted to do. Although all of the women remembered that when they were children they thought they'd be mothers when they grew up, they now saw this as an expression of a desire to be conventional, rather than as a true personal wish. Coming out as lesbians freed them from feeling obligated to have children. Typical of this group was one woman's recollection that "I got married and stayed in a relationship thinking of having a kid. I was real conscious of wanting a child because then I'd be like everyone else out there.... It wasn't until I came out, at 35, that I realized I didn't want one.... The desire to have kids was tied to my need to be normal and conventional—married with a family."

None of the five women expressed regrets or mixed feelings about her decision. Two of the women did not like children, although both needed to assure me that they did not "hate" them. The other three liked children and felt that their lack of regret about not having them was tied to their ability to have contact with children. All of these women mentioned how nice it was to be with children and not be responsible for them 24 hours a day. "I love kids, especially to have them for a certain period of time and then to give them back."

All five felt fulfilled in their lives and were pleased that they had not had to sacrifice things that were important to them. As one recalled, "I come from a working-class background and I've seen women struggle raising kids and tolerating men. I realized that there was no way I'd get myself in that spot. I watched them have no sense of who they were or what they wanted. I feel very privileged in this society that I've had time for myself." Perhaps because none of them felt that wanting children and having them is "natural," they didn't feel inadequate about being different. One said, "It's positive being different. The problem with this country is they don't want anybody being different. I always feel on the radical fringe of everything."

Group II consists of four women. Although they described themselves as having decided not to have children, contradictions arose during the interviews and it became clear that their decisions were more tenuous than first expressed. Two women seemed unaware of their ambivalence. For example, one began the interview saying, "…Practically speaking, I knew that I would not have a child. Kids are delightful, to hold them and play with them…(but when) they're not yours and you don't have to get up at night or worry about their getting sick…. I wanted to be free to do all the things I'd never done before in my life and not have to worry about a child." Later in the interview she said: "I sometimes think I could adopt a child if I don't have a mate." When I pointed out this contradiction she said: "Yes. I can't really say I dwell on it very seriously…. I haven't made any hard or firm decision. If I won Lotto tomorrow it wouldn't be the first thing I'd do but I would seriously consider it then." For her, money and relationship issues stood in the way of having a child. "If commitment were easier (if I had money and could stay home with a child), and have all the benefits of help, it would be a different thing; it's not reality. I doubt things will change enough for me to do this. If I make more money I'd still never have enough. And lesbian relationships are too ephemeral to count on the help of that."

Unlike this woman, the ambivalence of another was more on the surface. While she reported feeling that the "negatives outweighed the positives" about having a child, she still felt unsure about whether she might want one sometime in the future. "I can't say what will happen in five years, I may decide I want to adopt." The fourth woman was the most upset about not having a child. Although she had definitely decided not to have her own biological child, she wanted desperately to co-parent, aunt or grandmother a child. She was thinking about moving across the country for the opportunity to co-parent a friend's child. She had no friends or family members with children with whom she was in close contact and thus no opportunity for closeness to children.

The theme of closeness with children was important to this group. Unlike Group I, where the women who liked children reported that they had close, rewarding relationships with children, only one woman in this group said that she had close relationships with children. Unlike the women in Group I who expressed pleasure about not having children, only one woman in Group II mentioned feeling more positive than negative about not having a child. "I'm a late bloomer, coming to things later than other people. Maybe they were 'sated' in their thirties, but I want to experience learning more about my career, taking piano lessons, working with injured animals, traveling…. I feel sad about not having a child, but positive about the things I can do." This is in contrast to another woman in the group who also reported being a late bloomer but said "I am regretful that I wasn't brought up to feel good about myself and I had to spend time giving this to myself and not having a child."

A recurrent theme in this group was how hard society makes it for women to have children and how this had affected their decisions. According to one woman, "Although this society professes to being very child-oriented, there are really very few supports for people to have children, even for heterosexuals, and because of this you have to give up a lot. I wouldn't be willing to give up my career."

Group III consists of six women who had all considered having children, but decided against it. Four had wanted to have children very badly and had changed their minds when they pondered the difficulties that children of lesbians would encounter. According to one woman, "I thought of what it would be like as a sort of fantasy rather than in realistic terms.... As I went along I thought if you were really going to do this, you know, it's not a storybook, not a fantasy and I had to think of it realistically.... At this point I began to let go of the idea and started to think of other things more worthwhile to do."

Homophobia was mentioned by most of the women in this group as one of the primary reasons that they had decided not to have children. As one woman put it: (my being a lesbian would be) "particularly difficult on a child. For all the feminist thinking and feeling, when you think of it realistically: here I am in my neighborhood with my lover...it's not difficult for me to handle the reactions of society because to some degree I've handled it all along. But a child can't really have a choice about these things and has less of an understanding of them."

All four women expressed a great deal of regret. One woman said, "I really made a conscious decision and felt very bad about it. It felt like a tremendous loss to me." The loss has changed for her as she gets older: "It's less intense. I've resolved some of the feelings and the most important part is that I realize that I made a choice and that it wasn't something that just happened to me.... There's something about the freedom that's involved in not having a child that I really appreciate."

Unlike the four women described above, the last two women expressed less regret about their decisions. One of them had always had ambivalent feelings about having a child. Although she went through an intense exploratory process to decide whether or not to have a child, "it didn't come from a part of me that said I want to have a child. It came from a more exploratory and ambivalent part of me, than some woman who knows this is what she wants to do.... (Having a child is) a metaphor or fantasy more than reality. It's more about joining in a familial sense and commitment than about actually having a child.... It's also about marking yourself as an adult."

Although the last woman in this group had thought she'd have a child when she was younger, she changed her mind when she got older and found that she wanted to devote her time and energy to other things. Because she was able to satisfy what she described as her "maternal instincts" (she defined these as something that some people have and others don't, independent of gender) by being nurturant in close relationships with children, as well as in her relationship with her lover, she rarely felt sad about her decision. She, like so many of the other women who had satisfying contacts with children, described a feeling of pleasure arising from the freedom to be with children for a limited period of time and then give them back to their parents.

Several themes emerged from this exploratory study:

Women who don't like children, and don't feel that there is anything wrong with this, have the easiest time making the decision not to become mothers and don't experience regret, sadness or mixed feelings. Although only two women I interviewed admitted not liking children, it seemed evident that even they felt uncomfortable talking to me about this feeling. They seemed intent on making sure that I understood that they didn't "hate" children, that they're not "monsters" when they're around children.

Women who see having children as "something that women do," have the most difficulty coming to terms with their decisions not to become mothers. They experience themselves as being "different" in a pejorative sense and wonder whether there is something wrong with them. Women who associate having children with feminine identity seem to feel the most guilty and inadequate about not wanting children. Although they described themselves as having made a decision not to have children and seemed to feel certain of their choice, it seemed evident during their interviews that they hadn't made up their minds. They seemed unaware of this ambivalence. It was as though the decision were so laden with feelings and meanings that they couldn't think it through fully and had to disassociate part of it from themselves. It seems logical to assume that the more a woman feels that it's "natural" to have a child, the harder it will be to let go of the idea that she will have one.

Women who feel that the work they do is meaningful have fewer regrets about not having children and less guilt. While some women I interviewed felt content with their lives (e.g., career and artistic pursuits), other women seemed to feel that these priorities are less "meaningful" than having a child. Some women felt that having a child was the most important thing a woman could do and that they were selfish and odd for not doing it.

For women who like children, the opportunity to be close to children of relatives or friends is very important. Many women mentioned that their needs for contact with children were satisfied by having close relationships with children of relatives and friends. They seemed to relish the intimacy in these relationships with children, as well as the freedom to be able to give the children back to their parents at the end of the day. Women who like children and don't have contact with them seem to experience more sadness, feelings of deprivation and, for one woman, an almost desperate need to establish relationships with children.

Women who feel that they made the choice not to have children freely, seemed to feel the least regret. Although they had to work through feelings of sadness and loss, it was in a context of knowing that they could have chosen to have children and that they had decided against it by weighing all the possibilities. Women who felt that they couldn't have children because of circumstances beyond their control (e.g., not having a partner or financial stability), seemed to be the most ambivalent.

Life as Improvisation

MATILE ROTHSCHILD

Though I was in my early forties when I came out as a lesbian, I was naive about how coming out would impact on my children or how much my life would change. I believed that midlife would be a smooth continuation of the stability and security I had experienced in my thirties. When I came out, Liz, my daughter, was twelve and Chris, my son, was eleven. They were beginning to experience all the feelings teenagers go through, including a heightened awareness about themselves and sexuality. They also were being more demanding about the way they wanted everything to be at home.

My husband, Harold, and I always laughed at the idea of midlife crises. We thought they were inventions of generations before ours which were no longer applicable, or problems comedians and sitcoms grossly exaggerated. In any event, they would never happen to us. Then we each turned 40 and realized that we, like our adolescent children, were going through radical changes. We also had a heightened sense about ourselves and about sexuality, and for us it meant that more than any time in our lives we wanted to be more openly gay.

Harold and I had been having same-sex relationships within the framework of what appeared to our straight friends to be a traditional marriage. As long as the family was intact, our children didn't react very much to having gay parents; however, when we decided to separate, they began to face the difficulties it posed for them and I had to face a whole new world of being a lesbian mother without the protection of being married.

In an excitement bordering on euphoria, I tried to be both an "out" lesbian and a mother. I tried to be involved in a whole new consciousness about women and to be involved in the beginnings of an emerging gay culture. As I tried to find my identity, I found few role models. In the early '70s, a lesbian over 40 was very unusual—and certainly "old." After so many years of having been "in the closet," many lesbians over 60 didn't feel safe being "out" in the community and were, on the whole, not very visible. I was shocked to be considered one of the elders in a community of younger women. Sometimes I felt I'd put on twenty years just by coming out.

I faced my own midlife identity crisis on every front, not realizing what an uncharted course I had chosen. I didn't know anything about lesbians in midlife and, in fact, *no one* knew anything about lesbians in midlife with older children.

I truly didn't think it would matter to my children if I were a lesbian, trusting they would perceive me as the same mommy they had always loved. I thought their difficulty with me and my lesbian friends was because lesbianism was new to me, that if they had known me only as a lesbian, they wouldn't feel angry and rejecting. Since then, I've heard the stories of about 150 mothers with older children and I've learned that, with a few exceptions, most teenagers, especially in the years between twelve and fifteen, react negatively to having a lesbian mother (or gay father). Adolescents do not want to be aware of their parents' sexuality while they are just discovering their own. Liz, at fourteen, could explain very well that she felt more threatened by my being a lesbian than by her father's being gay because she felt more identified with me. The idea of my having a woman lover made me seem like a different mother to her. Her pain was also painful to me.

I didn't have any perspective about what was going on at the time. In the early '70s, during the early days of the gay liberation movement, the word "mother" and the word "lesbian" were considered antithetical to one another: to be a lesbian mother was considered as impossible as being a Jewish nun. Lesbian mothers had always existed, but they had not identified themselves yet as a group with common needs and problems. Actually, between 1971 and 1973, the first groups formed in New York and the term "lesbian mother" began to be used. The earliest groups raised money to defend lesbians in child custody battles. About 1972, Carol Morton organized Dykes and Tykes which focused on childcare, as well as lesbians who wanted to have children. The idea of a group of lesbian mothers was so extraordinary, they were asked to lead the first Freedom Day Parade up Fifth Avenue. In the midst of this totally new consciousness, I found it difficult to find much firm ground to stand on.

All teenagers go through identity problems and conflicts with their parents, but in retrospect I realize my children were often mirroring my own conflicts. Their negative reactions to having gay parents were impossible to separate from the grief and anger they felt about the divorce. They felt unable to escape being identified with us. It didn't matter which of us they lived with, they had to deal with homophobia. Chris once read a cartoon story in *Mad Magazine* about a boy with two lesbian parents pictured in short hair, jeans, plaid shirts and boots—looking rather butch. A counselor suggested that the boy live with his father to have more male contact in his life. The next frame showed the boy at the door of his father's house being greeted by his father and his male lover who were dressed exactly like the mother and her lover except they had long hair. When Chris showed me the story he said, "Mom, this story is supposed to be funny, but

I'm probably one of a really small group of kids that doesn't feel that way." He was almost in tears when he said it.

How our children react to us forces us to look at ourselves and have thoughts about ourselves we wouldn't have if we weren't parents. Liz and Chris felt the stigma of having gay parents; therefore, it played into my doubts. All the homophobia around me came flooding in. We had terrible angry times when they screamed with grief and pain about me and Harold. I felt so insecure and attacked, I found it difficult, and at times impossible, to give them the love and reassurances they needed. In the earlier years I didn't have a mother's group to turn to to get help with my children, but I did have lesbians who would validate my feelings about being a lesbian. Generally, I felt fragmented—torn between the positive feelings about being a lesbian I could get at meetings or concerts and the lack of support about being a mother. I did not know who to turn to for that.

Liz and Chris did not feel they had anyone safe to turn to either. They balked at the thought of counseling (and Harold and I had fears about finding a counselor who would not be homophobic). In an ironic twist, when the children began to speak with their school counselor, they learned she was a lesbian and lost trust in her because they felt she was biased. Liz and Chris had to risk judgments, if not outright rejection in "coming out" (to their friends) as the children of gay parents. Most of their friends continued to "hang out" at our house as usual, but a few parents stopped their children from coming over. Over time Liz and Chris tended to choose friends who were less conventional and more accepting.

We tried to keep some sense of family structure and shared time. In our small suburban town in New Jersey, I felt increasingly isolated from other lesbians and from the straight families around me and I worried about the long-term effects on me and the children. I decided that we might have an easier life somewhere else. I thought if I could feel more integrated in my life as a lesbian, I could be a better mother. Eventually, Chris and I moved to the San Francisco Bay Area, which had seemed like paradise every time I had visited. We lived with my friend Corky and her son, Larry, who was Chris's age. Liz chose not to move with us and later, when she changed her mind, I was not in a position to receive her. So the change which was meant to ease the stress in our lives, created difficulties between us which still have not been resolved.

As I look back, I believe that separatism heightened the homophobia Chris and Liz felt toward me. They had some rough experiences in the straight world and they were not generally accepted in the lesbian community. I understand separatism gave a lot of strength to the lesbian community as a whole, but older children were not taken into consideration in the "politics of separatism." Childcare was offered at many events for small children, but teenagers, even girls, were seldom included or welcomed.

This exclusion of older children also affected me. Some friends would not come to my house for dinner because they didn't want to eat with Chris and Larry and some would not allow them in their homes. On holidays, I usually had to choose between the children and my friends or make special arrangements to have earlier meals with the children and join lesbian friends later.

Because of separatism, I felt no validation for me and Harold and the children staying together in any kind of extended family. And among my lesbian friends, I got very little validation for having tried a different kind of marriage and for remaining close friends with Harold. One mother I recently became friends with in San Francisco was also married to a gay man. They lived in a duplex where each lived separately with a respective lover. They raised their children together in an extended family. On occasion, she and her gay husband together took their teenage daughters on vacations. Their arrangement was a creation of the '80s. If I had been able to imagine anything like that in the '70s, I would have tried to keep the family more intact. Older children need frequent contact and emotional support from both parents—if they have always known two parents.

In 1980 I started a support group for mothers of teenage and older children which lasted about eight years. It was the major support I had as a mother during the '80s. Most of the women in the group were in midlife (as happens by default when our children reach their teens and older). They provided much of the feedback and support I had missed in the '70s, when coming out in the midst of younger women.

The group sometimes had picnics where all the teens were invited. It was very validating for them to meet one another and I wish we had done this more often. Once Chris said he would attend only if he could bring all his friends with him. I was pleased that he felt open enough to do that. They had a great time and were the last ones to leave. Some years later, when he was in college, Chris told some of my friends how "weird" it had been for his friends to see all the lesbians together and especially the ones who took off their shirts. I remembered that day and the conflict I'd felt: wanting to support the lesbians to "do their own thing" and also wanting to make the youngsters feel comfortable. It was as though some of the women denied that the boys had any special needs at all. Somehow, in the midst of separatism, we didn't realize how hurtful it was to our children to treat them as outsiders because they were (usually) straight and often male.

In 1985 Jeanne Jullion invited all the mothers and children who had been a part of her life to celebrate her book, *Long Way Home, the Odyssey of a Lesbian Mother and Her Children*. On a small stage mothers informally sang songs and read poems about themselves. Some children spoke or sang. For Chris the celebration was exhilarating. It was the first time his struggle had been publicly shared. We need so much more of this for our children of all ages—even those who are adults. By validating our children's experiences in our lesbian lives, we validate our own lesbianism.

All the mothers in my support group had been in heterosexual marriages or relationships and several other mothers also had gay husbands (none had children through insemination). Lesbians today who are deciding to have children generally think they will have different experiences with their kids because they will never know heterosexual family life. Very few of those children are teenagers or adults yet and so we're not sure if these children will feel the stigma of having a lesbian mother as much as our children did.

Traditional celebrations which honor children like bar and bat mitzvahs, graduations, weddings, bris, or christenings are important for all families, but they take on special meanings for lesbian mothers. We struggle to make a celebration the way the child wants it and also have it reflect ourselves as lesbian mothers—to be able to be ourselves and feel comfortable at the event. These events were major topics of discussion in the Mother's Group. They held many areas of concern: Will lovers attend? What role will lovers play? Will former lovers attend? Will lesbian friends attend and feel free to dance together? How will ex-husbands, relatives and ex-lovers who have been co-parents behave? What should we wear to honor our straight children as they play out traditional roles?

My daughter's wedding, for example, was a traditional and beautiful occasion which Liz planned totally by herself. I didn't have a lover at the time and friends on the West Coast couldn't travel to the East Coast for a wedding, so I was worried about being the only lesbian present. As it turned out, Liz invited two friends of hers who were lesbians. Harold had invited a few gay friends and the groom invited a gay friend. Harold's lover of many years, who in recent years has lived with my children more than I have, chose to sit with friends rather than on the pew with me and Harold. No one acknowledged Tom as family and he was not included in the family pictures. I felt sad about that, but he seemed to want it that way. Toward the end of the dinner, Harold and Tom danced together—but very discreetly. I danced with an older lesbian and with some other people in groups. During one dance, Liz and I danced together with the older woman who was her friend. However, the setting was not comfortable for being completely open. Even though I felt very loved and supported by my brothers and sisters and Harold and Tom and our straight friends who were there, I felt alone in a way I don't think I would have if I had been straight. I wanted Harold and me to be able to be proud of who we are, a lesbian mother and gay father. I wanted us to be totally open at the wedding, but that did not feel right to Liz and we respected what she wanted.

When lesbians get together with their families, the question of acceptance usually arises, especially about relationships. Straight families are generally more accepting of long-term lesbian (or gay) relationships because they see them as more serious and meaningful—and more like marriages. We often want our older children or relatives to automatically accept our new lovers as a family member or to feel very involved with them. It is difficult for teenagers or adult children to love (or even fully accept) a woman who has been in our lives only six months or a year. If a teen has known several lovers in several years, she or he is not going to jump at a chance to get to know someone new. In addition, teens are usually wary of adults who may influence the way they are treated at home. They may be more than just wary, they may be actively rejecting; sometimes it comes out in a homophobic way. I don't think it is so different for straight mothers who get involved with new partners. For lesbian mothers, an older child's negative reactions, especially about a partner, feel like homophobia and are painful and difficult to deal with. We still know so little, including how changing partners affects children. Of the more than 100 mothers who were in the group, only three or four had the same lesbian partner during all of the child's teen years. Only one mother had the same lesbian partner from the time the child was very young until age eighteen. Recently I heard a sixteen-year-old say that until her mom's most recent relationship of six years, she didn't realize that relationships could be ongoing and that life at home could be so peaceful without the emotional cycles of new romance and angry breakups.

I chose not to have lovers act as co-parents for my teenage children because I thought they would not accept another parent while they were trying to gain independence. In fact, teens, with their emerging independence and sexuality, rarely accept or are even polite to a lover. Straight lovers and step-parents probably have similar experiences with teenagers. Trying to define what role a lover can play for an older child is a challenge.

From all the mothers whose stories I've heard, it seems that at sixteen or seventeen, most teens begin to be more accepting about having a lesbian mother. As children become adult it is even easier. Once they go away to school or establish their own homes, their identity does not rest so much with the parent's identity. My children are now 25 and 26. They have finished college and have full and interesting lives. While they are more accepting of my being a lesbian, homosexuality is a poignant issue for them right now because Harold has AIDS. Of course, they have been distraught at the thought of losing their dad. And I have been devastated at the thought of losing my dearest friend.

In the past, one of the assumptions about midlife lesbians was that they could move on into the later years with greater independence partly because they did not have to experience the "empty nest" syndrome. That assumption is certainly no longer valid, if it ever was. Whereas most of the mothers I have talked with eagerly awaited the day their children could live on their own, they still experienced the deep sense of loss once their child left home. I remember one mother in the group who complained about her son for several years and said she couldn't wait for him to grow up and leave home. When the time came for her son to go to college she broke into tears just talking about it. He had been born when she was twenty and she had raised him as a single mother for eighteen years. She couldn't imagine what her life would be like without him at home. I also expected to feel the loss for only a few hours—maybe a few days. Then it hit me: living with my children was over. All the mistakes, guilt, things never worked out totally absorbed me. I was very depressed for about six months. As more and more lesbian mothers are having children, maybe we will find ways to build special supports and to ritualize the end of nest time in our lives.

I know each mother has her own story. I know some, very different from mine, where mothers and children did feel supported. In one case, a dozen or so friends helped a mother raise two adopted daughters. In the '70s and early '80s however, most mothers did not have ongoing support as their children grew up. We were the pioneer mothers, because we were the first large identifiable group to figure out for ourselves and our children what it meant to be a lesbian family.

Literature often refers to women in midlife as the sandwich generation, caught between their children and their aging parents. As a lesbian mother, I felt caught between the needs of my children and the lesbian community. Other minorities, like Jews or Blacks, had for generations built the care and support of children into the fabric of their lives. Gay and lesbian culture has emerged only since the '60s and it has been only recently that families with children have become a significant part of the community. At the Jewish New Year's service this year, a member of the gay synagogue, Sha'ar Zahav, proudly announced that the religious school for children had about 50 children enrolled. We are just beginning to build a place for families and children and to have a greater consciousness about the old in our community.

I think my children suffered, not only because of my being a lesbian, but because they didn't have a sense of safety and normalcy either in the straight world or as a part of my life in the lesbian community. When my children felt bad or upset or angry about having to live with lesbian or gay parents, they had only their straight friends to turn to. I think their friends were understanding to a point, but how savvy can a straight teenager be about lesbian families? The lesbian community had, I believe, an oppressive attitude toward older children, especially boys. With more lesbians having children, I think it is crucial that we have holidays, events, rituals, picnics, dances, big celebrations about being lesbian families which include our children—males and females of all ages. I would like to see annual events celebrating our children. Somehow we must create more interactions and exchange between lesbian families and lesbians without children. Our community will be enhanced when more older children, older mothers and grandmothers are included and visible. During the past year Liz had a baby girl. I hope that her becoming a mother and my becoming a grandma will help us become closer.

I am 56 now and I am nearing the end of what is generally called midlife. I am older and my children are older. For several years I've taught a course whose title seems to me to say it all: "Life as Improvisation." That is what I have found myself and many other lesbian mothers learning to do in these mid-years. These years have not been secure and stable, as I would have predicted in my thirties. I have found myself searching in every part of my life—as a lesbian, as a mother and in my professional life—for my own identity, one that worked for me. I have come to believe that what really happens in midlife is the need to make many radical changes as we search for a deeper understanding and expression of ourselves. Sometimes I have felt that I didn't know myself—that I had been reborn a different person. At other times, I have felt my mind and body joined in a new way and I've become more whole.

Another View of Lesbians Choosing Children

ANGELA BOWEN

In 1976, Adrienne Rich said, "We need to imagine a world in which every woman is the presiding genius of her own body. In such a world women will truly create new life, bringing forth not only children, if and as we choose, but the visions and the thinking necessary to sustain, console and alter human existence, a new relationship to the universe. Sexuality, politics, intelligence, power, motherhood, work, community and intimacy will develop new meanings. Thinking itself will be transformed. This is where we have to begin."[1] Well, lesbians, we have begun. At least, the bringing forth of children as we choose has begun. It's the visions and thinking, the politics, the community—all that other business—that I want to discuss here.

I remember how resentful I felt when the true deal about marriage hit me and I realized that all the people who had been urging me along that path knew the truth about it but *no one had told me*. I'd asked all the women I could talk to what marriage was really like. And everyone—including those who professed to care about me—were under societal pressure to uphold the myth so they wouldn't disillusion young women. Didn't want people to accuse them of being bitter. Then when I made the discovery that I'd been rooked, and wanted to know was this all, what I heard was, "Oh, girl, of course that's what marriage is, you should know that, what did you expect? Don't be so naive." Accompanied by all those sly winks, the wise nods and the beginnings of the talk about men as those little boys whom you could coddle and make think that they're big and strong, etc. Well, I made up my mind that if anyone asked me, I'd sure as hell tell them all of it—including the few good things that I could somehow scrounge up for them—the truth as I saw it.

Lately, while I've been doing some serious thinking about trying to get at my truths, what struck me was that motherhood has been such a constant factor in my life for the past 25 years that I never even considered that I'm not heading out of motherhood, even though my children will be grown. It will be with me for as long as I live. It's a forever fact that never ceases to be. My firstborn died one month short of his fourth birthday in

1966. And I remember the first Mother's Day after he died, wondering if I was still a mother. Well, as it happened at that time, I had a foster daughter and a stepdaughter. So clearly I was still a mother even though my muddled grief didn't allow me to think so. But I believe now that even if I didn't have those older girls to mother, I still would have been a mother, because you don't cease being one even though you outlive your child. You're never again not a mother, just as you're never again a virgin once you have sex. Just as you're never again not conscious once you become a feminist. So you are never again not a mother once you have a child. It's the only really forever relationship. Even if you decide to no longer mother someone you've mothered in the past, it's still an ongoing relationship, if only one of refusal. You're only done with it when you die. Now, just think about that. I came to that realization only *two weeks* ago.

One week ago I was in Washington, D.C. at a lesbian conference on aging called Passages and the panel was asked, "What was it like being a lesbian of your age?"—which is 52—and we were told to define our answers in terms of being an activist, a feminist, disabled, whatever—and I chose to speak in terms of feminism, because it so totally transformed my life. Three times in my life I've felt transformed. Once when as a teenager I discovered dance, again when I was in my late thirties and discovered feminism and then at 40 when I became a lesbian. Now, I've heard women say that being a mother transformed their lives, but I can't say the same. I was a mother at 26, long before I felt the consciousness of feminism. But I felt reborn because of feminism and it is that feminism which has allowed me to even *begin* to question the whys of motherhood.

In my youth, women didn't much question the desire to be mothers, even when they didn't want husbands. I remember as a little girl saying, "I want to have children but I don't want a husband." And people would kind of think that was cute and laugh and I didn't know why they were laughing. Then when I was a teenager, they would try to make me explain how I would go about this. I'd say, "Well, when I'm about 28 (to me that was pretty old) and I finish traveling all over the world dancing (which I did manage to do), I'll pick out a healthy, intelligent man, have two children by him, he'll go his way and I'll take the children and go my way." And they would say, "Oh yeah, you think you're going to pull that one off?" But if I were a young woman today, that wouldn't be a farfetched plan—they're doing it all the time. Lesbians and non-lesbians. We're all doing it. We keep reading the papers about broken, single-parent families. But what the statistics don't tell us is that those families aren't necessarily broken—a great many are quite deliberately planned that way.

But why do we plot and plan to have these children? What do they offer? What does motherhood offer to lesbians? Is it really worth it? Why do we do it? Is it maternal instinct? What is maternal instinct, really? Is it a response to societal conditioning? Are we exhibiting rebellious defiance, showing that as lesbians we can have children without your participation or approval, you men, so up yours? Is it the wish to create that perfect childhood we never had for ourselves? Is it the ego of perpetuating ourselves? Is it simple curiosity? Or the yearning to have the experience every woman feels she has the right to? But if so, where did that yearning come from? If it's instinctual, why doesn't every woman have it? And if these aren't enough questions for you, what are yours? And after all those questions, as lesbians, we still have to go out of our way to acquire children. But today's technology assures us that we don't have to go as far as we used to. These days we can make the choice to have babies if we want to.

In the excellent new anthology on lesbian parenting, *Politics of the Heart,* Jan Clausen says, "We don't move by rules, we move toward what we love. We don't have or not have them for political reasons. Having kids, being with kids, looking toward a new generation is part of being human. And in one sense I think the current public and publicized interest in having babies is another way the lesbian feminist community has of stretching into a newfound sense of its rights to the full range of human and female experience."[2] Now, what about that full range of human and female experience?

Well, being pregnant is a unique experience and after three births, I can tell you that in each of my completed pregnancies, the first trimester, the last trimester, the birth and postpartum experience didn't exactly thrill me. There is something to be said for the second trimester, though. There's a private little feeling between you and one other little being that no one else can feel and the movement of the baby inside is quite sensuous once you get used to it. Now I may be strange, but out of this whole sacred, mystical feeling that I've seen written about in such glowing terms for so many years, that's about what I've got to say. Let's hear it for the second trimester.

After the obvious anxiety of the pregnancy, waiting to see if what came out of you is a complete, viable, healthy human person, then begin the years of seeing that they eat enough, burp enough, poop enough, sleep enough, air enough, bathe enough, exercise enough, walk, talk, smile, play, recognize, stimulate, or separate from you enough. You've got to see that they have playmates, develop manual dexterity, don't kill that playmate, are polite enough, get inoculated, know their numbers, colors, ABC's, read, dress themselves, pick up their toys, don't run into the street, get good marks, listen to the right music, go to a decent school, impress the teachers, don't eat sand—or doo-doo, etc. Then, when they get older, it's school, cultural development, the right companions, dating, talking about relationships, drink, dope, sex, condoms, AIDS, college, marriage, grandchildren, etc. And all the while you're trying to have a life. And you're trying to affect the future of this world to assure that life goes on for yourself and for them and for theirs. And all the while you live with that constant, lurking anxiety about your children that you who are not parents can't even begin to conceive of.

Now here's another in that range of human and female experience. Most of us who had borne children would never consider giving them away, even though in some cases we know someone who would do a better job than we could. And of course we love them, so that counts for everything. Well, sometimes we do—and sometimes we don't. I don't mean that in the trivial sense of exasperation that overcomes us periodically when we say, "Sometimes I really hate that kid." I mean sometimes parents have children that they really don't, simply can't, love. But who admits it? Just last week a woman spoke a cliché to me I've heard over and over. She said of her seventeen-year-old son, "I love him but I just don't like him very much." I smiled. What could I say? I've used those same words myself, as so many of us do. But lately I've been wondering what they mean.

The myth abounds that we love our children. Well, we are bound to them, we're responsible to and for them, but it's not always possible to feel that automatic love for a child that we are assured comes naturally to every mother. We're all born with inherent differences, our personalities don't necessarily mesh, no matter how hard we try, and you may happen to get a kid you just don't like or love and who doesn't love you. And don't be so sure it's that unusual either. This may just be one of the best kept dirty little secrets the world over. As Marilyn Murphy says in *Politics of the Heart,* "As a love relationship, motherhood bears some resemblance to that of an arranged marriage, wherein a woman chooses, or is forced, to enter a relationship with a person she does not know, but whom she is expected to love and take care of until one of them dies."[3] So if you seek motherhood to experience the full range of human and female experience posed by Jan Clausen, you'd be only fair to yourself if you included the realities I've just mentioned. We, of all people, don't need to romanticize motherhood.

Motherhood was named an institution and examined by Adrienne Rich in her comprehensive, *Of Woman Born.* It is at one and the same time the most revered and most reviled of institutions. Lesbians notoriously have refused to live in institutions. That's why we're right out here being our sweet lesbian selves. Yet many of us who read Rich's classic work, along with other books on motherhood from the '70s, such as *The Baby Trap,* lesbians who've analyzed and agonized, still have found themselves craving the experience of motherhood. So they've plunged right in, many others follow and it's growing. Still, if we're going to do motherhood, it's good to be able to talk about how, in our own honest lesbian ways.

It's quite clear that you newer mothers will have far more support for your choices than we old-timers had. You have the groups you've formed while talking about choosing children. Lesbian choice groups lead to lesbian birthing classes, lead to lesbian children's play groups and on to lesbian mother and children communities. But who is part of those communities? How do you form your household? Some of those questions are being dealt with all over the lesbian feminist communities here and abroad. What model of childraising will you initiate or imitate? Nuclear, extended, interfamilial, multicultural, mothers, partners, other mothers, child-free friends? The possibilities are bounded only by our imaginations. But we're lesbians, so of course we can break the mind boundaries set up around childraising, right? Do you expect that you'll bring together groups of mothers and children who live in the same neighborhood, houses, apartment buildings, apartments? Will you share parenting with other mothers and some child-oriented single women? Will only your lovers have access to your children? Will your ex-lovers have access to the children you have nurtured jointly? Will grandparents, aunts and uncles be included as we are more out to our own families? Will you create networks of diversity for them, people with different ethnic and class backgrounds, who are trying to overcome the variety of internalized "isms" we're all infected with? Children raised this way would be choice children indeed.

But you know, I have to say that there is something about the notion of choice children that's a bit off-putting. Does the title "Lesbians Choosing Children" mean that other women did not choose to have them? Does it mean that by definition the children of the new lesbians are somehow better than the children who came here in the time before all these new choices were available? As a Black woman, I feel a gut rejection of the notion of choice children. And here's another question I have—being a Black woman who had children the old-fashioned way. For those of you who took up the banner of true feminism, how will the babymaking and childrearing choices you are making now affect the work you've already put into coalition building, into self-examination, into throwing off the shackles of your own racism, classism, homophobia, ableism, ageism? What do you do with the children you bring here in defiance of the patriarchy, which says, "You don't deserve to have children, since you've chosen this life style?" What will you teach them? Whose allies will you raise them to become? To whom will you be trying to prove yourselves worthy? Your families, neighbors, teachers, social workers, employers, the corner grocer, the postman? And who or what will you sacrifice to prove yourselves worthy? Me, my children, your integrity, feminism, your own soul? Yes, we have some ethical child rearing choices ahead as more children of lesbians enter our community of women.

Were you around during the last ten to twenty years making women who had children the old-fashioned way feel as if we should hide our children away, not mention them, leave them at home while we attended women-only events? I somehow don't expect that will happen in this new environment of lesbian choice. Were you among the brave new women of the '70s who set up those cruel "only girl children acceptable" parameters, making us choose between leaving our boys at home (if we could find sitters), or staying at home with them, rather than joining our sisters in shaping our movement? I hope we've come too far for that, even if so many lesbians today weren't choosing to have children. Did you ever support a sister with children by offering to babysit, by including her children in invitations, or even by simply inquiring after them, giving her an opportunity to acknowledge that they just might be as important to her as the demonstration, the mailing, the rap session? It's still not too late. And for those of you just beginning to raise children, do women of color, poor women, disabled women now have the support of you *and* your children in our struggles? Or do you have more important concerns now that you have your child's welfare at stake? In *Politics of the Heart* a woman is asked how having a child affected her being out as a lesbian and her reply was, "If anything, I went back into the closet a little more. Before, I didn't compromise my freedom…but after…it wasn't just me at stake. I didn't really go back in the closet, but I'm not willing to get in trouble or…make her life harder. There is something I love more than my own freedom and that's her."[4] But Pat Parker, in the same anthology, says, "We had had to do some serious consciousness-raising among family and friends. We simply made it clear that anyone wishing to participate in this child's life had to accept the premise that she had two mothers. The school got it that she would be picked up by whichever of us was available, that the permission slip was signed by whoever remembered to do it, that potluck food was prepared by whoever had time. And I still had to go to the school after her first Mother's Day there and make it clear that she should come home with two Mother's Day gifts or none at all."[5] What will *you* teach your children? To align themselves with heterosexuals, becoming yet another source of oppression against us? Or will you teach them to assume that our fight is also their fight? Will you be trying to raise people who can be your own friend and ally later in life, radical little warriors in the battle? Or yet another bunch of greedy yuppies mixed and matched and blended with the offspring of heterosexuals so that they won't have to suffer any slight discomfort by being considered different? Do my children, my grandchildren have future allies in your children? Or when they've all grown up will mine need to start from scratch to teach your children and grandchildren the ground rules about racism, ableism, classism because you have been so busy blending and hiding for the sake of your choice children that my children can't even find allies anymore?

Among the women who joined the second wave of feminism in the late '60s and early '70s, there was a commitment to address racism and classism as well as sexism. That commitment drew many women of color into feminism. Now, once consciousness dawns, you don't choose or not choose to be a feminist; there's no choice about it. Still, it was difficult for many of us who were born into communities of color because it meant rebelling against our root communities, which insisted that feminists were white, middle-class women looking to advance themselves into the existing structures of a racist and classist society. That argument still abounds today, although it recedes gradually—very gradually—as the skeptical communities of color see where principled feminists come down on most of the issues. But the struggle, begun two decades ago, to hammer out our difficulties so that we can identify and acknowledge our differences, assuage the hurts, hear one another's oppressions and work together to confront our common enemies, has only just begun, really. We can't expect in these very few short years to overcome hundreds of years of separation, divide-and-conquer tactics by intransigent men and unenlightened women, as well as our own internalized terror and self-protection. So for those of us who've already stuck our faces out the door, rather than retreating into the closet to protect our children, we need to work to develop surroundings conducive to cushioning our children from the hostility of heterosexism by finding competent, loving allies among lesbians, gay men and progressive hetero-sexuals who will know and honor who we are. By hiding, we're not helping our children. And putting our lesbianism on hold until they're grown is no solution. We can come up with more creative solutions to mothering than retreating into a closet.

Just recently, I figured out one way to provide more support for my daughter, my life partner and myself. Tomorrow, four loving women, one who has a child and three who do not, will participate with us in a bonding ceremony between them and my daughter. These are women we've come to know and respect, who have talents, love and warmth to share with her; she's an absolute gem and can give something back to each of them in turn. No one person can or should try to be the be-all to another. We have so many resources in the community that mothers don't need to end up feeling the full burden of trying to do it all themselves. In fact, the more of us who share our children within the community, the better for all of us, single women with much to give and receive, and the children as well. As Sweet Honey in the Rock tell us, "Your children are not your children: they are the sons and daughters of life yearning for itself."

My mother, an immigrant from the West Indies, was aware of her need for assistance when my father died in 1938 and left her a widow with seven children. She sought out allies. We each had at least two godparents, some of us three. But as we grew up and began to identify the grown-ups we might bond with more naturally, she allowed each of us that connection after carefully checking out the people we had chosen. If she didn't like them, she let us know, but that didn't happen too often—we had pretty good judgment. So each of us had special adults and we're all the richer for it. Surround your children with the kind of people whose influence on them will please you.

I'd like now to get back to those lesbians who hide once they are parents. It's hard to answer people who think that their children are such delicate flowers that they can't undergo the trauma of having to face the reality of their parents being different from other parents. My daughter's fine about most of it, except that she can't stand for me to be on TV talking about being a lesbian. I tell her that I understand how she feels, but she needs to think about the children in South Africa or in the Palestinian camps in Israel if she thinks she's suffering because she sees my face on TV! That tends to put things in perspective a bit. And, although she may not like it, she does respect that this is my life and she'll have to choose later how to live her own. Children are strong, resilient and brave when they're given reason to be.

They also get grown and gone eventually and you're left with yourself to live with always. And they're left with the lifelong remembrance of you and what you told and showed them about how to live. Giving up your principles in the name of motherhood can be a pretty self-defeating choice. For one thing, you don't like yourself as much as you used to. For the children's sake you have become a bit less of a proud dyke than you used to be before you had them to worry about, so you resent them. Then, by hiding, you're telling them that if the larger society tells them to shut their mouths about anything that doesn't sit well with the power boys, you think they should go along with that.

And let's not forget too that kids watch and absorb our brand of integrity even if it doesn't seem to sink in at the time. I've heard my nineteen-year-old son saying something about me in pride to other people that I never hear him address directly to me. And I can't even count the number of times children, not just mine but others, have come back and told me that they appreciated my having stood firm in some piece of conflict we'd had where they had yelled, screamed and cried because they were being made to take a difficult path. But, quiet as it's kept, they also remember the times you took the other, not so noble path. Those aren't the times they tell you about, but they sure as hell remember them. Well, you watched your parents and you sure as hell remember what they did, don't you? I know I do. Still, when all is said and done, there are no guarantees. You can spend all those good years you've got and still not end up in concert with your own children. They might decide to become the epitome of everything you can't stand.

I'm going to close by answering the question so many of us mothers hedge about when we're asked. We don't feel we can answer, for whatever reasons. It goes, "If you had to do it again, would you have children, knowing what you know now?" My answer is no. Right now, I feel the weight of all the years of mothering that I'll never shake off. The trips I haven't taken, the books I haven't read, the solitude I haven't enjoyed, the books I haven't written, the women I haven't loved. Maybe if you asked me again in ten years I might feel differently, but somehow I doubt it. If I had it to do all over again, I'd mother children, as I've done; but I wouldn't have them myself. I'd take some off their mothers' hands for a couple of months at a time, or even a few years. One of my most positive mothering experiences in addition to my birth daughter, was with my teenage foster daughter for a period of three and a half years. That was over twenty years ago and between then and now, many children have thought of me as their mother—whether I wanted them to or not.

I'm only one voice among many, speaking my own truth to the best of my ability. The most helpful thing I can say is, if you have children, for your own sake and for theirs, don't hoard them to yourselves. Share them. And for those of you who choose not to have children, share in the nurturing of some other women's children. Our children, of course, are our future. But everyone else's children are our future too. So whatever else we decide, let's share the children in whatever ways we can: physically, spiritually, financially, mentally; let's take care of one another's children as well as one another. Because we've got a long way to go and we'll only make it by expanding our consciousness enough to create better ways of doing it together.

(Excerpted from a speech delivered at University of Massachusetts, Boston, in January, 1988. The complete version is published in pamphlet form by Kitchen Table: Women of Color Press as part of the Freedom Organizing Series.)

ENDNOTES

1. *Of Woman Born*, (New York: Bantam Books, 1977) afterword, p. 292

2. *Politics of the Heart,* (Ithaca, NY: Firebrand Books, 1987) p. 339

3. ibid, p. 126

4. ibid, p. 118

5. ibid, p. 99

Maintaining Our Equilbrium In Couples —Or Not

Pursuing Creativity Through a Twenty Year Interracial Marriage: Two Views

JEAN LOIS GREGGS
& ELFRIEDA MUNZ

Jean Lois Greggs

Erato, our muse, has many faces. She comes to me one way and speaks to Elfrieda, it seems to me, quite differently. When we first met in 1969, my constant companion was my drawing pad and pen. Whenever it was possible, I either drew or wrote. At this time Elfrieda had two young girls, ages five and three, for whom she was responsible. She was not actively involved with her piano. But from early on, I knew from our talks that we shared an enchantment: we were each stirred by the same Queen of the Soul, Erato.

My childhood school could not afford an art department. Throughout my school years, however, I was allowed to create displays of various kinds for special occasions, using whatever materials were around. When I was younger than school age, I ofttimes went with my dad to the construction company where he performed his janitorial chores. He sat me in the drafting room with pen and paper to occupy myself. Dad would sometimes finish his work before I finished mine and sometimes showed my drawings to the owner of the company. The kindly man wanted to be notified whenever I needed paper or any other tools they had around. With art, I grew up with the concept of making use of whatever materials were available.

I seemed to have known early in life that I could not maintain an inner balance without being involved in some process of creating. When I ignore these urges to write, to paint or to sculpt, everything within me rebels. My physical, emotional and spiritual bodies break down. My recoveries are slow and painful.

At age eighteen I left Monroe, Louisiana and a very protected childhood to attend college in Atlanta. Upon graduation from Grambling

University, six of us headed for Chicago to see the world and make our way in it. My friends had degrees in Education and knew within weeks where they would begin their teaching careers. I, on the other hand, was the only Fine Arts major in the class.

Directly before resigning myself to taking a civil service exam, I was urged by a friend to come to upstate New York to work for IBM as a commercial artist. She lived in the area, had just been hired by IBM and loved the job. At first, the opportunity of working commercially as an artist sounded exciting to me. At some point in the interviewing process, however, I realized that I didn't want the job. I feared that making art daily, with someone else commanding the product, would leave me little or no energy for creating my own images. I chose to work for Child Welfare, instead. I moved to New York City two years later and met Elfrieda while I was in my final year of social work school. By becoming a psychotherapist I had found a profession in which I could be creative, support myself financially and have space enough to continue my art work. At that time I was painting, drawing and writing poetry. I felt profoundly understood as an artist by Elfrieda.

Encouragement to procure art supplies is one of the major ways I receive support from Elfrieda. I may complain endlessly about a brush being less and less usable, but often it is Elfrieda who will suggest a quick ride to the art store. I now have a different consciousness; I can have an idea which is not dependent upon available materials for execution. This type of influence is difficult to explain. It provides a material base that nourishes an inner expansion, a larger arena in which to allow images to emerge.

Providing space is another way in which Elfrieda has been instrumental in my creativity. College classrooms were the only experiences I had of starting an art piece that could remain in one place until completion. Growing up, our kitchen table was my work bench. Shortly after we began our lives together, Elfrieda introduced the idea of a studio. I was originally reluctant, since I felt that having a studio would require a greater output and the marketing of my work. Elfrieda assured me that there were no expectations and no demands would be forthcoming. Along with some other renovations, we built a studio attached to our bedroom. With this new, permanent workspace my productivity increased greatly. More importantly, the quality of my work took an upward turn. I now had room to step away from it, to work out mistakes without a sense of urgency and to have a place where my art supplies belonged. This gave me the structure by which I began to identify myself as an artist, rather than someone who drew and painted.

I make art very slowly; three to four hours working on a piece seems a short time to me. Elfrieda's rhythm is faster than mine, partly due to lessons learned in child rearing, that interruptions were a given, no matter what the activity. Speeding me up is like accelerating a car to go 80 miles an hour when it is only capable of going 60. Whatever I'm involved in has my complete attention. This difference in tempo, along with not quite understanding the other's use of time and attention, remains an ongoing conflict between us.

Within our twenty year relationship our warring has taken many forms. We often disagreed about the time and quality of attention the children needed. I did not like continual interruptions while I was working; Elfrieda believed they were unavoidable. The children are now grown. They still require attention, but differently. There is more of a reciprocal quality in the relationships. We're not drained by them even when their situations are serious and painful. Our time is no longer governed by their needs.

While being open to Elfrieda's presence, I try to remain aware of the number of hours I am faithful to the muse. I try not to give Erato all of my best energy. It is difficult maintaining this balance in a continual way and I still sometimes find myself at one extreme or the other, although not as frequently as in the past. A poem I wrote in March of 1982 addresses this balancing act:

Elfrieda

Loving you like Spring
Like hidden Scents
Floating through nearly moist air
I am charmed to error
I neglect my muse
She grows jealous veiled.

My muse fears you
Coming like a scared mistress
Threatening never to return
Waiting for dismissal
You sometimes like her
Almost accepting her.

You and I, my love
Birth fantasies together
We grow the children up
Pretending we know something
We extend our visions beyond them
So we may continue with them.

I will not lose your presence
Spring is eternal beginnings
You anchor my dreams
Give patience to my thoughts
She, this muse of mine
Is the murmurings of my spirit.

She inspires me
You inflame me
You are the earth I touch
Rushing toward rebirth
She is the air I aspire to breathe.

You are my light for
Each new webbed and darkened tunnel
You are the dream
I awake to each morn
My muse is my reckoning
My life sustaining presentness.

Sweetness, I cannot
I must not choose
Earth and air exist
Each giving space, growth
I give back to you
What she gives to me.

In recent years, Elfrieda's reconnection and continual involvement with her piano studies has opened new doors of communication. We are now looking at ways to better share our practical responsibilities. She carries more of these tasks than I do, with a speed that I cannot begin to imitate. Elfrieda believes that I should do more; I believe we need to do less. I suspect that the truth lies in between. I need to develop a greater tolerance for attention to the practical aspects of existence. This is a difficult dilemma since I don't think of tasks and then reject doing them. Rather, many escape my consciousness. I have gotten better through the years, but not quite good enough. On the other hand, I believe that Elfrieda needs to redefine necessities of living to include more empty spaces, more blank canvases, as an essential nutrient of life. I don't know if this battle is ever meant to end or if it will just continue as one of life's ongoing lesson plans. There is something inspiring in the conflict. For one thing, it keeps creativity in the foreground. We frequently have long discussions on all aspects of making art. We struggle with language since both of our media are coded forms of speaking. I am learning to articulate more clearly and as a result of these discussions, I am gaining greater insight into my creative process. I better understand my passion to create in ways that allow me to feel in contact and clear, rather than defensive and muddled. I have come to realize how we both have dual marriages. No matter how close we are with each other, we are each at the mercy of the muse's beckoning. Erato recedes at times, seems almost to be asleep, but when she emerges, we attend.

Elfrieda Munz

"We bring to our music from our lives
and take from our music for the rest
of our living."
-Mildred Portney Chase
Just Being at the Piano

I have never been without a piano for any period of my life. New pianos, for me, seem to coincide with the imminent movings to new physical spaces and entering new eras of awakening creativity. At age 53, I am again at such a point in my life. Jean and I are planning to move to a new home and are considering buying another piano. Our living space is no longer ideal for our needs; the piano requires either major rebuilding or replacement.

This year we are celebrating our twentieth anniversary marking, for me, a period of reflection and self-examination on the important themes and issues of my life. I look at our relationship and wonder, in Tevye's words from *Fiddler on the Roof,* how "a bird and a fish make a home together?" Jean and I are as different and as similar as two women can be. She is Black, Southern and from a Catholic-Baptist upbringing; I am Caucasian, Central European by birth and reared in a Jewish Ethical Culture tradition. Jean comes from a large extended family and was raised in a small-town environment, where inclusiveness was the guiding principle. I am a Holocaust survivor whose immediate family escaped from Austria; due to "war circumstances" I am an only child. I was reared in a large city, isolated from and distrustful of neighbors. We belonged to a small circle of Austrian refugees who became "family" in a closed, protective network. Not only do Jean and I come from very different circumstances, our temperaments—born out of our backgrounds—are opposite in character. Jean has an easygoing, slow, accepting, meditative nature; I am quick energetic, busy and overly productive.

When we first met, twenty years ago this summer, a friend sent us a birthday card stating: "It's not that you're not different from each other, it's that you're so much alike!" Our first discovery of similarity left us each in states of disbelief: we were born on the same date, May 14th. From there, we discovered that on an external level we both loved to travel, yet were also "homebodies." We both delight in a well-cared for and beautiful home and are essentially "day" people by temperament. Jean and I enjoy the same types of activities, particularly theater, opera and concerts. Spiritually, we are both seekers of truth, each valuing and appreciating the other's journey. A deep and abiding respect for and love of the arts, is the major place where our paths meet.

And from there, collecting our similarities and differences, we had to create an intermediary environment, a space in which we could each function and take nourishment. This was not an easy undertaking as our Taurean natures often blocked compromise and resolution. We are both stubborn, quick to anger and we focus narrowly. To this day our struggles continue, but fortunately we share the same intense passions which support and nourish our souls; the love of and the making of art and music. Our participation in these arts feeds our relationship by teaching us "grounded-ness," inner balance and a pursuit of truthfulness. Our life together is about the seeking and uncovering of deeper and deeper levels of "telling the truth." In the process of "making art," we also learn about a quality of effort, work and struggle, which carries over into our relationship and the rest of our lives.

Jean and I came to this union as women who have always been involved in making art. Most of my childhood was devoted to studying and practicing piano—along with voice, drama and dance. I attended the Institute of Modern Piano Technology, a small private school for "gifted" pianists, where I only devoted two hours daily to academic study. From grades two to seven I attended a "one-room schoolhouse" on the fourth floor of an old brownstone building in upper Manhattan with four other children, ranging in age from three to eighteen. The rest of my day was spent practicing the piano in one of the many little practice rooms through-out the building. Most of the children were being prepared for a life of concertizing and nothing was as important as practice time. I believe that if my piano teachers could have eliminated school time or one half-hour of "playtime" after lunch, they surely would have. Although I had few peers my age at school, all the students shared a strong sense of community and common purpose.

My life continued to center around the piano when I left this school and entered the High School of Performing Arts. Here, for the first time I was surrounded by students my own age who were also brilliant pianists. I felt the awakening of a keen sense of competition and inadequacy. I'm not certain that I had ever entertained the notion of becoming a pianist, but at this time I certainly gave up any fantasies of such a career. The piano, however, was still the center of my life and the next four years were the period of my most intensive music study. In college, I continued to major in music, but my attention to the piano began to recede strongly by the third year. Then, for the first time in memory, I was not taking piano lessons; there seemed to be no purpose.

I bought my first piano when I moved out of my parents' home into my own apartment. I spent every penny I had earned from my summer job on the piano. When I married a year later, I moved this piano into our new apartment, where, over the next ten years, it deteriorated along with my waning interest.

An astrologer I consulted this summer, on the occasion of my twentieth anniversary with Jean, described the period of my first marriage as "a period of misplaced values," without knowing the facts surrounding the years she described. In many ways I felt like a lost child. I had two children and was still floundering for my identity and struggling to separate from my parents. My music was lost to me in a world overwhelmed with teaching, diapers, cooking, babysitting problems, ordinary illnesses and laundry. I was desperately trying to survive as a mother and a wife, while struggling with my sexuality in an "illicit" lesbian love affair which began before my marriage and continued throughout it. In deep sadness and total confusion of loyalties, my lover and I broke up one year before my marriage fell apart.

During those years when I longingly touched the piano, tried to play some music, it was always with the heavy feeling of a purposeless experience. Without perfection and performance as a goal, what reason could there be for practicing? I have always had difficulty with the ephemeral and intangible aspects of music. A musical work, upon completion, could not be framed and hung on the wall. Jean's art can be appreciated each time I walk through a room. But nothing I had recreated on the piano would remain after a performance; there would be no visible product for my efforts. My ex-husband never encouraged me to work through my creative emptiness and confusions, although he was an artist himself who found some time to make art during our marriage. I felt very lonely and depressed throughout those years.

When I first met Jean in 1969, fell in love and awakened into a new era, I felt reborn. My stars must have been in the right constellation for a year of change and movement out of the stage of "Scorpionic symbolism." This is the stage where the very primitive animal keeps self-destructing under pressure and stress. I was finally, after a long period of depression and tears, able to move out of this stagnant, heavy period to the "symbolism of the serpent" stage, where I was willing to shed some of the old skin and walk vulnerably into the new era. At this point, I summoned the needed courage (not an easy task) to leave my husband and begin a new life with a woman and my two very young children, ages three and five-and-a-half.

We had no lesbian role models to follow, as neither of us knew any other lesbians who were living together, let alone with children. Jean and I used to laugh, at first, at the fact that we were beginning our life together, each with three strikes against us in the world: I—a woman, lesbian and Jewish; she—a woman, lesbian and Black.

Within the first year of our life together, even before we moved out of the city, we bought a baby grand Knabe for me. It cost us a fortune at the time; neither of us had any money. And yet its importance loomed large, becoming the center, the focus, the symbol of a new creative beginning for me. Jean insisted that our money was being well spent on a very essential item; I was unsure but extremely excited and filled with anticipation. I began practicing and playing the piano again, which filled me with joy. Jean loved to hear me play the piano and would bring whatever she was doing into the living room in order to hear the music. Even the boring and repetitive practice of isolated sections of music did not irritate her; she often said that it helped her to understand the music better. The one difficulty I still had, however, was that once again a purpose or outlet seemed to be missing.

Throughout my child rearing years, in a suburban town just outside of New York City, I had a difficult time allowing myself the time and space in which to practice. There always seemed to be so many other pressing priorities after a full day's work. I sometimes felt jealous of Jean's "freedom" in pursuing her art, for during this period she was more prolific than at any time before. When the children were young I always permitted them to interrupt my concentration at the piano, because no other adult was home in the afternoons. Jean, a psychotherapist, came home only in the early evening. By then I was much too tired to begin any practice. As all children will, mine often interrupted me. I remember once leaving the piano a dozen or more times within one short practice session. When I even entertained the possibility of taking lessons again, I was stopped by images of interrupted practice time and, once again, by the uncertainty of purpose in the commitment. Practice and expression at the piano still seemed, for me, to be entirely connected to performance and an audience, which I did not have. Jean, at this time, was preparing for her first one-woman art show, an event that made a major impact on our lives. I spent a great deal of time framing her paintings, writing invitations and even hanging her art at the show. The "success" of the art show generated much excitement and joy in our family. We loosely targeted a showing of her art every five to six years.

About five years ago, at the time of the most recent art show, a close friend introduced me to another woman who was involved in a classical music group which met monthly at different women's homes. The purpose of CML (Classical Music Lovers) is for women to come together in fellowship and to share their love of music through live performances by the members. Willingness to share, enjoyment and participation are the guiding principles of the group. Performers range from newly studying instrumentalists to professional singers and musicians. The atmosphere is always informal and appreciative of anyone who is willing to share her musical endeavors. This group has given me the opportunity and the "purpose" to return to my piano studies. For the past five years I have been taking lessons from a professional pianist who is also a member of the group. Her loving support, inspiration and encouragement have once again awakened Erato in my life. I practice as much as possible, which still falls far short of what I feel is needed in order to make "real" progress, though Jean reminds me not to use an arbitrary standard of "real," or other people's expectations, as a measure of my unfolding. I am still plagued by the voices of my early piano teachers and my parents, in words such as "not being good enough," "perfection or nothing," and "trying to make real progress." I have heard these inner voices described as the "drivers" of our lives, which can only cause illness and despair. Health and happiness can only come from turning these "drivers" into "allowers." I realize that this is exactly what I have been trying to accomplish with my music. My piano playing teaches me that I don't have to be perfect (I can make mistakes) and I am good enough at any given moment (there are no outside standards to pit myself against). I have all the time I need, so it is not necessary to keep "trying harder." Of course, I always do battle on the thin line between permitting and accepting myself to be where I am, pianistically, and being highly self-critical. However, when I find myself at this latter place, it is usually the result of "judgment" based on comparison with others, or by the need for approval and recognition for accomplishment.

Midlife is a time of letting go of many worn-out values, particularly one's ego and notions of self- importance. I am learning that it is impossible to be conscious of the self and be involved in music at the same time. This becomes a barrier in reaching that place where the soul of the composer and the soul of the pianist meet. This place Robertson Davies describes in *A Mixture of Frailties* as "the mood": "The mood's everything. Get it and you'll get the rest. If you don't get it, all the exercises in agility…in the world will be powerless to make a good musician of you. The mood's at the root of all."

My astrological reading revealed that I am at the end of an era and at the beginning of a new path of refining my communications through words, expressions of my feelings and my music. This confirmed my own very strong sense of a new beginning (I've had many dreams of being pregnant and giving birth). I am planning to give my first adult recital next spring for friends who I feel will celebrate with me in the sharing of music. I have been very nourished and supported in my creative process by Jean and my CML friends. I now feel a strong desire to give something back.

The Knabe, which has been my close musical companion for twenty years, no longer seems to have the sonorities I long to hear. We will either have to rebuild it, or trade it in for another piano. We are planning to sell our house in the suburbs and move to a smaller and more appropriate living space. A new home, a new piano, are once again coinciding with a strong surge of musical interest and a certain amount of courage in risk taking. I feel a new creative era on the horizon.

Seedless Grapes and Brie

ANGELA VAN PATTEN

You tell me, over seedless grapes and brie,
how we will fight for our independence.
Is this a duel? Two strong women, with softnesses to cover,
making promises difficult to keep.
We are set in granite, earth and ashes,
standing rooted in our sensible shoes
to these claims we have staked
so many years at such great cost.
Could we agree to return each strong,
sure hug someday when the other needs it?
Loving both in weakness and in strength, perhaps,
careful not to disturb the balance.

Subtle Balances: Love and Work in Lesbian Relationships

MARNY HALL with
ANN GREGORY

A freshly minted and uppity twenty-year-old lesbian, I was undaunted by the fact that I would never have a husband to support me. I would, instead, capture the heart of an heiress, an updated Gertrude Stein or Natalie Barney, who would subsidize us in a moveable feast of love and art.

Years have passed. I never acquired my heiress. Those I met, industrious, sober and usually partnered with other hard workers, gave the *coup de grace* to my dreams of romantic indolence.

I find that most lesbians work. Even if our economic survival isn't at stake, our sense of pride and purposefulness is. Besides working for money, we work for existential meaning. If we are lucky, we work for self-esteem and pleasure. We also work to be our partners' equals. Our desire for egalitarian relationships makes it unlikely—even when it makes total economic and practical sense—that one partner will manage the home while the other goes off to her job.

The fact that vocational focus is almost as critical to lesbian identity as women-loving means that lesbians who are partnered typically contend with all the problems indigenous to dual career heterosexual couples. As well as the standard tensions between work, personal needs and domestic demands, lesbians often have the added stress of shifting regularly between very disparate private and public lives.

To understand more about how we manage this balancing act, I interviewed eighteen lesbians, nine couples, which I found through my friendship and career networks. The hour-and-a-half interviews, which were conducted separately with each partner, consisted of a series of open-ended questions about work and relationships.

The Interviewees: Similarities and Differences

Except for one Canadian couple, all the women I interviewed lived and worked in the San Francisco Bay Area. Twelve of the women had Anglo and/or Northern European backgrounds, four were Jewish, one was

African-American and one was Italian-American. The length of their current relationships ranged from two and one half to twelve years. The average length of the interviewees' relationships was about six years. Except for one woman who was 32, all were between 35 and 50. Only two were mothers, and they had semi-independent, college-aged children. All except two couples lived together. Three women were in managerial jobs, three were attorneys, three were in sales, two in arts-related professions, two were academics, two were ministers, one was a physical therapist. The last two were in transition: one, previously a corporate manager, had just started her own business as a body therapist; the other, previously a social service worker, was beginning a sales career.

Their individual yearly salaries ranged from $12,500 to $120,000. These women were at various levels in their current jobs ranging from novices to advanced specialists. The majority had postgraduate degrees.

Within work settings, the degree of openness about being lesbians varied considerably. Some, the ministers for example, served an entirely gay congregation. These women's particular careers hinged on the fact that they were openly lesbian. Most of the rest were open with certain clients and colleagues in particular situations, discreet in others. Others were entirely closeted at work.

Though this identifying information gives a general profile of the women who were interviewed, it doesn't capture the spirit of individual couples. The following sketches of two couples reflect, in more detail, the ways in which lesbian couples integrate intimacy and career. Certain identifying characteristics of these couples have been altered to protect the interviewees' anonymity.

DANA AND SUE

Dana and Sue seem utterly comfortable in their elegant, understated business suits. Their gestures, as they talk, are athletic and graceful. Here the parallels stop. Dana is dark, angular. She is tearful when she describes some of the difficulties they have weathered. Sue is fair, cherubic. Her description of her life is peppered with droll asides.

In their early forties, they have been together for twelve years. Over the years they have advanced in their careers as corporate executives and each currently earns between $70,000 and $80,000 a year. Sue, openly gay with most colleagues, sees herself as part of a large informal network of other gay co-workers. Dana, closeted, believes that it would not be wise to disclose her sexual orientation to all of her professional colleagues, although certain of them know she is gay. She prefers, she says, to keep her private life private.

Their work weeks are predictable: up at five-thirty in the morning, on the road by seven o'clock, they are both usually in their offices before eight o'clock. They spend the next ten hours in meetings with clients or staff, gathering or analyzing data, presenting or writing reports. They try to meet for lunch once a week. On other weekdays, Sue is more likely to meet friends for lunch, Dana to have business lunches. When possible, they talk during the day to coordinate evening schedules. On the two or three nights a week they don't have evening meetings or appointments, they come home, look over the mail, watch the news or read, discuss the day's events over dinner—often some fruit and cheese, since they have their major meal at lunch. They usually spend the rest of these precious evenings unwinding with a book or a video. Jogging, Twelve Step meetings, housecleaning, shopping, gardening and friends must all be squeezed into weekends. One of the casualties of this life style is sex. They have trouble making time for sensual intimacy in their relationship. They do, however, make weekly "dates" and try to schedule erotic interludes. They succeed sporadically.

Their major relationship crisis occurred seven years ago. Dana, against Sue's wishes, took a job that required her to travel two or three weeks a month. Sue felt abandoned, started drinking heavily and began an affair. Dana's drinking also escalated and on the rare times she was home, they fought bitterly. Finally, on the verge of dissolution, Sue confided in her mother. Her response was pivotal. "She told me," said Sue, "that I was in a marriage that I should honor. I should stick it out...get help from a counselor about our differences. I realized that my mother had sound values, that those values were also mine and that I wasn't living up to them." Dana and Sue did get counseling, but attribute the real turnaround in their relationship to their decisions to stop drinking and join a Twelve Step program. Dana got a new job and though their major relationship stresses continue to be time and job related, they are committed to each other and optimistic about their future.

JOAN AND DEBORAH

Joan, short, dark eyed and intense, has recently left a corporate career and started a new business. Deborah, blond, willowy and soft-spoken, is a free-lance photographer with a best-selling urbanscape book to her credit. The differences between these two partners go beyond first impressions and occupation. Joan, at 35, is nine years younger than Deborah. Joan comes from a working-class background; Deborah from a family who made it to the upper middle-class by a combination of ambition, hard work and professional orientation. Joan, who is task-oriented, frugal and takes nothing for granted, is sometimes dismayed by what she sees as Deborah's sense of entitlement. Deborah is extravagant, dream-oriented and tends to focus on overall projects rather than everyday tasks.

Though both women value long-term relationships, they do so for different reasons. Joan feels most content when she is in a primary relationship. Eventually she would like children. Deborah, not as interested in parenting, values her relationship because it is a "way station where you get revitalized for your signficant contribution," i.e., your work. Joan would like to live together at some point. Deborah, who "has done all that" no longer feels she has to prove anything by conventional relationship formatting. She enjoys living alone, not having to accommodate to another person's domestic idiosyncrasies. Joan likes to spend quiet time together. Deborah likes to socialize, go to bookstores, events, out to dinner. When Joan and Deborah became lovers, they earned the same amount of money and, consequently, had similar life styles. Even that area of mutuality has shifted. Recently, Joan, who left her job as a manager of a bank's credit department, has begun a small massage practice and started studying kinesiology. As a result her income has plunged. Deborah, who because of her recent successes is more in demand, earned an unprecedented $60,000 this year. Central to Joan and Deborah's relationship is a dynamic exchange of values and support about their careers. Deborah had had some work setbacks, for example, when they got together. It was, she says, Joan who restored her confidence. Later, when it became apparent Joan was not happy with her career, Deborah encouraged her to venture out on her own. Deborah has continued to support her by listening and advising, recommending books, picking up some of their extra recreational expenses and some of Joan's tuition. Joan, in turn, has helped out in various ways with Deborah's photography assignments.

Both partners agree that Joan has also introduced Deborah to the mysteries and pleasures of the here-and-now. Joan has enticed Deborah into hiking, biking and backpacking. Where bridges could not be built between them, they have learned to tolerate each other's differences. Deborah has come to accept Joan's introverted style at parties; Joan is less critical of what she sees as Deborah's procrastination about housecleaning and other domestic projects. Ever true to form, both partners see the future of their relationship differently. Deborah cannot picture being together with Joan—or anybody—indefinitely; Joan can. Since neither partner forces or expects harmony, they seem, in quite surprising ways, to have achieved it.

Major Interview Themes: Approaches to Relationships

With these two couples, and the other seven I interviewed, significant common themes emerged involving relationship attitudes, work values, self-sufficiency issues, stress points, sexual frequency and coming out. It seems worth noting that the attitudes and values of these particular women —for the most part white, career-oriented, living in the unusually tolerant social climate of the San Francisco Bay Area—may not be particularly representative of a more inclusive population of lesbians.

RELATIONSHIP ATTITUDES

Like most lesbians in this age group, all the interviewees had had previous significant relationships and most had had several. Eight women had been in heterosexual marriages. Between or within past lesbian relationships, (and often within their current relationship as well) the interviewees had experienced ruptures—divorces and separations, infidelity, illness and other vicissitudes—which had tempered original expectations that they would find one partner with whom they would live "forever after." One woman who had left her husband because the relationship had only been 80 percent okay, gave her current relationship the same ranking. Now, however, twenty percent away from perfect was reason to stay, not to leave. Another said she had played around enough. She was through with that phase. Another said that her past mistakes had made her cautious. She was no longer willing to ride into the sunset with a beloved for whom she would sacrifice everything. Her current relationship, if less romantic, was much more of a stable, equal partnership. Another said, "I don't think in 'rest of your life' terms…four or five years seems fine." In some cases this one-day-at-a-time philosophy was reinforced by participation in Twelve Step programs.

WORK VALUES

As a result of their experiences the interviewees tended to see romance, if not relationships, as transitory. In contrast, most of the interviewees had high expectations about vocational fulfillment. The majority of women were strongly identified with and stimulated by their work. Job-related tensions—incompatibility with co-workers, the strain of secrecy, the pressures of deadlines, long hours—were compensated for not only by increasing status and salary, but also by a sense of empowerment, acknowledgement from others and an overall sense of achievement and self-direction. In addition to these work-generated gratifications, most had been groomed for such career focus from childhood.

Despite considerable variation in the socioeconomic status of their parents, all had embraced the values of education and hard work. Although there was some evidence of sexism, almost all the women's parents had expected them to go to college and, if not to be career oriented, then at least to "have a career to fall back on in case your husband dies." According to the women, this mandate either accompanied or supplanted messages about the desirability of marriage. All saw their parents as hardworking, although not all saw them as happily married. About half the respondents' mothers had worked outside, as well as inside, their homes.

"I remember," said one interviewee, "my mother working all day, coming home and doing all the cooking. If you tried to help, she shooed you away. She could do it all herself."

Even those mothers who had stayed home, however, were no slouches. One woman said her "unemployed" mother "was out building a compost pile right now.... When she comes to visit, I'd better have ten days' work for her to do. She doesn't sit around and jabber."

Still other interviewees remembered their mothers helping out with their fathers' businesses or supplementing household duties with volunteer work. None, according to the interviewees, had led leisurely lives. In addition, several women had been influenced by the careers and economic independence of "maiden" aunts or other female relatives.

Messages, direct and indirect, about relationships and intimacy were much more equivocal than those about the value of hard work, self-sufficiency and success. "Marriage," one woman's mother confided to her, "can be a misery."

SELF-SUFFICIENCY VERSUS DEPENDENCY

To call self-sufficiency a value of lesbians understates the deep psychological commitment most of the women felt to their financial independence. The prospect of any lapse in this independence was unthinkable and usually frightening to many of them. Most said they would be willing to take care of their partners, but could never allow themselves to be taken care of. When one partner earned significantly more than the other, as was the case for half the couples, adjustments were necessary. Sometimes one partner paid for more of the recreational expenses, fronted the down payment for a house, or paid more than half of the mortgage. In these cases, the benefited partners always seemed to compensate by doing extra services, running errands, or taking over more of the household chores. Despite services rendered, the receiver of the financial assistance always claimed more discomfort in these transactions than the giver, whom it "didn't bother at all." Economic differences which were "understandable" or temporary usually helped to ease the discomfort caused by any inequities. For example, if one person was younger and beginning her career, she could "remind" herself that she couldn't yet expect to earn as much as her partner.

In relationships where partners earned about the same amount, they tended to keep close accounts of what each had spent on household expenses during the week or month. Balances were rectified at regular intervals. In one situation, where partners claimed not to keep close accounts, expenditures, when actually calculated, turned out to be almost equal. Both were surprised and concluded they had been keeping an unconscious tally all along.

In three instances, partners had become unexpectedly ill during the course of their relationships. Each ill woman expected her partner to be resentful; however, to her surprise, her partner was solicitous and loving. This inadvertent break in what amounted to a dependency taboo in these relationships seemed, as the relationship continued, to strengthen the bond between these partners.

STRESS SOURCES

"I don't have enough time to do all the things I want to," was a recurring refrain among the women. Sometimes both partners lamented work obligations which kept them from pursuing independent activities, seeing friends or taking care of household chores. Though some couples could work out partially satisfying solutions to most of these problems—the hiring, for example, of a part-time housekeeper—they found it more challenging to wrest intimate time together from their busy schedules. Often, it seemed that the partner whose work obligations were less demanding felt this stress more keenly than the other. Partners handled a scarcity of time together in several ways. Some tried to even out the differences in their schedules. One woman, for example, who was just beginning the same career in which her partner was already well-established, said that instead of relaxing when her partner was performing some work-related function, she, too, would dig up work to do. Another interviewee did the household shopping during the time her partner was commuting. The less busy partner was also more likely to complain about the lack of shared time and to initiate negotiations about redressing the imbalance.

When the differences between partners' commitments to work became too great, they tended to polarize—one focusing on the relationship and the other, on her job. Perhaps by inclination, or perhaps by default, the less work-oriented partner became more relationship-oriented. Her time, unclaimed by work, tended to be more devoted to the maintenance of the relationship; her partner's, to the outside world. The work-oriented partner was likely to see her partnership in terms of renewal—a resting place on the way to career goals. Her partner was more likely to see the relationship as the goal itself. These differences in definition, because they were usually accompanied by differences in incomes and status—the more career-oriented partner having higher income and perceived status— challenged the egalitarian ideals which prevailed among interviewees. The stress created by any perceived inequality was more bearable if both partners believed the situation to be temporary, i.e., that the less work-oriented partner would find her work niche eventually, or the less relationship-oriented partner would someday cut back her work schedule. If partners were not convinced of the transitory nature of the imbalance, they tended to consider the relationship itself transitional. Significantly, such a feeling of impermanence did not actually lead to a shortened relationship or even painful tension. In fact, the acceptance of such an "out" probably allowed partners the relief they needed to stay in the relationship.

SEXUAL FREQUENCY

As might be expected, partners, when they were not working, seeing friends or pursuing other individual activities, spent time together in a variety of ways—had dinner together, watched the evening news, went for walks, exercised, meditated, or lingered in bed, reading the paper. All but one couple cited infrequent sex as a problem. If both partners had demanding schedules, they claimed that lack of time together or the impossibility of "scheduling" sex accounted for the decline in their eroticism, even though they might be able to schedule an evening together. Less tightly scheduled couples were also dissatisfied with the lack of sex. They attributed it to other sources: fatigue or partners' inability to shift from work focus even when they had ample time together.

It was work, in fact, that accounted for most of the couples' intimacy. Most partners spent more time together conferring about career projects, problem-solving, arguing about, debriefing from their jobs than they spent doing any other mutual activity. Sometimes this was a satisfying mutuality that ebbed and flowed over the course of the relationship. Sometimes, it represented the battle lines of the relationship, the area of little satisfaction and considerable disharmony. The public domain of work comprised more of most couples' private domain than the reverse: the couples' private lives, even if they were not closeted at work, rarely intruded into their work worlds.

COMING OUT AT WORK

Except for those lesbians who worked primarily with gay colleagues or clientele, most women were constantly deciding who, when, where and under what circumstances they could reveal their lesbianism in their work setting. Nor were such choices consistent. One instructor came out to one class because she was confident of their high regard for her. She remained closeted, however, with most of her classes and colleagues.

Women who worked in large corporations had generally tapped a semi-submerged network of other lesbian/gay employees with whom they could be candid. No one, however, felt that they would be fired if their lesbianism came to light and none said they would explicitly deny their gayness if questioned. Yet, they did believe that such a revelation would interfere with their chances for promotion. Already feeling like unwanted newcomers in previously male-only territory, they feared their sexual orientation, if acknowledged, would constitute another strike against them. One woman said that gay men in her previous company had been quite open and had not suffered reprisals even when they displayed pictures of their partners on their desks. But the lesbians in the company were secretive, feeling that such disclosures on their part would be weighted differently because of their gender. Thus, sexism and homophobia seemed to interact synergistically, each maximizing the effect of the other.

Conclusions

It is tempting to conclude from the interviews that there are two types of lesbian couples: those who are more polarized—one partner advocating work and the other, intimacy—and those who are more aligned in their allegiance to work. Instead, it seems to me that lesbians, within couples, are always forming new, subtly interactive balances which at times seem to emphasize work, at times intimacy. The interaction between these two spheres serves as a crucible for our relationships. The career-related concerns of both partners and, in particular, the time constraints imposed by work, may comprise a background from which post-passionate intimacy and dependency can emerge in a nonthreatening way.

Without reflections from the dominant culture or acknowledgements from family and colleagues, lesbian couples feel consigned to invisibility. If we cease generating our own romantic meaning, with its accompanying sexual passion, we certainly have no institutionalized roles to lend other form and meaning to our relationships. Because the dominant culture has no models for our various intimacies, it is hard for us to perceive our relationships as anything more special than briefly sexualized friendships, further devalued because they are between women. When both partners, however, are grounded in work, they are embedded in a meaningful, socially recognized structure. A certain amount of tension is involved in integrating this formal career role with a more improvised lover role. Lesbians' attempts to resolve this tension, in concert with our partners, sculpt our intimacies, lend form and, over time, meaning, to our relationships. Irresolution, conflict and trial arrangements are all part of this intimacy-sculpting process.

Even if each partner takes a characteristic stance—one more in favor of time together, one more preoccupied with her own work—their mutual belief in the value of work keeps them from extreme polarization. If they are within negotiating distance, they will usually be able to resolve the recurring tensions between commitments to work and intimacy. Phone calls during the day, morning commutes on the same bus, weekend getaways together, evenings wrested from busy schedules—each represents a way of sculpting intimacy. Women had, in fact, designated such interludes as "sacred time," "spontaneous time," "date night," "Sunday morning rituals." These arrangements were, to some extent changing and still under negotiation even in long-term relationships. Over time, however, most partners seem to have worked out more polished, satisfying routines that involve less conflict. Seasoned partners had come to expect that their relationship would emerge from the landscape of work in fairly reliable, fulfilling ways, even if they could interact intimately only one or two nights a week. This outcome is most likely if both partners' levels of work commitment are similar, if not identical. Thus for certain lesbian couples, the tensions of combining work and intimacy may provoke mutual and frequent re-engagements which continue to define and invigorate partnerships rendered indistinct by an unreflecting universe.

(Thanks to Jeanne Adleman, Jane Futcher, Richard Hall, Diana Russell, Celeste West and the women who were willing to be interviewed, for their contribution to this article.)

Single Lesbians Speak Out

CLARE COSS

Single lesbians I have known have raised profoundly interesting issues. At first it seemed that the very concept, single lesbian, was drawn from the heterosexual world: married or single. The term had an unfamiliar ring. To my knowledge, other than a section in *Our Bodies, Ourselves*, no one has written specifically about the range of emotional issues single lesbians face. Most psychological writings focus on lesbians in relationships.

My pursuit of the subject led me to interview eight women I know who range in age from 24 to 61. They spoke of being lesbian and single in the context of their work, their history of relationships, intimacy, alcohol, race, class, health and the future. The narratives of the four women in midlife, excerpted here, only begin to reflect and celebrate the adventurous diversity in our community.

It was particularly interesting to me how expectations differed between the younger women and the older women interviewed. The younger women (24 to 37) are looking forward to, and expecting to be in, a relationship sometime in the future. Three of them foresee living with a lover as a committed couple. As a result of the lesbian and gay movement, they have grown up with the assumption that this is now an option in our society. "That's really different from the way it was in the '50s. Living together openly just wasn't something we even thought about," Audre Lorde commented on reading the interviews.

Perhaps that is in part why several of the women over 40 present a more philosophic attitude toward the single life. They didn't come out or come of age with the expectation that they would be part of a long-term committed couple sharing a home together. As several of them say in the following interviews, at this point having a relationship would be welcome, but only if it "fits in" and isn't disruptive to the satisfying balance they have achieved in their work and social lives. Their past relationships soured, whether through alcohol, co-dependency, or intimacy issues. And now they prefer to navigate solo rather than jeopardize that balance with a rush into coupledom.

These four midlife women are all privileged in that they are working in fields of their choice: writer, gym teacher, college professor and alcoholism counselor. While the families of origin of the total group of eight cut across class, ethnic and racial lines (three African-Americans, two Jewish women and three white Anglo-Saxon Protestants), all savor their lesbianism and have forged careers that are fulfilling and gratifying.

One black woman discussed the problems of becoming involved with white women and another discussed racism in the lesbian community. The white women noted that their lives rarely intersect socially with the lives of women of color. While there is a great deal more consciousness and action about bridging differences within the lesbian feminist community, several of the interviewees noted that this is an area that requires the concerted attention of white women.

The struggle with alcoholism in the lesbian community has impacted heavily on three of the women. Allison now enjoys sobriety and is getting to know her new personality. Maua and Ann have relinquished the enabler/co-dependent "dyke drama and trauma" days for an evolving stability. More and more women are taking advantage of the structure and support provided by Twelve Step programs such as AA, Al-Anon, ACOA, and Sex and Love Addicts Anonymous, all with gay and lesbian meetings.

One area of deep concern is health. Ann is robust and a strong opponent on the tennis court. But because of a mastectomy several years ago and the vicissitudes of age, she is fearful of what the future may hold. Maua is challenged by having lupus and the threat this presents to her future ability to care for herself. The empowerment from being single and independent is offset by the fear of aloneness and isolation that failing health could bring. In the age of AIDS when a massive mobilization has taken place within the gay and lesbian community, the plight of the aging lesbian still goes largely unaddressed. Senior Action in a Gay Environment (SAGE) in New York City and plans for lesbian retirement homes are movements in this direction, and the National Lesbian Conference in Atlanta in 1991 has designated housing, health and care of aging lesbians as a priority.

The subject of being single and lesbian engendered large responsive audiences when I read from the eight interviews at Gay Women's Alternative in New York City. Hundreds of women exchanged exciting and passionate insights on the advantages and disadvantages of the single status, the concept of "dating" in the lesbian community and the bittersweet pain of falling in love at first sight only to have it come crashing to a halt after two or three months. How can we keep someone's interest long enough to let an intimacy develop *before* we start living together? To allow ourselves to date without becoming involved in an instant commitment is an entitlement we deserve.

These dimensions of freedom and choice enlighten our understanding and appreciation of the single status. As one of the interviewees noted, "Our interviews will be important for people, both gay and straight. No matter

your sexual orientation, many people dread being alone. These interviews
will provides a kind of strength for women to draw on to be able to live
without a partner—to be content with it."

In this preliminary effort to understand the spectrum of choices
among single lesbians, the four midlife women profiled here represent
distinct and heartening models of how to be.

Allison, a writer, doubts she would ever want to live with a partner
again. At 61 she is successful in her profession and comfortable with her
network of friends.

I've been in nine relationships. I can't imagine I'll ever be coupled
again. Never say never, but I can't imagine it. That's not choice, it's
probably circumstance and you adjust to circumstance. Because I've
stopped drinking since I've been single, I have this new personality that I'm
not quite familiar with now. It's a whole new way of looking at life.

Somebody who's been in a long relationship is stranger in the gay life
than people who've been in and out of them. And if and when they break
up, some of these 26 year, 16 year relationships, then you hear all these
stories as they complain about what their life was like. Somebody comes
along and breaks them up and they're ready to break up and there's a catalyst
and then you hear that they never had sex, they never got along, they never
did this, they never did that. I always think the very long relationships have
been: "Let's not risk what's out there. This is steady." I think the longest
one I ever had went on because we bought a house together.

I met somebody the other day and she's been in and out of relationships as I have. She said, "You know, I'm so jaded now I think if I ever got
into a relationship it would be about six weeks." I said, "That long?"

I was seldom single when I was younger. It's hard for me to imagine
what it would have been like younger. I probably would have been uptight
and nervous if I didn't have somebody. Because if you're young, living in
New York City, you feel the world is going by if you're not coupled. That
you should be out looking for somebody; you should have somebody in
your life. I don't feel any of that now.

I hate the idea of working hard on a relationship. I can remember
when mine would be sort of faltering, then I thought, I don't want this to
work. I know it's a sterling thing to have, but for me—move on. Working
hard on a relationship calls up all sorts of awful things.

The main thing it calls up is that I lose interest sexually. I really don't
care to try to rekindle that flame. I'm glad I moved on because I always
liked what came next. One of the wonderful things about gay life is that
you stay friends usually with your old partner. You see them go on to better

things too. Working on a relationship to me, I have other things to do, I can't do that. But I know that's very shallow.

Sex comes and goes when you're single. Choosing your scene and your partner. And there's always masturbation. There's probably more sex when you're single than when you're coupled. At least for me. It's like living near the Statue of Liberty. You'll get around to it eventually. Or maybe you don't. But if you're going to go visit New York, you're going to visit the Statue of Liberty.

I can't imagine changing the life style I have now. It just seems perfect. To accommodate somebody in my house? I might have a relationship but I wouldn't live with somebody again. It's just too hard. The only goals I have are work goals. Most people my age are coupled and I'm not interested in younger women. I'm not looking. Really, whenever I have time, I see old friends. I don't see any problem living alone. I like it. I'm not lonely by nature. I live alone and do a lot of things alone. I'm not lonely, or unhappy or depressed. If I'm depressed, and I can't remember the last time I was, it's usually got to do with work. So I can't think of any disadvantages of living alone. I have a good network of friends, old friends.

Ann is an alcoholism counselor in a town in upstate New York. She has made a choice as a single woman to be intimate, platonic friends with a married woman and feels content and at peace with herself for the first time in her life.

When I came out in 1961, I was 29. Before that I had no idea. It hit me just like a bombshell when a woman seduced me. Much to my delight. I had never thought about it for myself.

I've been in a series of disastrous relationships that continued right up until I went into therapy. Each one seemed to be with someone who really couldn't give me anything. It always kind of turned around that it was my fault and I was selfish. Those were relationships with alcoholic women, some of them were almost disturbed in their behavior. They were wretched and drank to mask their pain.

I was an enabler. I didn't even realize they were alcoholics. I knew that they were drinking an awful lot and had problems. It was as though I had blinders on. I didn't want to see a lot of stuff. Just didn't. Because I became emotionally involved and wanted the relationship to continue, I just blocked out vast amounts of things that were going on. It wasn't until I got into therapy with a very good therapist that I was able to get myself healthy enough not to do this any more.

I don't know if I'm single by choice or if I've had it thrust upon me. I would much prefer to be in a relationship. It's so much better in so many ways if it's a good relationship. It's better emotionally, financially. There's no way I'll ever get a house of my own. I'll probably be renting the rest of my life if I stay single, which I'm pretty sure I will. Emotionally it's very hard sometimes not to have someone around at all if you're feeling upset or feeling happy. Someone to share vacations and Thanksgiving and Christmas and all that. But I much prefer being single to the relationships I had.

I have become very close friends with a woman that I met in a karate class. She's married with children, a pillar of the community. There's no hint of any sexual thing. We're just close friends. She's good company. We go out once a week and do things together. Plus I see her in the on going karate class. That has become very satisfying to me because she is a good friend. If I need something she's there.

We share a lot of things. I find I enjoy her much more than a good many of my lovers. We don't fight. She's never going to leave me. She's never going to cheat on me. All of that is taken care of. It's not a problem. She's there. She's available. She likes me. I like her. We're fond of each other. And to me it's the perfect relationship. That probably sounds a little weird, but I get a lot out of it. And I've been a lot happier since we got close. It's very remote that it would turn into something else because I know her pretty well. I don't have those hopes. I just like her company.

I've been up here three years now and I've made it my business to know a lot of people. I have a lot of people I can call on. Having cancer also affected me. It makes you feel that whether you've got 1 year or 30 years you want to spend that time where you want to be, doing what you want to do. That's really why I moved up here. I just didn't want to be in the city any more. My counseling work is very rewarding—I couldn't imagine doing anything else.

The biggest pressure about being single is the feeling that there's just me. If I get sick, for instance, I'm really in trouble. I'm fine this way as long as my health is good and I can work and I can go out and play tennis and do whatever I want to do. So that's a pressure, that's something I worry about.

The major difference between my life today and when I was in relationships is that there's tranquillity in my life now. Life was a roller coaster. Now everything's on an even keel. That's a great blessing. Nothing's going wrong, no terrible screaming fights and things being thrown. Life is predictable. I wouldn't trade it for anything—wouldn't take on a relationship that disturbed that tranquillity for anything. That probably guarantees that I'll be single forever. There are worse things than being single. You can make your life quite pleasant and it's yours. If it gets messed up, you're the one who's messed it up and you can fix it. When I was in my thirties and forties, if I wasn't in a relationship I was wretched. But now I feel free from searching.

I don't think it's as hard as it once was to be a single person in this society. It depends on the individual person and on your inner resources. I'm relaxed and content with my life. My happiness used to revolve around someone else. It doesn't any more.

Maua is 57, a college professor now on sabbatical writing a book. While her social energy and activism keep her busy and involved, she misses the intimacy of a relationship.

How I feel about being single depends on what day you ask me. On certain days it feels very, very sad and I have a lot of grief for relationships that I don't have or for ones that I've had in the past. That's how I felt Saturday, lonely and disconnected. The moon was full. A beautiful moon. It's still the same moon but it's completely different when there's nobody to share it with.

I've been coupled many times. There was a lot of dyke drama and trauma, but through all the craziness there was still intimacy. And I have to look at who I was at the time. Active in so many addictive ways, drinking, getting high, running the streets, compulsively romantic, always having two and three affairs going on at the same time. I didn't know it could be any other way but the insanity I was used to. Good old dyke drama.

I have been with some beautiful women, beautiful inside, beautiful outside. Many of them I remain good friends with. The only regret is that we couldn't be for each other what we needed to be at that particular time.

My health has taken me to the position of really having to take care of myself. When you are single you know that you can't rely on somebody being there for you. If it's anything extended or devastating, friends burn out unless there's some kind of commitment to you.

Lupus has taught me a clear lesson. You can't not take care of yourself for a minute. You can't think that somebody else is going to think about it. It's forced me into not being able to enable. It's helped me get on the other side of that. I've had lupus for nineteen years. The doctors consider me a miracle, but I've worked at it, had good help with ancestors and the higher power and the goddess is looking out for me. I've had some excellent medical help as well as holistic stuff.

I really do miss intimacy. I'm very used to having it. I miss sex. Because I'm in a place now in my own recovery where I just won't sleep with a woman for sex. I did that all my life. It hurt a lot of people. They thought it was a matter of love. I thought it was love until I got honest with myself.

It was very much part of the times and part of the culture but it was also very much part of my own personal issue. The whole thing kind of played out together with a certain amount of ego that goes with a reputation, being a dynamite person in bed. But certainly it was also a reflection of the times. Just like abstinence is very much a part of these times. Now there is a clear need for safe sex. At that time there was a clear need to free up sexuality. I graduated from high school in 1950. Things were repressed. Sexuality wasn't supposed to exist.

When I was younger I really felt that being single was a temporary state. I was always falling in love and there was always somebody ready to fall in love, too. And there were always women ready for sex. You could meet somebody, zap, pick up, and you're home in bed. That's different now.

When you're older, whatever physical attraction you had is diminished. I'm not physically attractive to most women now. A woman of 45 may be more interested in a woman of 35. A woman of my age—I don't know any of them. I don't know where they've disappeared to.

If you live long enough and you're single, you've had a lot of lovers. I've been involved with maybe only three white women. Black women would catch hell for being involved with a white woman. But my creator is such that whenever I think I've got that all worked out and this is all arranged, she'll throw something else on me. She'll say, "Oh yeah, you don't deal with white girls? Well, try this one on." And that's what happened a few years ago. Everybody knew that I didn't date white women. I've had a zillion girl friends who are white and who I've been friends with for years and years, just good friends. Next thing I know I was best friends with this white woman for about six months and we'd see each other every day and then we realized it was more than that. And there we were, phee, off and running.

I do find it easier to relate to black women. There are so many things about me they understand, where it comes from, what it's about, so I can cut across a whole lot of stuff. But for me it's just a question of, I fall in love with individuals. One of the things that attracts me about a woman is her politics. If she doesn't have any politics I'm not even interested in her. You can just forget her. My main criteria is some kind of emotional maturity and energy for living, for dancing, for life, for people. I love to be in love and when I love love, I love loving. I really miss that very much. I shed tears about it. And then sometimes I say thank you to the goddess for not letting me get involved in that which I thought I had to have.

Marge, 49, is a gym teacher with a family real estate business. She attributes some of the ease with which she had adapted to the single life to her financial affluence. Open to being with someone, she is unwilling to rush into anyone's arms just to dispel loneliness.

I don't really mind being single. You can do just about what you want. You don't have to consult anyone else. "Can we go here? Can we go there?" That kind of sappy consultation.

I've been in three or four relationships. The last one was about two years. I decided to leave it before I found somebody else. Some people do that. They hang on, stay with it, it's not good, it's not what they want but they don't want to be alone. So until they find somebody else who piques their interest they hang onto this uninteresting party. I can't do that. I'm too honest with myself.

I like to be alone. I like to have short-term meetings with people. Do you want to go to the movies, or play tennis? That means you don't commit yourself to a whole day of agony. Small talk.

I like being romantic. I like wooing, I like being wooed. It's very enjoyable. First of all, I have plenty of time for this. For this I've got time. I make time. I like knowing the songs you like, knowing what kind of food you like, going shopping and picking out the clothes I know you want.

Sometimes you feel lonely momentarily, so you go to a movie, you go shopping, you do something like that. As far as tying yourself up with somebody so you don't feel lonely, you could feel lonelier when you're with somebody then if you're alone without somebody. Seriously.

You also have to have someone who is in your corner. Somebody who's really for you. When you start a relationship you have somebody who is your ally. And you know it's over when that person is no longer your ally. Fighting or disagreeing all the time, or precipitating situations when you are not going to be at your best.

When you're single, sex is hit or miss. You find somebody now and then. You have old friends you call up who have liked to go to bed with you before and they go to bed with you again. Even if they're with other people sometimes. Because they know it's going to be nice. You don't get pregnant from it. Adult movies help sometimes, especially the ones with what's-her-name, Crystal. They're not dirty, just erotic and fun.

I get calls from time to time. From old friends who are in relationships that are not very interesting. It's not blatant calls, like come over and let's go to bed. It's like "What are you doing tonight?" "Oh, I'm just watching TV." "Why don't you come over and watch with me?" This is only with people I've known and been to bed with before.

You want to hear the strangest ones? I know people who are together for years but they haven't been to bed together. They may sleep together but they don't have sex together. Can you believe this? I wouldn't be with somebody a week if we weren't sleeping together. I swear to God, why bother? Why bother taking all this shit from somebody if you're not going to sleep with them? And people hand out the shit left and right. I wouldn't turn around the corner. I swear to God I wouldn't. Nobody tells me no. Tell me no, take a walk. What kind of no? It's not fun anymore, then leave. I'm serious.

I'm just happy I'm here. I've got a nice house. I'm in a very privileged position, I know. I'm financially very secure and that makes a big difference. I enjoy myself. It's summer—I go swimming in the ocean. I go swimming in the pool. A big kid. I'm happy I'm alive.

(Many thanks go to the women for their forthright interviews. With the exception of Maua, their names have been changed. Also in appreciation for their insightful comments, my thanks go to Blanche Wiesen Cook, Sonny Stokes and the women at Gay Women's Alternative.)

Our
Changing
Bodies

Ripening

ROBYN POSIN

Eight years ago, at 42, after two intense, difficult and isolating years in Indiana caring for her family, my partner and I returned to California. Coming home to the Santa Barbara women's community in which she had spent most of her life and I'd spent the preceding seven years, I was startled to see how visibly so many friends and acquaintances had aged. All of them had the wrinkles, lip lines, the general softening and loosening of flesh that had for me, always and lovingly, been associated with the teachers, aunts and grandmothers who had been the primary source of warmth and love in my life. It was strange and disconcerting to see my contemporaries showing signs of aging that I had yet to notice in myself. Still, as always, there were the familiar heart-melting, loving feelings that overcame me, unbidden, when I noticed those outward signs of a maturing womanliness in these women friends.

Within six months of our return and in the midst of overwhelming anguish, I had literally to tear myself out of the seven year relationship with my partner. I, and she, felt in pieces; broken, bereft, confused and devastated.

After two years of an intensely painful breakup, I finally, at 44, found myself fragmented, emotionally exhausted and trying again to begin a life of my own. With much help from the Goddess I found an enchanted rental house on a very magical piece of land in the midst of the wilderness and orange groves of Ojai. Here I began the journey of recovering and reclaiming myself.

At the same time, I began the process of noticing in my own face and body the changes I had already witnessed in the faces and bodies of my friends. First I noticed the wrinkles and lip lines that, quite visible in photos from the preceding years, had already been there without my being able to see them. My immediate reaction was to feel intense guilt; somehow, because I'd sunned so deliciously and indiscriminately over the years and because I'd begun smoking again, without a filter, I had not taken good enough care of myself. A flash of outrage immediately followed the feeling of guilt. For years I had been working with myself and women clients who had eating and weight issues in order to break free from the societal swindles around body image and to learn to love and cherish our natural bodies. I couldn't believe that I was feeling guilty about these natural changes in my body; here I was feeling that somehow I was "bad and wrong" for not having prevented those changes. Quick on the heels of the rage at having been swindled into such feelings came an extraordinary wave of grief. Clearly body image consciousness made one no less vulnerable to the powerful brainwashing that leads us to feel upset at any signs of aging.

We all, lesbian or not, are daily bombarded subtly and not so subtly by the swindle, the intense brainwashing of patriarchal media constructions in which anything other than a twelve-year-old face and body on a woman is unacceptable, offensive, shameful, pitiable and blameworthy. It's a construction of reality in which everything (at least in women) must stay relentlessly unblemished, young, able and "perfect;" a construction in which the second half of the sacred, natural life cycle of birth, blossoming, ripening and death-before-rebirth is always and inevitably denied and certainly uncelebrated.

As I stood there looking at myself through the waves of feeling, I found myself letting go of those "outside eyes." I stood there remembering that I was not to blame for this natural unfolding of changes in my face. I stood there also remembering the powerful healing richness of those endless hours lying naked in the warmth of the sun, knowing that I wouldn't and wouldn't have done one moment differently. My eyes softened their looking and I felt the loving, melting feelings I feel when I see any other woman's wrinkles. I felt that loving for my own wrinkles. They were mine, a sign of my deepening into my own aging, mellowing process.

When I first noticed the dimples appearing in my thighs, I again (!) experienced a reflexive surge of guilt as though I'd been irresponsible in not being involved in some intense exercise regime. Again, the guilt was followed first by outrage that I had been brainwashed into such a response and then grief over the way all women are abused into feeling that our aging bodies (just as our fat or differently abled bodies) are a sign of our personal failure, negligence, slothfulness or intention to offend the sensibilities of others. And, as I sat there, my eyes and heart softened. I continued with my morning ritual of massaging lotion into my body, being especially loving as I lotioned my thighs. I forgave them for showing the inevitable signs of being part of my temporarily able, almost 50-year-old body. I thanked them for their strength and dependability, for serving my mobility so long and without complaint. I thanked them for enabling me still to delight in my yoga, tai chi and daily wanderings in the canyons. Rather than launching into some program to change them, I lovingly included my thighs, dimples and all, in my life as I continued putting my time and energy where it feels the most appropriate and rewarding at this stage of my unfolding. I go on learning to unconditionally love and mother all the aspects of my being, making the space and safety in my world for me to reclaim the long ago abandoned little child-self inside of me.

Slowly, and sometimes not so slowly, as the wrinkles multiply and deepen, as the dimpling increases in my thighs and buttocks, as the flesh under my upper arms gets softer and looser, as the little folds of skin emerge over the crooks in my elbows, as the skin between my breasts gets all wrinkly when I put on a bra and as the skin sags above my knees and gets all puckery everywhere, I can see when I come down from a shoulder stand, I notice. And, now, each first time and all the other times that I notice, I feel an overwhelming tenderness for this occasion of seeing my body become like my grandmothers' bodies. A heart-melting feeling of love fills me. My body is becoming like the bodies with which I've always associated great, unconditional, compassionate loving and vitality. (One grandmother just died after thriving until 95 while her 75- and 85-year-old "baby" sisters still lead active and busy lives!)

Over the past six years of coming home to loving all of my selves, I have come more and more deeply into loving this body I live in just exactly as it is and also as it is becoming. Sometime over these past few years I've given up the last vestiges of the "nineteen-year-old Southern California Naked Beach Frisbee Player Girl" against which I once saw my own dear body. When I look at myself in mirrors these days (my house is filled with mirrors and I like to wander about without clothing), I see the beautiful, soft, voluptuous body and face of a grown woman of almost 50 long and richly satisfying years of growing. It's a comforting body that nourishes, supports and holds me as I continue becoming ever more deeply aware of the wise woman and the child that live comfortably together within me. It's a body that often these days remembers lots of ancient terror and trauma as I work at healing more and more fully into inhabiting it. I'm as fascinated with the ways the outside of me is changing as I am with the ways the inside of me is changing. I am growing paradoxically older and younger at one and the same time.

I've become so much more gentle with myself emotionally and psychologically as I've felt freer, without criticism or judgment, to become conscious of my inner limits and frailties. So, too, I find myself responding to the outer limitations imposed by my aging (and often not as forgiving) 50-year-old body with an increasing measure of similarly compassionate gentleness and acceptance.

With each day and year, I am more and more willing to allow myself to be just exactly however I am, even when how I am is some way that an earlier me would have been appalled to be. It seems no coincidence that I'm growing more vibrant and vital in my being, more in touch with my own deepening wisdom and vision, more intolerant of any and all externally or internally imposed restraints. I will not steal from my deepening process the endlessly increasing amounts of energy it would take to try to hold back the relentless and gentle decaying of this bag of flesh and bone within which

I live. I will not consider having my face or breasts lifted; my eyelids, tummy and buttocks tucked; or my arms and thighs liposuctioned because the inside of me feels so much younger than the outside of me looks! I will not waste my time, my energy, my attention or my money shoring up—in whatever fashion—the outside of me at a time in my life when the real work is taking care of my health and responding to the depths of my insides. Those insides beckon me to healing, to freedom from meaningless pursuits and, most importantly, to claiming and sharing the wisdom of my almost 50 years of living.

Who We Are: Health Concerns of Middle-Aged Lesbians

JUDITH BRADFORD
& CAITLIN RYAN

A Report from the National Lesbian Health Care Survey

A priority of the National Lesbian and Gay Health Foundation is to establish a comprehensive agenda for improving lesbians' access to affordable and high quality health care. As a starting point, the National Lesbian Health Care Survey was developed and distributed throughout the country in 1984. Response to the survey was overwhelming. Nearly 2000 lesbians returned completed questionnaires, from all over the United States. Many wrote down their personal stories; all answered several hundred questions about many aspects of their lives. Information was gathered about the health of lesbians, broadly defined and encompassing the various dimensions of physical, social and mental health. These women shared information about past experiences and current needs and provided a wealth of data about the very individualized ways in which they live both in the "real world" and in alternative worlds of their own making.

In this article, we report information from a special group of respondents to the National Lesbian Health Care Survey—women from 40 to 60 years old, in the middle years of their lives. These women, vulnerable and yet remarkably resilient, live everyday lives in heterosexual society with the support and caring of mostly gay people. Although these women are not receiving economic rewards equivalent to the responsibility they carry, they express overall satisfaction with their lives and know how to care for themselves.

Characteristics of the Midlife Group

Most of these lesbians a got their questionnaires from a friend (56 percent), a health care provider (eighteen percent), or from an organization (seventeen percent). Of these midlife lesbians, 90 percent were white and ten percent minority (including African-Americans, Latinas, Asians and others). Unlike women their age in the general population, among whom 45 percent were not in the labor force, almost all respondents were employed.

Occupational choices of lesbians were also quite different from those of all American women. Within the general population of working women (55 percent of women 40-60 years old), twelve percent reported professional or technical occupations, sixteen percent managerial or administrative occupations and 29 percent clerical. Midlife lesbians were four times as likely to be employed in professional or technical roles (56 percent), considerably more likely to work as managers or administrators (22 percent), and much less likely to occupy clerical positions. Other occupational groups represented in the sample were craftswomen, service workers, skilled and unskilled laborers.

Consistent with their vocations, most respondents were highly educated. Forty-eight percent had completed a graduate or professional degree and 24 percent had graduated from college or completed some graduate work. Only fifteen percent had not been to college at all.

Although these women were very well educated and typically worked in professional or managerial positions, many are economically vulnerable. Almost half earn less than $20,000 per year and fourteen percent earn less than $10,000. Only 25 percent earn as much as $30,000, with ten percent earning in excess of $40,000. Clearly, the earned incomes of middle-aged lesbians was not commensurate with their educational preparation and professional experience.

Despite the fact that most were employed and very few were receiving any form of financial assistance, economic uncertainty was a familiar experience for this group of lesbians. A third had received unemployment benefits at some time in the past and fifteen percent had received food stamps. Six percent had been on welfare, four percent on Aid to Families with Dependent Children (AFDC), four percent on Medicaid and six percent on Social Security Disability Insurance (SSDI).

About three-fourths of the women were living in large cities at the time of the survey—66 percent in cities with a population of more than one million and eleven percent in cities of a half million or more. Twelve percent lived in smaller cities or urban areas; the remainder lived in small towns or rural areas. Almost everyone (95 percent) had been born in the United States and at the time of the survey their residences were fairly evenly distributed around the country. Fewer than one in ten (eight percent) were still living in the city or town of their birth.

Lesbian Identity and Openness

Two-thirds of these women had sex with another woman before they were 30, with most having their first experience during their late teens or early twenties. A very small number (eight percent) had sex with another female during childhood (before they were ten years old) or between the ages of ten and seventeen (seventeen percent). Except for respondents who had this experience before they were ten (when same-sex experiences may be inherently exploratory), the longer ago the experience had occurred, the more open respondents were about their lesbianism in middle age. Least "out" were those women (eight percent of the sample) who had their first sexual experience with another woman after 40.

Sexual orientation was assessed by asking respondents to place themselves on a seven-point scale, from heterosexual only (1) to bisexual (4) to lesbian only (7). Well over half the sample (61 percent) described themselves as lesbian only; 93 percent rated themselves as 5, 6, or 7—at the lesbian end of the continuum. Outness (degree of disclosure about their sexual orientation) was assessed by having respondents estimate the proportions of individuals in four different groups to whom they were open about their lesbianism: family members, gay friends, straight friends and co-workers.

Overall, 60 percent of midlife lesbians were out to more than half of the people in all their networks. Only seven percent were out to *everyone;* an equal proportion were out to *none.* Patterns of disclosure varied with respect to different groups of individuals. For example, midlife lesbians in our sample were most likely to be out to their gay friends; 88 percent had come out to all these individuals and fewer than two percent had come out to none. Proportions who had come out to all family members and to straight friends were quite similar, 24 percent each, although much lower than for gay friends. However, only seventeen percent were out to all co-workers.

Two obvious concerns are raised by these data. First, large percentages of middle-aged lesbians appear to be hiding their lesbianism from most or all of their family members, straight friends and co-workers. To live with this behavior means they must be dissimulating with and perhaps actually lying to loved ones and regular acquaintances. It is in this area of life that gay women are undoubtedly most affected by their lesbianism. For most of these women, daily life and family relations *usually* include at least some degree of deception or over-rationalization.

Degree of disclosure was also related to where respondents lived and in what types of communities. Those who lived in the Pacific states reported a higher degree of openness than did respondents in any other area. Next most out were women in the Northeast. Women in the Southern and Mountain states were most closeted and those in the North Central only a little more open. Women who lived in the town or city of their birth were more open than were those who had moved away. Women who lived in small communities (from 2,500-49,999) and in the largest metropolitan areas (of more than one million) were more open than were those in mid-sized cities (50,000-499,999).

A majority of midlife lesbians were involved in a relationship with another woman. Sixty percent of respondents described themselves as being in a primary relationship with another woman and fourteen percent as single but involved. Nineteen described themselves as single and uninvolved. At various times in their lives, many respondents had experienced a variety of relationship styles. Thirty-four percent had been married to a man, whereas only four percent were currently living this way. Nine had lived with a male lover without being married.

Although 74 percent were involved either in a primary relationship or with someone they were dating, 27 percent were living alone when they completed the survey. Midlife lesbians appear nearly twice as likely to be living alone as are women in the general population, of whom only seventeen percent were living by themselves in 1985. Sixty-nine percent of all women were living with their spouses, compared with only half of lesbians (51 percent) who were living with their lovers (65 percent of those who were in a significant relationship). Sixteen percent were living with their children; others lived with a roommate, or with their husbands, parents, or other family members or boarders. Six percent lived in households where another woman's children were also living.

Having or wanting to have children was very much a part of life for a significant group of these lesbians. Forty-three percent had been pregnant and 37 percent were actually mothers. Among those who had not been pregnant, nineteen percent said they wanted to be. Adoption was the chosen method for most who wanted to have a child; 86 women (24 percent of the sample) said they would consider adoption. Sixteen percent would choose to co-parent. For those who wanted to be pregnant, 73 percent would choose artificial insemination with a known donor. Other acceptable methods were having sex with a man (71 percent), artificial insemination from a sperm bank (31 percent), or insemination from an unknown donor (24 percent).

Social Connections

Most of the midlife lesbians in our sample were at best marginally connected to their surrounding communities. Only half had as many as five people they could talk to about a personal problem; eight percent had only one such confidant. Similarly, only 41 percent had as many as five individuals they could count on for a ride; eleven percent had only one such person or could think of no one. For well over half our sample, most of their close women friends were also lesbians (64 percent) and of the same ethnicity (58 percent). Half of the respondents with close male friends said they were all or mostly gay; for 25 percent, however, all of their close male friends were straight.

Affiliation with regular community activities and institutions was limited. Only thirteen percent participated in neighborhood associations, fourteen percent in minority political groups (not specifically gay) and 22 percent in other political groups. Other frequently reported groups or activities included health centers or clubs (eighteen percent) and groups related to the needs of respondents' children (ten percent). Nearly a third attended some form of union or professional group meetings.

Most frequently reported activities were either supportive, social, or gay rights oriented. A third of the sample reported regular participation in some form of social group and about the same proportion attended women's support groups or women's rights groups. More than a third were active in lesbian and gay rights organizations (37 percent); women who participated in these groups were more likely to be open about their lesbianism than were women who did not.

Although participation in regular community activities was limited, most of our sample reported access to activities specifically designed for lesbians and most attended lesbian-only events regularly. Fifty-two percent attended these events at least once or twice a month, sixteen percent once a week; only six percent attended less than once a year. For at least two-thirds of the sample, one or more of the following activities were available in the communities where they lived: lesbian bar or nightclub, lesbian counselor or therapist, lesbian support group, lesbian softball or other athletic team, lesbian concerts or other cultural events and/or a lesbian and gay religious group. Other gay community resources were not as widely available but did exist for the following percentages of respondents: lesbian health care center (for 38 percent), lesbian healing circle (22 percent), lesbian-feminist bookstore (61 percent), lesbian social club (50 percent), and/or a lesbian hotline and information center (52 percent). For twenty percent of the sample there were no local resources; of these, eleven percent had resources within a 50-mile radius, four percent between 50 and 100 miles away and five percent at a distance greater than 100 miles.

Changes over time were quite evident in the religious lives of our sample. Almost everyone attended a religious institution while they were growing up; only five percent had not. However, religious affiliation was no longer characteristic of our sample at midlife; two-thirds of those who responded were no longer church members. In fact, the percentage of respondents who had no adult affiliation was nearly thirteen times the percentage of those who had no affiliation during childhood. Among those who did attend a religious community, half described their attendance as rare. About one in five attended weekly; about one-third went at least once a month.

The distribution of respondents among various religious denominations had also changed considerably; only 30 percent of the sample reported current affiliation with the same denomination as in childhood. Half had been raised in Protestant churches, but only 23 percent of these women were still affiliated with Protestant congregations. Thirty-one percent had been raised as Catholics; as adults, only 28 percent of these remained affiliated with Catholicism. Jewish women were much more likely than non-Jewish women to retain their religious affiliation; only 30 percent of Jewish women reported no religious affiliation at midlife. Seventy percent reported ongoing affiliation with a Jewish congregation.

There were other shifts in the religious groups with which these lesbians were affiliated as adults. Several denominations were grouped on the basis of their liberal attitudes toward homosexuality and/or sanctioning of gay marriages; these included Unity, Unitarian, Quaker and "Gay Church." The proportion of respondents affiliated with these "liberal" churches was five times as large during midlife as it had been in childhood. Conversely, affiliation had decreased with denominations known to be conservative in their views toward homosexuality. Two percent of respondents at the time of the survey were affiliated with churches in which none had participated as children: pagan, witches; Buddhism; and Islam.

Most gay women believe they have been treated differently because they are lesbians, in ways that are often indirect and hard to be certain about. Nearly half our sample had experienced *overt* discrimination because they were gay. Most often reported was verbal attack—42 percent had experienced this. Smaller percentages reported other forms of discrimination which they knew were associated with their lesbianism. Ten percent had lost jobs and three percent believed the quality of health care they received had been adversely affected. Eight of the women had been discharged from the service because they were lesbians and 23 women had been physically attacked.

Nearly half the sample (49 percent) had experienced physical or sexual abuse at some time in their lives. A third (34 percent) had been abused *either* sexually or physically when they were children and eight percent had experienced *both* forms of abuse. Sixteen percent had been involved in an incestuous relationship when they were children. As adults, 25 percent had experienced *either* physical or sexual abuse and seven percent had experienced both. Lesbians thus appear as likely as other women in the United States to have experienced incest.

There were 56 women in the sample (sixteen percent) who had experienced incest while they were growing up, almost always with a male in the family. For most middle-aged lesbians, their father (23 percent), uncle (25 percent), or brother (about 29 percent) were involved. Sixteen percent had had sex with a stepfather and seven percent with a grandfather. One-half of one percent (three women) had had sex with a female member of the family, one with her mother. Only 38 percent of those who had experienced incest had ever told anyone about it. Of those who did tell, 43 percent had talked with their mothers, 24 percent with counselors and fourteen percent with their fathers.

Alarmingly, 29 percent of the sample had been sexually attacked or abused. Nineteen percent had experienced this as children and thirteen percent as adults. As with incest, almost all sexual abuse was perpetrated by males. All but two women who reported being sexually attacked as children said the perpetrator was either a male relative (27 percent), another male they knew (48 percent), or a male stranger (28 percent). As adults, most had been attacked either by a male stranger (38 percent) or by a male they knew (53 percent). A majority of those who had been sexually attacked *had not* asked anyone for help; only 44 percent had sought assistance.

Thirty-eight percent had been physically abused at some time in their lives—23 percent as children and eighteen percent after being grown. Respondents abused during childhood were more likely to report male abusers, but a significant proportion had suffered physical abuse at the hands of women. Sixty-two percent had been abused by a male relative, 48 percent by a female relative and twenty percent by a male non-relative who was known to them. Most who had been abused as adults identified the abuser as a lover (36 percent) or a husband (44 percent). Twenty-seven percent had been physically abused by a male stranger.

Common Concerns

Worry was a common experience for well over half of these lesbians, suggesting that midlife lesbians are more likely to live with disabling stress than are other women. Among the general population of women, 53 percent reported that stress had affected some aspect of their health within the previous year. Among lesbian respondents, 24 percent were often too worried or nervous to accomplish routine tasks; for an additional 40 percent, worry or nervousness had at least sometimes gotten in the way. Midlife lesbians appear more likely than women in the general population to experience worry and more likely to have their daily lives affected by the extent of their worry. Patterns of concern for lesbians also differ from those of the general population; midlife lesbians appear at least five times as likely as other women their age to have money problems. The percentage of respondents who were concerned about job or school problems was about twice as high as that of the general female population.

The most common concern was money; 55 percent of respondents were experiencing current distress because of money problems. Several other problems were reported by about one-fourth of the sample: problems with their jobs or school, with a lover and with too much responsibility at work. Smaller percentages reported current distress with these other concerns: problems with others in the family, job dissatisfaction, worry about illness and/or death, problems with children and worry about being found out as a lesbian.

Most concerns of midlife lesbians thus appear related in some way to economic aspects of life. As noted earlier, our sample was surprisingly vulnerable in this area. Despite their high levels of education and professional work lives, most simply do not earn a salary commensurate with their qualifications. This contradiction between what should be predictable and what really happens is usually reflected by emotional distress and worry. At a time in their lives when financial security should be the norm, a majority of lesbians at midlife are concerned about not having enough.

Use of tobacco, alcohol and/or marijuana was reported by substantial proportions of the sample. Alcohol use was most prevalent; 82 percent reported at least occasional use, although 58 percent drank alcohol less than once a month. Fifteen percent were worried about the extent of their drinking. One-third of respondents smoked daily and 67 percent of smokers were worried about their use. Marijuana was used by 29 percent of the sample but usually on an occasional basis. Well over half of those who reported use of marijuana (64 percent) said they used it less than once a month and only eight percent were concerned about their use.

Despite the wide use of alcohol, lesbians in our sample do not appear to have greater dependence on alcohol than do other women in the American population. Among all women in the general population, 91 percent reported alcohol use at least sometime within the previous year. Sixty-three percent of all women reported alcohol use at least once in every one of the previous twelve months. Available data on smoking are not directly comparable, but 59 percent of all American women in this age group in 1985 reported being current smokers.

In addition to alcohol and tobacco use, many respondents expressed concern about other potentially harmful substances and about eating patterns. Thirty-seven percent of respondents worried about the amount of caffeine they consumed and 33 percent worried about their use of sugar. Two-thirds of the sample said they overeat at least sometimes, 24 percent often. One in four reported sometimes, or often, undereating. Almost seven percent of the sample had overeaten and vomited afterward, though most did so rarely.

Given these high percentages who reported serious concerns about their emotional and financial lives, and many additional concerns about substance use and eating habits, it is not surprising that most of the sample (73 percent) sought out mental health counseling at some time in their lives. Reliance on counseling had been short-term and situational for most; a majority had seen either one counselor (33 percent) or two counselors (24 percent).

Although concern about financial issues caused these lesbians most of their worry, it was primarily because of emotional distress and relationship problems that they actually sought out mental health care. Of those who received counseling, 68 percent did so because they were feeling sad or depressed, 62 percent because of problems with lovers, 39 percent for problems with family members, 36 percent because of feeling anxious or scared and 32 percent for personal growth. Twenty-seven percent of midlife lesbians had needed mental health care because of difficulty with their lesbianism. Twenty-four percent of those who sought help did so because they were lonely and twenty percent needed help with alcohol and/or drug problems. For twenty percent, it was problems at work that caused them to seek help and for ten percent it had been problems with their friends. Four percent needed help because of experiences with racism.

Among respondents were 56 women (sixteen percent of the total) who had tried to kill themselves. The most frequent method used was drug overdose, by 64 percent of those who had tried to commit suicide. Ten percent had used a razor blade and much smaller percentages had used other methods. At the time of the survey, seventeen percent reported thinking about suicide at least sometimes.

Most respondents who received professional mental health counseling had seen a private counselor (93 percent), but other professional sources of care were also reported—eighteen percent had been to a clinic and five percent to a school counselor. Twelve percent had been hospitalized for mental health care. Over 60 percent relied upon non-professional sources of counseling, primarily from friends, support groups, or peer counselors. Nine percent had consulted psychics and seven percent religious counselors.

Overall, those who sought help for mental health concerns were satisfied with the quality of their care. Respondents who were receiving counseling help at the time of the survey reported higher levels of satisfaction than with the care they had received in the past. Most respondents (87 percent) expressed a preference for seeing women counselors; nearly two-thirds preferred counselors who were lesbians. Sixty-nine percent said ethnicity was not an issue for them, but 31 percent preferred to see a counselor of the same ethnicity.

The most frequently reported difficulties experienced in past counseling situations were finding it hard to talk to the counselor, believing that the counselor gave wrong information, or feeling that the counselor would not listen. About one in ten of those who sought help felt they really couldn't tell their counselors they were gay. Among respondents who had *not* sought mental health counseling, the most typical reason was simply having felt no need to do so (33 percent). Nearly as many, however, felt they should get help but had been putting it off for a variety of reasons. Eleven percent didn't know where to go and eight percent felt counselors would not be able to help them. Ten percent who needed help but hadn't gotten it reported that financial need was the reason.

Health Concerns and Experiences with Care

Ninety-two percent of respondents had been hospitalized overnight at some time in their lives and 84 percent reported having some type of surgery. Many midlife lesbians had fairly serious health needs which did not appear to be adequately met. Further, there were indications in the data that a substantial number were not getting care because of limited access to appropriate services.

Respondents were asked very specific questions about health, what types of problems they had experienced in the past and were experiencing now, and how they were dealing with their needs for care. Health conditions were divided into two groups: general health problems and ob/gyn problems. For some conditions, comparisons can be made with information available about the general population from the National Health Interview Survey. For most of these, midlife lesbians appear to report problems with about the same frequency as do women their age in the general population.

Nine percent of lesbians reported current high blood pressure, compared with thirteen percent of all women of the same age. About two percent of both groups reported current diabetes. Eight percent of all women and a similar proportion of lesbians (five percent) reported current heart and/or circulatory problems. Lesbians, however, appeared more likely to suffer from arthritis (23 percent of lesbians and nine percent of all women) and from hemorrhoids (seven percent of lesbians and one percent of all women). Conversely, women in the general population were twice as likely as women in our sample to consider overweight a current problem (63 percent of women in the general population; 30 percent of lesbians).

As a group, respondents were more likely to be receiving care for some current problems than for others. For example, all or almost all who had current thyroid problems or high blood pressure were getting help. Smaller proportions reported receiving care if they had other problems, such as migraine headaches (70 percent were getting help), back problems (65 percent), or arthritis (45 percent). Only 38 percent of those with current weight problems were receiving professional care.

For five problems where chronicity or recurring illness may occur, ongoing care was reported by a number of asymptomatic individuals. Included in this group were alcohol, other drugs, cancer, long-term depression and constant anxiety. Proportions of middle-aged lesbians who reported current problems with these varied from ten percent for long depression and six percent for constant anxiety, to smaller percentages for alcohol (four percent), other drugs (one percent) and cancer (one percent). It was reassuring to find an awareness of the need for continuing care, but the other side of the picture was not as positive. Although some asymptomatic individuals *were* continuing to receive care, *most* were not. With respect to treatment for alcohol problems, for example, the 43 women who were receiving care represented one-and-a-half times the number of women who reported a *current* problem, but were only one-third of those who had had an alcohol problem *in the past*.

Questions about ob/gyn problems were asked in non-medical terminology and results cannot be compared to national statistics. Respondents were asked if they had past or current experience with ten different problem areas and if they had current problems, whether or not they were receiving care. Problem areas included: lumps in the breast or vagina, irregular bleeding or cessation of periods, vaginal or nipple discharge, cramps, premenstrual syndrome and cancer. Three problems were of current concern for at least ten percent of the sample: twelve percent reported very bad cramps with their periods, ten percent lumps or growths in their breasts and ten percent PMS. For about half of the ob/gyn problems, a majority of women with current symptoms were receiving care, including cancer, breast lumps, discharge between periods and interruption or cessation of periods. For other problems, a majority were *not* receiving care. Included in this group of symptoms were various menstrual problems, such as irregularity or abnormal bleeding and PMS, as well as nipple discharge and vaginal lumps.

Eleven percent of the sample had had an abortion and twelve percent a miscarriage. Three women (one percent) had experienced stillbirth. Quite a few (fourteen percent) reported worrying about sexually transmitted diseases (STDs) and nearly as many reported that the fear of acquiring an STD kept them from performing certain sex acts. How well informed these women were about STDs was unclear, however. Only about a third had received any information from a health professional (30 percent) or a health clinic (four percent). About the same proportion (31 percent) had received their information from either lovers (fifteen percent) or friends (fourteen percent). Other sources of information were gay organizations and gay media (fourteen percent) and other health or medical journals (sixteen percent).

Respondents were also asked about two recommended preventive behaviors—Pap smear and breast self-examination. Only two percent reported *never* having had a Pap smear. About half (55 percent) had had this done within the last twelve months. Eighteen percent last had a Pap smear between 12 and 24 months ago and the rest more than two years ago. Most respondents examined their own breasts at least once a year; however, fifteen percent said they never did.

Although a large majority of these middle-aged lesbians preferred going to a private office for care of any type of health problem, 69 percent for ob/gyn problems and 74 percent for other health concerns, they were less likely to do so than were all women. Eighty-nine percent of all women report that they usually go to a "doctor's office" for health care. Substantial numbers of respondents also went to women's health centers and community clinics. However, nine percent received no professional ob/gyn care and eight percent received no professional care for a broad range of other health problems.

About three-quarters of respondents reported that their usual health care provider was a medical doctor, 79 percent for ob/gyn and 81 percent for other care. Twenty-one percent reported that they received most of their health care from a chiropractor; nurses were also identified as primary practitioners for a substantial proportion of these women. However, for many health problems, respondents simply cared for themselves. Nine percent said they cared for their own ob/gyn care needs and 24 percent for other health problems.

Overall, most of the sample were at least somewhat satisfied with their current health care. Eighty-eight percent considered their general health care to be either very good (44 percent) or good (44 percent). Satisfaction with ob/gyn care was a little lower but still quite high; 42 percent described their care as very good, 39 percent as good. These ratings were higher than for past care. Only 64 percent rated past ob/gyn care as good or very good and 71 percent rated past general health care as highly as what they receive now.

Consistent with these mixed reviews of quality, respondents reported a number of specific difficulties with getting adequate care. These difficulties varied both over time and with respect to the type of problem for which help was sought. Most frequently reported past problems with ob/gyn care included: providers' assumption that the respondent was straight (for 13 percent) and difficulty in communication—because the provider wouldn't listen, was hard to talk to, was physically rough, or was someone the respondent couldn't come out to. Other difficulties related to poor treatment and included providers who gave wrong information, wouldn't tell respondents enough about the problem or how it should be handled, or gave the wrong treatment.

When reporting on ob/gyn care specifically, the three problems named are particularly significant for lesbians and middle-aged women. Six percent reported that their primary provider was hard to talk to, thirteen percent that they couldn't come out to the provider and seventeen percent that primary providers assumed they were straight. Although our sample felt they had found providers who delivered higher quality services than some they had seen in the past, many had still not found providers who delivered services equitably to lesbians.

Many of these same difficulties were reported with general health care services. In the past, sixteen percent of respondents had received general health services from providers who assumed they were straight; 25 percent reported this as a current problem. Fourteen percent had seen providers they couldn't come out to and eighteen percent were still seeing such providers at the time of the survey. Five women (one percent of the sample) had encountered racial discrimination from providers. Some reasons for not receiving professional help were more troubling. Nine percent said they couldn't afford general health care, six percent for ob/gyn care. About three percent had had negative experiences in the past, including being mistreated at the office or having providers with whom they could not communicate well. Others felt they could not trust the staff at the places they were familiar with, or were embarrassed or afraid to ask for the help they needed.

Given a general theme of compromised relationships with the health care system, it is understandable that many respondents would seek professional help only when problems were perceived as serious. Overall, respondents appeared to be conscious about their health, while having an explicit interest in learning about self-care. Many learned how to care for themselves from members of their families; 40 percent from their parents or grandparents. Learning about self-care became even more salient for these women during their adult lives. Well over half (59 percent) reported learning about self-care from friends and about half learned from health care workers or in newspapers or magazines. Non-medical methods for promoting and maintaining personal health were reported by large proportions. Over two-thirds (68 percent) relied on diet and/or exercise to maintain good health. Nearly as many reported regular use of vitamins. Among menopausal women, 75 percent were involved with some sort of treatment: thirty-five percent were receiving hormone treatment, 28 percent nutritional treatment and twelve percent herbal treatment.

Many lesbians indicated an active interest in learning more about various aspects of health and other areas of their lives. Three health topics were most often mentioned as areas in which they would like to have more information—menopause, PMS and aging; each of these areas of concern was mentioned by about a third of respondents. Smaller but still substantial proportions wanted more information about breast cancer and vaginal infections. Other concerns mentioned by at least one in ten of the women were mental health concerns, digestive problems and strokes.

Many women also added comments or references to issues of specific concern to gay people. Half of all respondents expressed a need to know about their lovers' rights to medical power of attorney in the event of their illness. And 56 percent were already affected by the AIDS epidemic in ways which ranged from heightened awareness, to concern for their friends and other gay men, to altered sexual behavior, getting involved with AIDS organizations, having friends die of the disease, becoming personally afraid of infection or concerned about safe personal contact. Eight percent of respondents expressed a need to learn more about the epidemic.

Summary

Middle-aged lesbians who participated in the National Lesbian Health Care Survey seem to have worked out an approach to life that is both realistic and creative, taking into account society's continuing resistance to full acceptance of gay people, while preserving the individual's right to choose her own life whenever possible. Women in our sample had little to do with traditional social institutions but a lot to do with personal relationships, family life and alternative communities.

Social institutions of childhood have been largely set aside. With the exception of Jewish women, who retain an association with Judaism if not with a specific congregation, most women who were raised with a religious affiliation have simply left the church. Few women participate in community or neighborhood activities, except for those specifically for gay people or for women. Only about one in four are open about their lesbianism with all or most family members. Only a few are open with their co-workers.

Over a third of midlife lesbians (37 percent) know someone else in their family who is gay or lesbian. For 25 percent, this is someone in the same generation, either a sibling or cousin.

Although their private lives are often quite hidden from family members, co-workers and the larger community, lesbians have found ways to create full lives for themselves. A large majority have a primary relationship and a very large proportion also have children. Over a third are mothers and an additional nineteen percent want to be. Although some of those are too concerned about the responsibilities and difficulties involved, quite a few appear to be actively considering various ways to become mothers.

Social time is spent primarily with other lesbians or in mixed gay activities. Almost everyone attends lesbian-only activities and many attend such events quite frequently. Three-fourths of the sample live in communities where at least some lesbian activities or support services are available. About a third participate regularly in groups devoted to lesbian and gay rights issues and nearly a third belong to some sort of professional or occupational group.

Being lesbian has had a negative impact on the lives of most of these women. A large majority have experienced at least verbal harassment and significant proportions have suffered actual losses because they are known to be gay. Coming out to others is generally considered to be a healthy step for gay people and, for survey respondents, this undoubtedly was the key to finding a partner and a place within the gay community. However, many middle-aged lesbians in our sample have suffered tremendous distress because of disclosing their lesbianism. Disclosure of their sexual orientation is significantly associated with long-term use of mental health counseling, as well as with increased connection with other gay people.

Although most women were engaged in a primary relationship at the time of the survey, almost all report a history of multiple relationships and of substantial distress with their partners. Having a primary relationship is clearly very significant to middle-aged lesbians but just as clearly involves ongoing stress. It is extremely difficult for gay people to maintain a committed partnership without the larger support of family and community available to heterosexual couples; midlife lesbians in our sample are clearly not exempt from this reality.

Respondents worry a lot, more so than do women in the "general population" of the United States, but lesbians may not be any more likely to seek professional help when they are concerned. Seventy-three percent of our sample had sought mental health counseling at some time during their lives; among the general population of women, 63 percent had sought help for stress during the previous year.

Although half of midlife lesbians report that money is a primary concern, in the general population only about one in ten women of the same age say they have concerns about money. The percentage of lesbians concerned about job or school problems is about twice as high as that of the general female population who report concern about their own or their spouse's occupation or business. These data are quite consistent with the relative lack of wealth that women have, compared to men; and with the relative lack of social integration that lesbians experience, relative to heterosexual women.

Extensive educational preparation and professional employment are insufficient to protect most middle-aged lesbians from financial insecurity. Even the economic situations of lesbian couples differ profoundly from those of heterosexually married women of similar backgrounds. Lesbian couples typically have much less income than could be earned by a heterosexual couple with comparable education and types of employment. Single lesbians have to be particularly concerned about financial needs, for most are utterly dependent on what they earn to support themselves, and typically work within situations where exposure could result in loss of employment.

With regard to physical health, most women in our sample present few if any complaints; four out of five consider their health to be excellent or good. Again, lesbians appear very similar to all women of the same age, both in general health (88 percent of women their age in the general population rated their general health from good to excellent) and in the prevalence of typical problems, such as heart and back trouble. Most common health problems of middle-aged lesbians are weight, arthritis, back trouble and allergies. Although quite high proportions report a past history of emotional distress and/or drug use, at the time of the survey relatively few reported significant difficulty in these areas. Nevertheless, among the sample are ten percent struggling with long-term depression and six percent experiencing constant anxiety. Four percent struggle with alcoholism, one percent with dependence on other drugs.

Among lesbians who have serious health problems, most are receiving care. However, many who appear to need professional care are *not* receiving it. Preventive health care is costly and may not be readily obtainable. A substantial proportion of respondents experience difficulty in receiving and/or being able to pay for high quality care, particularly when they try to be open about their lesbianism. Too many seem to elect to care for themselves when professional care would be better. As a general characteristic, their self-reliance is undoubtedly a positive adaptation but raises questions about the timeliness with which professional providers are sometimes consulted.

Within the survey sample as a whole, several age-related trends can be observed which place special emphasis on the middle years. Overeating and concern about weight are reported much more frequently by the older group. Mental health concerns are greater for middle-aged lesbians, although long-term depression and anxiety appear less often. Worry about money, family, jobs and relationships remains fairly constant for all ages; but lesbians in midlife experience greater worry about illness and too much responsibility. While concerns about being gay are lessened in midlife, use of alcohol and tobacco are more pronounced.

For these lesbians, between 40 and 60 years old in 1985, overall health was clearly possible but not easy to achieve. Serious concerns are apparent for midlife lesbians at risk of developing age- or stress-related, chronic and possibly degenerative diseases—conditions which require ongoing and costly care. Based on the experiences of our sample, many middle-aged lesbians can expect to have real difficulty in finding and paying for such care, especially from providers who can be sensitive to the special needs they present.

Limited financial resources will significantly affect the ability of these women to afford preventive or essential health care. Seventy-three percent have health insurance, but all others would have to pay for health care in another way. Of the uninsured, 23 percent would pay cash, on a sliding scale if available; others would make time payments or could accept only free care. Access to professional help is thus compromised, in terms of economics, as well as in the availability of providers who can give appropriate care. Perhaps in partial response to these factors, many lesbians appear to be more self-reliant than they should have to be.

Our review of the data from midlife lesbians results in a picture both heartening and disturbing. A very large majority of the women in our sample are in good or excellent overall health, socially, mentally and physically. But this health has been hard-won and accomplished with the support and help of counselors and other gay people, rather than through the social institutions which provide safety and structure for heterosexual individuals and couples.

Cuttings

ADALAIDE MORRIS

She was tall and thin and, from where I lay, her long precise forelimbs, canted head and fixed gaze gave her the air of a praying mantis. Her touch was firm, however, and possibly kind. When she was done, she extracted her hand, stripped off her glove, stepped round the table, sat down and said, "I think I'm going to have to refer you to a specialist."

I slid my feet out of the stirrups and sat up straight.

"Last year your uterus was slightly enlarged, but still well inside normal limits. This year there's a large mass. It could be a fibroid, but fibroids usually grow slowly. What concerns me is that I can't find your ovaries." She paused briefly. When I looked up, she went on: "I want you to make an appointment for an ultrasound scan to take along to the specialist. Is there a gynecologist you prefer, someone you've seen before?"

The word she didn't say was "tumor," but I found it in the dictionary right after "tumid" and "tummy." Tumor: "a swollen or distended mass that arises without obvious cause from cells of preexistent tissue and possesses no physiological function." I had noticed a tumid tummy, rounding out when I lay on my back, pressing in when I leaned forward, but I'd diagnosed it as yet another awkward effect of pleasure and prescribed the standard middle-aged cure: eat less, exercise more, exert eternal vigilance. Tumor, two syllables, just like terror.

There were two possibilities—a fibroid tumor or an ovarian tumor— and, being academics, Wendy and I looked them up in every handbook we could find. One was bizarre, almost, in fact, comic; the other was sinister. Fibroids are tough muscular tissue, strange fruit that burgeons on the uterine wall or sprouts along a stalk but generally stays benign. Like melons on a vine, they swell but they do not spread. Ovarian tumors spread: they poke into surrounding tissue, send cells through the blood and lymph streams, set up colonies, kill. Not always but often. That's why the ultrasound operator, propelling her scanner back and forth across my belly, was searching so assiduously for a pair of almond-shaped ovaries. Almond-shaped would mean all right.

She was young, maybe in her early twenties, and she watched the screen as she sent sound pulses to track the elusive ovaries. A kind of body sonar, these pulses propagate through a full bladder, hit the shapes submerged between the bladder and the rectum and send back echoes: shouts from the body cave, noise that shows up as a blotch on a screen. As she worked she decorously blocked my view of the screen, but she needn't have bothered, so fierce was the pain that flared each time her scanner crossed the bulge of my bladder. The radiologist who arrived to read the ultrascan confirmed the shadowy blotch I couldn't see. Nothing almond-shaped like an ovary. Nothing pear-shaped like a womb. A mass.

We have so many bodies in our lives. I had had a quick and skinny girl's body, a body puffed and tufted by adolescence then plumped by the stifled sensualities of college. I had had a slowly unstifled newly married body, a body that expelled one unformed baby then formed another so extravagantly that I bumped through the ninth month with the drag and lift of a hot air balloon. I had had a body readied by the rhetoric of the early women's movement to respond all at once to a baby's suck, a husband's sex and the strange seductions of women. Then I had a lesbian body, first awkward, then alert and eager, and now finally faithful, except, that is, for its recent stirring and shifting in response to the prolonged solicitations of gravity. A plural body: physical, social, historical, mythological. But now, this body: traitor.

Robot too. The school year was about to start and I went in my body to meetings where I looked out the window, I sat in my body at a desk where I stared at the pages of a book, I stood in my body in front of an open refrigerator and gazed at the shelves of food. When the physician called to say that the Pap smear had returned, indicating precancerous cells, I laid my body down again, put my feet in the stirrups and let the specialist snip a piece of my cervix.

The biopsy confirmed the Pap smear, but it didn't much matter. The cervix was history anyway. It had been decided. The family physician, the specialist who would be my surgeon, another specialist called in for a second opinion, all agreed. And I assented: take it out, take it out, yes, whatever it is. Like Molly Bloom at the end of *Ulysses,* I was in a hurry.

"Okay, okay," I said as I sat in the surgeon's office next to the woman with whom I'd lived some nine years of difficult, ordinary life. We had bought a house, planted perennials, raised a child, loved, fought, cooked dinner and made our wills, but this was new. The surgeon was our distant friend, the friend of friends we had, just the weekend before, helped to move into a new house. She and I had pretended nothing was new, but as we jointly settled a set of box springs into the bed of a pickup truck, I got nervous: "Watch your hands," I said. Now in her white coat she was ticking off the list of perils so I could sign the official assent form: a nick in the intestine, a tear of the bladder, permanently impaired orgasmic capacity, cancer advanced enough to bind the organs into one glutinous mass, massive hemorrhaging, copious transfusions, AIDS. I signed. We set the date.

Roland Barthes says the most erotic parts of the body are the places where garments gape: the flash of skin between the glove and sleeve, at the neck of an open collar, along the ridge of a waistband. Such sudden uncoverings are a promise of intimacy, like lips that open into the mouth's dark interior or the hole of the ear that plunges in toward the brain. But it is terrible to think of a long cut slitting the sinewy garment of the skin, to consider the prying apart, the damaged depths never meant to surface. As I cancelled my classes and put my desk in order, I tried to think instead about sutures: how splits are stitched, how severed edges fold back together to form the long tight seams of scars.

For example, my mother/myself. I pursued this dim memory: it was the last summer of my college years, I was on Cape Cod waitressing from dawn to late velvety dark to make money to take myself to Europe and one morning I called her. Ours was a WASP estrangement: curt but civil. I hadn't gone home at the end of spring semester and planned only a diplomatic stop before school began again, but I'd heard she'd had an operation.

"How are you?"

"Okay." I remembered how she jerked her shoulders back whenever she passed a plate glass window. "Stand up straight," said the harsh voice inside her head.

"And Dad?"

"He's gone camping."

"Camping?" I said, not asking but accusing. "He left?" She started to cry. I was good at anger, rigid and merciless, but I don't remember asking if she was scared or in pain or even what sort of operation she'd had, why it had been so sudden, what it meant. Now, however, as my life doubled hers, I found I knew.

When I called to ask, she confirmed my suspicion. She'd gone in for a yearly exam one day, been admitted to the hospital the next and on the third lost everything—tumor, uterus, ovaries, cervix and all. When she woke the doctor said, "I've sent it to the lab. We'll know in a week or so." That's what she remembered now: his brusqueness, her fear. But it was benign, a fibroid.

DNA twisting in an elegant double helix made my fingers as long and now as creased as the fingers I remember flattening the fabric in front of the iron's hot tip. What set the cells in my belly to multiply? I who had for so long been so proud to be different now knew myself to be also so much the same. My daughter, with her long fingers and clothes that drooped and puckered, listened to the talk of these long days with a dream of difference, a dread of similarity. "Will I get it?" she asked. "Maybe," I said, "but I hope not." Three of us cut from the same fabric, sutured with spiral stitches and long scarred seams. Divided and adhering.

The code of the cleaver. To cleave: to divide by or as if by a cutting blow, to split, to separate into distinct parts, especially into groups with antithetical interests. I remembered the years I scorned what I took to be my mother's triviality, her concern for surfaces, her devotion to convention. Wearing jeans and black turtlenecks, wreathed in a haze of smoke, murmuring the long lines of ecstatic poems, I was not trivial but profound, bound to an antithetical set of conventions and thereby still as tied to her as black to white, as day to night. The line that held us apart also, like a hyphen, drew us together. To cleave: to adhere firmly and closely, loyally and unwaveringly.

The afternoon before the surgery, while Wendy worked and Ellen was at school, I drove to the hospital for the requisite check-in rituals. I slipped the car into a slot at the ramp, recited my name and numbers to the receptionist and carried my file through a maze of corridors toward the rooms reserved for souls in gynecological limbo: not the upper world of the nursery with its sleepy fathers and shambling mothers, not the netherworld where chemicals drip slowly into the bloodstream, but the abode of those hovering between miscarriage and delivery, between biopsy and diagnosis—malignant or benign. It was the hundredth birthday of a poet I loved, a day I'd been scheduled to give a paper at a celebration in her hometown, but here I was unpacking a knapsack of good luck charms into a gray steel locker.

I shed my street clothes for the inmate's striped bathrobe and looked sideways at the women who were pushing their i.v. trees past my door and looking sideways at me. I told the nurse who perched at the foot of my bed that I was single and had no religion, answers that were accurate but nonetheless untrue. Where was the box for "Unmarried Partner," for "Admirer of Mystics"? In the pamphlet she handed me, a fatherly physician warned a woman in a housedress that for the next six weeks she must curtail her vacuuming. "Your Hysterectomy," it was called. Not mine, I thought. I said hello to the surgeon; I said yes, no, maybe to the anesthesiologist who jacked up the bedside table, draped himself across it and didn't listen; and I said okay to the bright, exhausted head resident who pulled on a surgical glove, banged her head on the hanging lamp and executed one last pelvic exam. Then it was time to go home for supper.

Together in our kitchen, sheltered from the oncoming dusk, we repeated the comforting formulas of family life: "How was your day?" "Anyone hungry?" "Any calls?" Reports: Ellen's from high school, Wendy's from the office, mine from the ward. No one's hungry. Some calls. I leaned on the counter watching the long loopy movements Ellen made as she unpacked her knapsack; I listened to Wendy talk on the phone. Out the window a few yellow blooms magnified the last available light. Then it was time to go back to the hospital.

The surgery was scheduled for the next day at noon. That night my roommate dragged her i.v. tree back and forth to the bathroom, crashing into beds, banging into chairs, so she told me, but I slept the sleep of the drugged and knew nothing. In the morning the paring down began: the fasting, the shaving, the purging. We had agreed, the surgeon and I, that instead of a general anesthetic I would have an epidural block and a valium drip, the first to numb the region, the second to ease the mind. Between the terror of coming to consciousness in the midst of surgery, which was possible with the valium drip, and the terror of a lingering suspension of the brain, which was possible with a general anesthetic, I thought I preferred the nightmare of knowing.

Night after night, I had had this nightmare: lying on the operating table, I see nothing, but I hear a voice in the air above me murmur "oh no" and then, to itself, after a long hiatus, "look at that!" and I know, there on the table, the despair of my long death coming. Night after night my heart thrashes in my chest like a caught fish and my eyes open into a depthless dark, iron dark and no one there, only water weeping over cheekbones and the harsh scrape of breath.

But it wasn't like that. That day in the midst of surgery I floated up from the drug into rich blue folds that hung from a curved aluminum bar and divided my head from my chest. On the other side of the curtain, inside a small circle of brightness, I could see the surgeon, the resident and a number of nurses. Their heads were down; their hands were busy. Then the surgeon stepped around the curtain and I saw her eyes between the surgical mask and her silly surgical hat. She said my name; she said, "It looks good"; she said, "fibroids." Then I asked the anesthesiologist who stood by my shoulder to hold my hand and in his warm dry grasp I sank back slowly into sleep.

Two fibroids, one slightly used uterus and a battered cervix were gone. The fibroids were the size of oranges, the texture of cantaloupes and, between them, like fists, they had clutched the lost ovaries, ovaries free now to pour hormones into the bloodstream, swell breasts to signal the periods I would no longer have, release eggs for babies never to be born. Release them, where? Alarm clocks ringing in an empty house. Vagina folded together at the top, sewn with a little cuff: cul de sac, road to nowhere, dead end. I was grateful, but it was a long time before I came back into my body.

Lying on a gurney in the recovery room: a mannequin split up the middle and stapled together again, fixed to drip through tubes, drain into vials and pouches. Wired-up cyborg with a stop switch, a start switch. Not alone: bodies parked like cars in the bays of a repair shop, each with its team of attending mechanics. "Where'd you get your haircut?" asks my mechanic. Haircut? Wheeled through the halls. Slid back into bed. A big pancake on a cold white plate.

They hover. Poke. Pry. Fold the sheet back. Uncap the vial and drain it. Blood and pus, thick cloudy liquids. A pouch of urine dangling from the tree: measure it. In the mouth, a green taste—bittergreen. Blow into a tube, push the ball up with your breath: the nurses believe in this, a god that keeps water out of the lungs.

But cool hands. Wendy's here. I fall asleep to the wash of her voice, wake into her gaze. She sits in a chair by the bed. I leave the real world to her. She answers the phone, tells the story, talks to the surgeon, takes the flowers, tugs at the sheets, talks to the nurses, talks to me. I lie still. When she leaves me, I sleep. She comes back, always.

After school, Ellen hurries through the long corridors to see for herself what the message delivered to her classroom had said: that the surgery is over, that it went well, that I am okay. I am better now seeing her, good fruit of my gone womb, odd girl grasping a flower from a street-side garden. As I rise and fall all afternoon, she hauls out her school books, kicks off her shoes, drapes her legs across a chair and pokes her long fingers into a sack of potato chips, licking the tips carefully afterwards to tongue away the salt. When the sun hits the bottom of my bed and the two of them are there, I am happy. I make a tentative move back toward my torn body.

Where does the soul go when it leaves the body? The body, flung doll, asleep in an armchair, sprawled at the accident site, laid out on a slab. Vacant. In sleep, the soul goes off, fast traveler, vision-quester, pursuer of phantoms; in death, the soul goes out, moving, so they say, faster and faster and with joy down a tunnel of light toward the ones who've gone before. But in the suspension of surgery—not sleep, not death—where does it go? I don't know, but I remember this: it was love that pulled me back, a fierce drag of love for the two beings who sat in the chairs by the foot of my bed.

The room filled up with flowers: ambassadors, bearers of greetings from a distant world, helpers. Not easy gestures, not customary courtesies— not at least to me: I greeted them as stand-ins for the spirits of their senders. I was glad to see them. But I didn't want to see any of the senders. Not one. Not yet. No one with the cold air of fall in their clothes, and in their eyes and limbs the hurry I had left: fast time, two-things-at-once time, jump-ahead stay-ahead hurt-your-head time. Poked by nurses, prodded by interns, I was awash on a distant tide. Where I was, water heaved and rolled and far below the surface whales sustained a long antiphonal song.

When your attention contracts to the edges of the room, to the margins of the bed, through a thin barrier of skin and in toward the rich drift that is letting go, the nurses tilt you up and pitch you out of bed. They take out the catheter and make you stumble to the toilet, they tape plastic over your wound so you can shower and they send you forth so that slowly the parameters of your world push out again: to the end of the hall, to the nursery where the babies sleep and cry, down the corridor past the waiting room for intensive care, past the ward where the patients are radioactive, into a passageway where you can stop and look into the windows of the rooms below, in one, a bone-thin man sprawled out in a breeze from a tall standing fan.

But hot, I was so hot. Wendy had flown to Chicago to celebrate her parents' anniversary, Ellen had glided from work into the arms of her boy friend and the friend who sat with me through the long afternoon now closed her book and bade me goodbye. A new crew of nurses circulated through the ward, nurses I'd never seen before, the night nurses condemned to care for us while somewhere in a rosier world waiters snapped stiff linen across tables for two, shined up the wine glasses and put a match to the candles.

There I was, bobbing over my bland dinner, eyes scraping open and shut like the eyes of my old doll that cried real tears. The night nurses take my tray and then take my temperature, they take it again and again and it's rising, and soon over the bed looms a figure in a green scrubsuit. Her black hair stretches straight back from her broad flat cheekbones as if to pry her eyes open, as if to yank her alert. She's in charge here. Night after night, women have twisted and moaned and babies have dropped screaming into her large hands. Now this.

"We'll have to run some tests," she says.

"Okay," I say. But she's gone.

I blur away and wake again when a man in a white coat comes carrying a wire basket of bottles. He picks up my arm, sticks in a needle, sucks out blood, clatters away. It's the milkman, that's who, en route to Vampire City: now he's going down the stairs and when he gets outside he'll slide open his panel truck, rack the basket and make a little note on his pad. Up and down the hall sleepers shift and snuffle. It's night's no-time. The thermometer reads 104° and rising. The night nurses glide by on their gumshoes wishing they were somewhere else.

When orders come for more tests, they tilt me out of bed, plump me in a wheelchair and push me off to X-ray. "Maybe there's fluid in your lungs," says the nurse. "Should've blown harder on that tube." We round a corner and graze a gurney ferrying an old man from surgery to intensive care. "Oops," she says, "sorry." His eyes are open, his skin the color of old city snow. I'm cold and so tired that when the radiologist stands me up and pushes my shoulders back against the black plate I start to cry. "Stand still," she says. On the way back in the wheelchair I fall asleep.

Two nurses stand by my bed holding needles, tubes and an i.v. bag. "We can't wake her up," says the skinny straw-haired one with weasel eyes. "She hasn't slept for days." They're talking about the resident.

"But I don't know how to do it," says the black-haired one whose arms are sausages tied tight once at the elbow and once at the wrist.

"Palpate a vein," says the skinny one, "then pop it in. I've seen her do it."

"No," I say, "no," as she picks up my arm. "Don't, don't." She fumbles, misses, tries another vein, misses again, then shoves it in and I don't care who hears. "No," I'm yelling, "no, no!"

"What was your operation?" asks the straw-haired one, cutting her eyes from my twisted face to the black-haired nurse and back again. "They take your ovaries?" I shake my head. "Well, then, they handled them, didn't they? I can always tell."

When Wendy returned, we consoled ourselves by turning this episode into a tawdry paperback, *The Revenge of the Night Nurses,* a thriller in which vicious women in white wreak vengeance on a hysteric who happens to be me. The motive for their cruel capers: rage, rage at being left alone on the night lovers everywhere clink glasses and sink into each other's eyes. But, of course, truth be told, *we* were the ones who were furious: one of us had been alone and afraid, the other had not known, there was nothing to be done about it and it wouldn't be the last time. "They handle your ovaries?" we asked each other knowingly. "I can always tell," we said, as we walked arm in arm down the hall pushing the i.v. tree before us.

When the infection healed, the nurses unhitched the i.v. tree and slowly the range of my rambling extended: through the passageway where I'd seen the bone-thin man, along an atrium lined with mirrors, out onto a roof where patients basked in the late fall sun and enjoyed a little privacy, a little autonomy. Then one day the resident took a shiny L-shaped tool and pried out the staples that tracked down my belly, a nurse reminded me to curtail my vacuuming and we packed the car with flowers and drove back home.

"Six weeks," the surgeon said, "and you'll be good as new." Good as new? "Like new," says the man on TV pointing to a row of reconditioned cars, a stack of recapped tires. That means the splits, the cracks, the flaws that could kill have been patched up, covered over, hidden from sight. Cover them over, hide them as I might, I now had a rough raised scar that ran from my navel to my pubic bone and a sense of vulnerability sharper and deeper than my relief that this time, at least, I had escaped.

I was in no hurry to resume the long days and longer nights of a dutiful professor's life. As elemental and fierce as the fear of death is the dream of recovery, of being wonderfully restored to ourselves and the world. I wanted to move back beyond all that had blunted me, to meet again some part of myself I seemed to have lost. What was it? And where?

I had had some clues lying there in bed, dispersed and fragmented clues: stray surges of love, the afternoon sun on my feet, a rhythm slower and deeper than breath. The body knows how to take you back, how to make you start again. I sat still as Wendy drove me past double-parked delivery trucks and through the students streaming to class. Near our house, the streets were empty. It was 10 A.M. Wendy was going back to work and I was going to climb into bed and pull the new flannel sheets up over my head.

Cocoon: a safe and silky place for the worm to turn. I curled up tight and waited. The sun crossed from the foot of the bed to the head and when it sank the moon rose. I slept swaddled in blankets and stepped like a toddler up and down the stairs: right foot, rest; left foot, rest. The days took their time. After the morning clatter, stillness returned like punched dough rising. While Ellen took her tests and Wendy met her deadlines, I drifted with the cat from window to window and nodded in the sun. I looked at pictures, I listened to music, I learned again to do one thing at a time: when I picked up the wooden spoon, when I stirred the soup for supper, when I sipped its salty broth, that's all I did. Gradually my mind began to clear.

Friends brought with them on their visits a familiar arrangement of arguments against other arguments, music to the intellectual ear but to me now noise from a distant battle. With effort I could follow the intricate orchestration of Wendy's office and Ellen's high school, but the rhythm that held me was a slow two-stroke, a systole-diastole steady as a wing beat, urgent as a heartbeat. The fear and release of surgery, the rise and fall of infection and now the hunch and stretch of recovery: I gathered my forces; I opened the door and walked out in the world.

The cool rain drifted underneath my black umbrella and I drank it in at every pore. Wind that pulled leaves from the branches and sent them scraping down the street tugged at the edges of my jacket. The sun burned down through the air and ignited the tops of maples; crows floated to the ground like heavy flakes of ash and rose again in the wind. Like Thoreau I became a surveyor of my neighborhood, an inspector of radiance alert for leaks and surges. Light shone through the rich yellow leaves, leaves spun through the shimmering air, wind snaked through the grass on the ground. In the gardens cornstalks shook and late tomatoes swelled and split on the vines. Around the trunk of a tree a mound of impatiens glinted like the shards at the bottom of a kaleidoscope tube. On bright windy days clouds raced up over the horizon and rolled the shadows back into the trees like snapped window shades. In the late afternoons when the wind fell the landscape grew mysterious, all contrast, and the shadow of a motionless tree had the force of an omen. The wind poured through my head. I rang with life.

"How wondrous, how mysterious!" the old Zen masters said, "I carry fuel, I draw water." As I walked home in the dusk in the fall of the year, I noticed how light clings to the earth as darkness sweeps over the skies. I saw the flowers in my garden glow like great yellow globes. I opened the door, I reentered my home.

Menopause, Hysterectomy and Sexuality

SUSANNE MORGAN

In addition to being interested, as a sociologist and a lesbian, in changes in sexuality at midlife and the ways that this particular generation may experience midlife differently than earlier generations, my personal interest arises in part from my own hysterectomy and ovariectomy from an IUD-related pelvic infection, which left me, at 30, physiologically post-menopausal.

Hysterectomy remains, despite consumer information and pressure, the *most common* major operation in the U.S.A. for women who are in midlife today. Statisticians predict that perhaps half of all women alive today will have a hysterectomy and studies show that up to one-third of the women over 60 already have. Despite this evidence, I have heard lesbians say that hysterectomy does not happen to us. This attitude is based on the incorrect idea that hysterectomy is always a result of childbirth or contraception (as if no lesbian ever had a child or used contraception)—and/or the chauvinistic belief that our bodies are "better" than heterosexual womens' bodies and therefore are not subject to these ordinary problems. We women must not abandon one another with such foolish attitudes.

It *is* true that some of the more common reasons for hysterectomy are directly or indirectly related to childbirth or contraception. Pelvic infections are often caused by IUDs, fibroids grow more rapidly when stimulated by estrogens such as birth control pills, and uterine prolapse may be more likely after several pregnancies. Many lesbians, of course, have used contraception at some time in their lives or had children, although the percentage is lower than that of the general population.

On the other hand, some conditions requiring hysterectomy are more *likely* to affect women who have not used contraception or borne children, and thus could be more common among lesbians (although we do not yet have studies of these frequencies). Endometriosis, for example, is a disease which frequently leads to hysterectomy and it is often more severe among women who have had no children. Recent studies show that birth control pills, despite all their other problems, may reduce the risk of uterine or cervical cancer.

Since hysterectomy is so very common and since women are enormously resilient and able to survive the most devastating ordeals, we tend to trivialize it. Hysterectomy is *not* trivial: it is a major operation which entails risks of minor or major complications or even death. Compared to other similar operations, hysterectomy is associated with higher rates of complications and depression and with longer recovery time.

Women are generally not warned about the risks of having a hysterectomy. In particular, women are not told about the sexual changes which occur after hysterectomy. In a misguided attempt to reassure women that they will not be devastated, doctors (most of whom are notoriously uninformed about sexuality) assure women that they will experience no sexuality changes after hysterectomy.

This is nonsense. The uterus is a strong, muscular organ which is involved in every phase of the sexual response cycle. It engorges with blood on arousal and grows to twice its unaroused size, contracting vigorously in orgasm. Pressure on the cervix and uterus is an important source of stimulation and orgasm for some women. It is ridiculous to suggest that no change will occur if these organs are no longer there.

Change does not necessarily equal problem, however. For many women, uterine response is not an important part of sexuality. For others, the hysterectomy eliminates a medical problem which had been interfering with their sex life. For many other women the experience is bittersweet: it is a relief to no longer be unwell, but there is a loss which is very real. There is little good research on the nature, cause and frequency of sexual problems after hysterectomy, although the few existing studies show that one-third to one-half of women report reduced sexual pleasure after hysterectomy.

Because of the confusing messages about sexuality after hysterectomy ("There will be no change", "You will be devastated"), all women deserve support from other women for whatever their experience is, positive or negative. Because of the confusing messages in the lesbian community ("It doesn't happen to us", "It won't affect us if we do not want children"), lesbians deserve particular support from other lesbians to express the feelings they do experience.

Simply being told that physical changes do occur can be enormously reassuring. Some women find that their arousal and orgasms seem less deep; some women for whom deep penetration has been important find that their primary center shifts to the clitoris; others find that stimulation of the area known as the G spot or the urethral sponge is especially important in the absence of the uterus; and some miss the sensuality of their menstrual periods.

For many women hysterectomy includes, in addition to removal of the uterus, ovariectomy, removal of the glands which produce estrogen and androgen. Ovariectomy is surgical castration and parallels removal of the testicles in men. According to one large study, one-fourth of *all* women in this country can expect to experience ovariectomy, or surgical menopause. I call it menostop since it is so very abrupt and it is a far greater trauma to a woman's system than hysterectomy alone.

After ovariectomy a woman will experience all the physical sexual changes which occur during and after natural menopause and additional changes as well. Natural menopause involves gradual changes in hormone balance and menstrual pattern; it is marked by the absence of a period for a year and typically happens around age 50. Surgical menopause, on the other hand, involves a very sudden drop in all ovarian hormones, removing entirely the estrogens and androgens which the post-menopausal ovaries continue to produce in small quantities.

The most typical sexual change that results from ovariectomy or natural menopause is vaginal dryness, although not all women experience this change. After menopause the wetness in a woman's vagina is less copious, thinner in texture and takes longer to produce. This change is due to reduced estrogens and to changes in the cervical mucus.

Although lubrication is usually discussed in terms of being able to accommodate a penis without pain, lubrication for a woman is often the first signal of arousal and is in that way parallel to erection in a man. Thus the use of an artificial lubricant should be seen specifically as an aid to arousal. The menopausal woman's lover should know that the substance makes stroking the vulva and clitoris more comfortable and facilitates penetration, but the woman's own juices will gradually appear.

Women are very resourceful about substances they use in love making, including sterile jelly such as KY Jelly, which feels cool; natural oils such as wheat germ or vitamin E oil, which may stimulate a woman's own estrogens; coconut oil, which is firm when you apply it and melts deliciously; and special products such as Kama Sutra Oil, which feels hot and tastes good but may irritate the urethra. If both partners are certain not to have HIV infection or active cold sores they can use saliva. If your lover is very wet and does not have yeast, trichomonas, herpes, or even a remote chance of HIV, you can use some shared juice. Be very cautious, however, not to transmit infection and also be alert to an allergic response to various substances. In addition, be careful about fingernail hygiene (short and clean) as a menopausal woman's vaginal tissue may be thinner and scratch more easily.

Less noticeable than vaginal dryness is the fact that after menopause the vaginal tissue is thinner and less elastic, the vulva tissue less fleshy and the general tone in the pelvic area more relaxed. These changes, referred to by doctors as "senile vaginal atrophy," parallel other more visible body changes. Since we know that, although we are not the same as we were twenty years ago, we are still vibrant, alive and sexy, we certainly don't want to adopt that negative attitude about our aging!

Changes are a natural part of our increased maturity and wisdom, but they also may alter our sexual experience. Particularly after surgical menopause when the changes are more abrupt, or in intergenerational relationships where the differences are more apparent, we may need to pay more attention to them.

There are several sexual implications of thinner vaginal tissue. Penetration may be less comfortable, particularly if the woman has not experienced penetration for awhile; a sharp fingernail may scratch or be more irritating. The sensitive areas in the vagina known as the G spot or urethral sponge may be less easily stimulated. As the vulva grows less fleshy it may be more important to stroke the clitoral area itself, since stimulation of other parts of the vulva are less readily transmitted to the clitoris, but the glans of the clitoris itself is less protected so vigorous stimulation may be uncomfortable... stay gentle and aware.

The tissue surrounding the entrance to the vagina also may become thinner and less elastic. This has implications for penetration. Many lesbians do not like penetration, but for those who do, her lover needs to allow for the possibility that she should enter more gradually, beginning with one finger, very gently.

Generally reduced resiliency in the pelvic tissue means that both arousal and orgasm may feel physically less intense for some women. Our tissues are still hormone-stimulated and still respond to sexual contact, but perhaps with less urgency. Other women find that sexual response is more intense after menopause. Multiple orgasm remains physically possible and for some women more frequent. For many of us these physical changes are unnoticeable, or welcome because they allow us to relax our sexual pacing and tune in to our bodies more intimately.

After menopause, some women find they have more frequent yeast overgrowth conditions (sometimes called yeast infections, but really a proliferation of naturally occurring vaginal bacteria). This is probably due to changes in blood hormones which make the vaginal fluids less acidic and the vaginal tissue "sweeter." Lesbians are generally less likely to get vaginal infections than women who relate sexually to men, but yeast can be passed from vagina to mouth or vagina to vagina on fingers or directly. Many women find that they are less likely to get an overgrowth of yeast if they restrict their sugar and alcohol intake.

More visible changes as we age also can affect our sexual self-image. Breasts become softer and may "droop," and they may also be less sensitive to stimulation. In some women nipple erections seem to be more pronounced and last longer after menopause. Pubic hair and other body hair becomes more sparse and may turn gray and for some women this is a difficult body image change to adjust to.

There are several ways of dealing with physical problems which might result from hysterectomy and/or menopause. Reduced estrogen is the most discussed physical change and estrogen drugs have been promoted for use by women in menopause. In addition to estrogen another ovarian hormone, androgen, the hormone of sex drive or libido, also has a key role in female sexual experience. Many women who have surgical menopause from ovariectomy experience a severe loss of sex drive following surgery. It is not known what the implications of androgen reduction from natural menopause are. We do know that sexual energy is affected by hormone levels and hormone levels are affected by sexual activity.

So it appears that many of the sexual changes after menopause are related to androgens and not to estrogens at all. Therefore, women who take estrogen pills or cream for sexual problems can expect help with dryness but not with sex drive or tissue changes. Recent research on older women's sexual physiology also showed that women with higher androgen levels had less "vaginal atrophy." Some women who have had surgical menopause and who are having severe sexual problems are seeking out androgen implants, a controversial and possibly dangerous, though possibly effective treatment. Others are investigating ways to promote androgen production by strengthening the adrenals, another source of androgen.

Estrogen drugs will probably help with vaginal dryness, will help reduce hot flashes and may be effective in preventing osteoporosis, a condition in which the bones become brittle. Estrogen, however, has been shown to greatly increase the risk of endometrial cancer and is increasingly implicated in breast cancer and perhaps in gall bladder disease, fibroid tumors and blood clots and arteriosclerosis. Many women are trying to use estrogen only if necessary and then for a short time and with progesterone, a hormone which, though yet untested over time, is thought by some to reduce some of the risks of estrogens alone for a woman with an intact uterus.

For dealing with hot flashes, women find "dressing like an onion" and eating a hypoglycemic diet, perhaps including vitamin E supplements, to be very helpful. For osteoporosis prevention, calcium/magnesium supplements (up to 1500 mg of calcium a day with 700 mg of magnesium) and regular weightbearing exercise have been shown to be nearly as effective as estrogen. Not only is this not dangerous at all, but the "side effects" can be very beneficial.

I have already discussed some substances women use to compensate for vaginal dryness, but if we understand the ways estrogen is produced in the female body we may be able to actually increase our estrogen level.

These approaches are detailed in the chapter called "Home-brew Estrogen" in my book *Coping With a Hysterectomy* (New American Library, 1985).

What I call home-brew estrogen is estrogen produced elsewhere in the body. Both fatty tissue and adrenal function are crucial, so we can assume that women who carry a little extra weight as they age may actually increase their estrogen level. In addition, we can use what we learn from holistic health about adrenal function: any ways of coping with physical and emotional stress are helpful; coffee, alcohol and drugs deplete the adrenals.

Physical fitness has both general and specific effects on sexuality. Regular exercise increases the blood supply to the pelvic area as well as serving as a fundamental anti-depressant. Too much alcohol interferes with sex as well as other parts of our lives. A good diet and supplements, including vitamin E and the B vitamins, can help prevent hot flashes and vaginal dryness.

More specifically, we can improve our sexual muscle tone by doing Kegel exercises, which involve contracting the muscles identified by stopping the flow of urine. Kegels are known to women who have had childbirth classes in the past fifteen or twenty years and are extremely helpful as we grow older. In addition to helping with sexual function, they also reduce mild urinary incontinence, an extremely common difficulty for older women. Specific instructions are found in *Ourselves, Growing Older* (Simon and Schuster, 1987), a useful source written in cooperation with the authors of *Our Bodies, Ourselves.* In addition, activity which gets us breathing and moving in the pelvic area is excellent exercise, so keep on dancing!

The general perspective that we should take is that as we move physiologically past menopause, the pacing of our love making may need to change. It may take longer to become aroused; certain kinds of touching may be too rough; our arousal and orgasm may be less intense.

For women who experience surgical menopause this transition can be especially hard. Many couples develop a love making "script" which leads to arousal and satisfaction. When suddenly the script does not work, both partners may be alarmed and, without information about physical changes, may blame themselves or the relationship. Especially after "menostop" I advise people to go back to "courtship" and explore again the touching, talking and caressing which makes love making spontaneous, sensitive and communicative. Some women agree to spend a period of weeks being intimate and sensual together but not genitally sexual. This can provide a time to get reacquainted without a focus on orgasm or performance, and can be a wonderful time to remind themselves of the many ways they can make love together.

I always speak of masturbation and love making as physical therapy and there is no doubt that continued sexual activity helps: women who are sexual regularly lubricate more quickly and appear to experience fewer changes in their vulva and vaginas. Research shows that sexually active women have higher levels of androgens, so sex may also keep our hormones flowing.

The phrase "use it or lose it" has been a way to remind us of the beneficial effects of continued sexual activity, but it can be used against us as well. Some of us may want to "use it" but not be able to due to discomfort with masturbation and the absence of partners. In addition, some women who have not "used it" for a period of time may feel that they have "lost it," and may not pursue options which could be wonderful for them.

We are all aware that some midlife women are lesbians and that lesbians grow older and still are sexual. But ageism does exist in the lesbian community and we should be alert to it. In response to the negative stereotypes of lesbians and of older women, we have reminded ourselves that women are sexual all the way through old age. This is certainly true, but if in addition to our invisibility as lesbians we ourselves contribute to the invisibility of sexual changes, we contribute to our own oppression. In *The Joy of Lesbian Sex* we read "Women never have to worry about getting it up, so at an age when men begin to fret about difficulties with penile erection women's sexual equipment remains blissfully unimpaired." This leaves a woman who *is* having trouble "getting it up," becoming aroused and lubricated, feeling like there must be something wrong with her.

It is certainly true that the physical changes I describe do not make lesbians sexless. "Reduced sex drive" can facilitate long, relaxed love making and many women are relieved not to have menstrual periods. Women may be able in the middle years to appreciate their accomplishments in work and life, and confidence certainly enhances a sexual relationship.

The generation of women who are now entering midlife has the potential to explode the myths: the myth that older women are sexless (look at all the women in the media celebrating their aging) and the myth that there are no sexual changes as we age. This generation has been the culturally dominant generation since the '60s and has continued to redefine sexuality, femaleness and aging, primarily by talking with one another and making our voices heard.

Desire Perfected:
Sex After Forty

JOAN NESTLE

Mabel Hampton, an African-American lesbian in her eighties, recently said to me, "Joan, there are some women I can't touch because the desire burns my hand like a blue flame, those women, those women!" We both laughed, but I was also humbled by the depth of Mabel's erotic feeling in the ninth decade of her life.

This knowledge of our own desires, perfected over many years of lesbian loving, can be one of our most enduring comrades in the later years of our lives. I say "can be" because I recognize that not all lesbians have been able to or have even wanted to fully explore their sexual selves. But for those who have been inspired by trust or need or opportunity to push at their sexual boundaries, the years after 40 can provide a canvas for perfected pleasures.

I am not writing about sex as a sociologist or as a psychologist; I am speaking as a 50-year-old woman who has been sexually active with women since I was ten. My own sexual journey began in 1950 when I became best friends with Roz, the butcher's daughter. We incorporated sex play into our relationship when I first shared with her the wonderful secret of masturbation. Then in weekly bouts of fantasy sex play, ensconced in her parents' double bed, we enacted such scenes as "The Sheik and His Harem," with Roz and me playing all the parts. In the year 1950, I put my head between her thighs to use my mouth to give her pleasure and I can still remember the softness of her skin against my cheeks. Our relationship changed in high school when Roz took commercial courses and I took the academic route; she married early and I found Greenwich Village.

Over the years, I have explored butch-femme sex, androgynous sex, intergenerational sex (where I lusted after much older women), S/M sex, group sex, back room sex, sex for money and, in a ten year relationship, domestic sex which included much of the above. I have made love when I was in love and when I was not, for many days and for one night. I do not mean this list to be flaunting; when I came out in 1958, one of the most important freedoms I was choosing was to move my body into the world under my own control. In those days, the vice squad made sure that we never forgot we were obscenities, but their harassment and the general intolerant social atmosphere did not impede my erotic progress.

I have used every day of my lesbian life to exercise this independence of desire. I think, in some way, many of us have made the same choice— to be the guardians of our own bodies and the explorers of our own desire. This erotic self-possession is one of the gifts of our lives in exchange for the loss of societal privileges of heterosexual marriage, the domestic sphere and other "normal" protections of womanhood.

Having a lot of sex or being comfortable with sex does not mean that the body is always one's friend or that aging does not offer challenges that change the erotic terrain. Issues like physical well-being, body size, menopause, emotional fragility are always there, waiting to be incorporated into daily moments of intimacy. I have always been a big woman and now I am bigger. Sometimes I'm caught up in the old battle of hating my body for its fullness of flesh, that will show the effects of aging in a more dramatic way because there is more of me to show it. Menopause is a natural occurrence and so is the feeling of loss that can accompany it. I cry and yell more than I have ever done. I feel a small moment of victory when my wandering period returns. Because of a chronic illness, I often do not feel physically safe and I think a lot about death.

And yet, in the face of all these challenges, I have a comrade to strengthen me—my developed knowledge of what gives me pleasure in love making and my willingness to put my body into play. Even when I am most at war with biology, I can find the life force to take all I have learned about loving and once again be the adventurer, the discoverer of new worlds, as I move down my lover's belly. To my old-time sense of sexual bravado have been added the woman-loving-woman insights of lesbian feminism that have helped me to value myself more as a woman, making aging an honored process.

We will all find different ways to keep our erotic identities alive as we change, different sources of inspiration and stimulation. I found mine in being open to what new generations of lesbians were doing with their bodies. I went to sex parties, talked to leather women and saw clearly what I could do and what I did not want to do. Then when I was 47, fighting the depression of illness, I found the ground I could stand on. Gay Women's Alternative of New York asked me to read some of my erotic stories. I realized that I did not want to read about sexual desire in everyday clothes, that I wanted some way to mark the specialness of the language, so I decided to wear a black slip and black stockings for the reading. I wanted the audience to see a large older woman's body as I said the words of sex. This wearing of the black slip publicly became my signature. I had found a way to transform perceived losses into newly acquired erotic territory.

I wanted the public revelation of my aging larger body to be a statement for all older lesbians; I wanted to proclaim our image and with it, our knowledge. Sexual self-discovery and issues of self-presentation do not stop at any decade's door. The desire I experience as a 50-year-old lesbian woman is not the same as the passion I pursued in earlier years; my desire has deepened and I experience it as a gift I bring to my lover. Stretched out on the bed, waiting for her, I sometimes feel as if I am bursting with sexual knowledge, that carried in the fullness of my breasts and hips, is all the wisdom I have gleaned from pursuing the touch of women for half a century. I do not feel arrogant or invulnerable to rejection, but I do know the ground I am lying on. I have never traded sexual desire for security; I have no economic or legal monuments like a twenty year marriage to mark the end of lust and the beginning of safety. I do have my own person, my own body, that has led me to a lifetime of new places, new resistances, new compassions. This accumulated wealth of sexual self-knowledge that many of us have is not often discussed in our communities and, thus, we are still learning about the political and personal implications of our sexual wisdom. We need more discussion of our lesbian sexual vitality and explorations at all ages to stimulate our desires. Not a discussion that will make any lesbian woman feel inadequate because she did not "do that" or doesn't "want that," but discussions that allow each woman to put new value on the moments of desire she has experienced.

As I have come to enjoy my own middle-aged sexual wisdom, I have also come to recognize it in other older women I see around me. Gray hair and textured hands are now erotic emblems I seek out. As I curiously explore the lines on my own chest running down to the valley between my breasts, I caress those same lines on the chest of my lover. I still want strong love making, I still want to play and pretend and seduce. But a moment comes when all of me is stark naked in body and imagination and then I know all of who I am and who I am no longer and I rise to offer this honest older self to my lover.

As if to return the gift of acceptance, my body has rewarded me with new sexual responses. I now have multiple orgasms, a delightful occurrence that did not begin until my mid-forties; I have jettisoned leftover feelings of shame and some youthful reluctance to accept oral love making. I allow myself much more time to look at my lover's body, to stroke her and caress her. Part of this tenderness comes from my sense of our combined years—almost 90 years of life between us—and thus even time becomes an erotic ally.

I have learned to incorporate safe sex techniques into my love making in a way that preserves my desire and recognizes the agony of this time in our sexual history. I keep packets of condoms at the side of our bed along with a large tube of KY jelly, one for the dildo play we enjoy, the other for the occasional dryness that makes greater lubrication necessary. The first time I faced my lack of wetness and realized that my internal desire would no longer always have an external marker, I was deeply distressed. I had always loved the gush of wetness that was the body's own voice and, at first, I was ashamed at this change of language. I had to find the words to ask my lover to help me. As she anointed me, I felt a new sense of seriousness about love making, similar to the sense of taking responsibility I feel when I am smoothing a condom down over our dildo. These conscious acts taken to allow for a spontaneous physical pleasure become spiritual moments of sexual reclamation.

While I have felt fear and change and loss, I have, even more, felt a glory in my love making in my fifth decade. The glory comes from knowing I am using everything my 50 years of living as a lesbian has taught me, not just about our bodies, but about the wonder of our risk takings, the strength of our autonomy, the courage of our choices.

Lesbian Sex at Menopause: as Good as or Better Than Ever

ELLEN COLE
& ESTHER D. ROTHBLUM

"Sex after menopause has brought
more pleasure than I ever experienced.
More wisdom, and a *fantastic* lover."

Considerable research has addressed the relationship between sexuality and menopause, but most studies rely on clinical samples of women who seek help. For some of these women, sexual problems existing prior to menopause were exacerbated, but for most of the women, problems developed during the years immediately preceding and following menopause. They included decreases in desire, arousal, frequency, clitoral responsiveness and orgasm and increased pain and sensitivity to touch. Moreover, the subjective experience of sex seemed to be a very negative one for the majority of these women. It is unclear whether or not these findings have any relevance at all for a general population.

Nearly all studies of sex at menopause fail to address women's feelings about the changes they experience. Moreover, to the best of our knowledge, every published study about sexual functioning and menopause assumes that women's sexuality is intercourse-based and heterosexual. Our study attempted to get a fuller picture of sex at menopause: to avoid the pathological bias of a clinical sample, to elicit not only descriptions of changes, but feelings about these changes and to look at a population that has not been studied before—the lesbian woman at menopause.

We developed a questionnaire designed to assess changes at menopause in sexual behavior and attitudes. We asked about menstrual history, partner characteristics, sexual behavior, changes in and quality of sexual activity, sexual problems, favorite sexual activities, sexual desire, sexual excitement, orgasm, pain with sex, sexual response of partners and other perceived positive and negative changes in sexuality since menopause.

Finally, we asked each respondent to complete the following sentence: "Based on my experience, sex at menopause is..."

Forty-one women responded to notices in local and national lesbian newspapers and to questionnaires distributed at two conferences. The mean age of the women was 51.5 years (the average age of naturally occuring menopause is 51.4), with a range from 43 to 68 years. One woman indicated her race/ethnicity to be Lebanese, the remainder were caucasian. All women indicated that they were lesbians, except one who was bisexual and two who did not indicate sexual orientation. One said, "Lesbian at present, probably bisexual."

On average, the women had their last menstrual period just under five years ago, but the range was considerable; from two years to 41 years ago. Seven women (sixteen percent) had had a hysterectomy. The mean age of hysterectomy was 42.7 years, with a range from 28 to 58 years. The most frequent menopausal signal for which the women sought professional advice was hot flashes (sixteen women, or 39 percent). Other signals varied widely and were described as tender vaginal mucosa, night sweats, osteoporosis, vaginal dryness, excessive bleeding, headaches, dizziness, irregularity of menstrual periods, insomnia, vomiting and diarrhea during menstrual periods, fatigue, mood changes, cramps and bloating, urinary leakage, epilepsy and diminished libido.

Fourteen lesbians (34 percent) were taking hormone replacement medication and one was taking homeopathic remedies. Although hormone replacement medication alters the menopausal experience, we have decided not to report the results separately for the two groups.

Twenty-three women (56 percent) were currently in a committed relationship with a partner, the average length of which was 7.28 years; ranging from eight months to 27 years. The mean age of the partners was 43.1 years, with a range of 30 to 60 years; on average, women were 10.1 years older than their partner. Only four lesbians in this sample were younger than their partners. Thus, most of the women's partners were younger and still menstruating.

Of the total, 41 women were currently engaged in sexual activity with other women. Frequency of sexual activity ranged considerably, from one to two times daily to monthly or rarely.

Nineteen lesbians (46 percent) stated that frequency of sexual activity had remained the same since the onset of menopause; six women (fifteen percent) stated that sexual activity had increased and eleven (27 percent) that it had decreased. We asked women if there had been a change in the *type* of sexual activity in which they engaged since menopause. Ten women (24 percent) indicated that there was. As one said: "More exploration—orgasms increased greatly as time went on, for me and for her. And the *affection* was almost constant—when we were together."

Some lesbians also responded that there was less genital involvement and less deep kissing. One woman said she and her partner choose to only embrace and deep kiss now. Another woman said her changes have more to do with wisdom than hormones. Two others indicated that they were more sexual since menopause, had more partners and more quantity and quality of sexual activity.

We asked specifically whether there were kinds of sexual activity that women *used* to prefer but no longer do, or that they now enjoy but didn't prior to menopause. Twenty-nine (71 percent) indicated that there was no change in the types of activities they had enjoyed since the onset of menopause. Of the twelve (29 percent) who did notice a difference, comments included increased interest in rougher sex with penetration, ability to sustain orgasm for a longer period; increased holding, hugging, cuddling; increased sexual communication due to experiences with other women from previous relationships; more manual and genital sex; decreased time spent in sexual activity; and a greater focus on safer sex. Several lesbians indicated that changes in their sexual activity were not necessarily related to menopause, but instead were due to such factors as "the timely mellowing of our relationship."

We asked specifically about the *quality* of the sexual experience since menopause, including the level of enjoyment, pleasure and satisfaction. We wanted to know how women explained these changes. Twelve lesbians (29 percent) indicated no changes or no regular sexual activity, eleven (27 percent) indicated some decrease in perceived quality. Some comments included references to changes in physiology:

"Orgasms are not as intense as in the twenties and thirties and even forties."

"Pleasure still the same but I hate not getting wet."

Other comments referred to possible negative consequences of hormone replacement therapy:

"I am having sex less often but it is probably a function of hormone therapy and not menopause."

Some women referred to their partners sexuality as a contrast:

"Yes, it takes longer to be aroused. I desire more foreplay and tenderness during love making. I don't understand these changes. I am very disappointed in myself and feel guilty that my lover feels rejected (in) my lack of desire. Could have something to do with my feeling older and my worrying about losing my attractiveness."

There was a feeling of loss:

"Greater enjoyment in affection and quiet sensuality. Some regret at loss of passion and enjoyment that went with it."

And from a woman in prison:

"No. My libido has not diminished—it's just damnably hard in here to get anything in besides a 'wham-bam-thank you-mam.'"

Twelve women (29 percent) expressed an increase in the quality of sex since menopause. Their comments indicated that sex was better and more fulfilling:

"Since menopause my sexual desire has increased, and so has the electric shock. I have never had so many orgasms in my life."

"Changes seem to have more to do with what is going on in relationship than menopause. Have had a recent resurgence of sexual activity after going to a lesbian sexuality workshop. Also doing better as a couple in our communication."

"No change—sex is still enjoyable *and* I look forward to my sixtiess."

"Sex is evener since menopause; less emotional up and down. I experience sex more as a part of life now than as an altered state. It's definitely different, but not better or worse."

"All of my sexual experiences with women—even prior to menopause have been *quality*—unlike the same with men, who I must admit that in my twenties and thirties I had more quantity…meaning, I was much more promiscuous with men (quantity) versus the quality of sexual intimacy since 1977 exclusively with women. Since menopause, my orgasms (whether from vibrator, self-stimulation or with a partner) happen more quickly and more multiply.

We asked women to indicate whether they felt that they have a sex problem and whether this is new since menopause. The overwhelming majority of respondents (31 women, or 76 percent) answered "no" to this item. Of the ten who said they did have a sex problem, comments included being dry and taking longer to reach orgasm. Nevertheless, many women indicated even here that these were not really problems to them, only differences since menopause.

We asked whether their favorite way to have sex changed since menopause and how their partner felt about this. While there·was a great variety of favorite ways to have sex, only one of the lesbians indicated that there had been a change since menopause. Thus, current favorite ways to have sex also reflect their younger adulthood.

Women were asked who initiates sex and whether this had changed since menopause. Of the 37 who answered this question, seventeen (45 percent) indicated that initiation is mutual, or that they take turns initiating. The remainder were evenly divided between those who initiated sex and those whose partners did. Only three women indicated that these patterns had changed since menopause.

"My partner always initiated sex in the past (but *I* controlled the encounter). Now I initiate sex about half the time—and I have less and less control" (followed by a smile symbol).

We also asked whether women had noticed any differences in their sexual fantasies since menopause. Thirty women (73 percent) indicated that there had been no change in their fantasies; some of them had never fantasized and others continued to fantasize as much as before menopause. Four women (ten percent) had noticed a decrease in sexual fantasies since menopause. One woman wrote:

"I used to depend more on fantasy but the ones I had appeal to me less and less and I don't have substitutes."

"Unfortunately, I have noticed that sexual fantasies are fewer—and that I'm far more selective."

Finally, five women (twelve percent) indicated an increase in sexual fantasies since menopause. Two wrote:

"Yes, I have fantasies and more since menopause because I masturbate."

"For some reason my fantasies seem kinky (fist fucking), bad, etc."

Women were asked about changes in their *interest* in sex since menopause, in their level of desire. Sixteen lesbians (39 percent) found no change in desire since menopause.

"I am more selective and seem to be less interested in sex overall (i.e., I'm not thinking about sex every waking minute), but my level of desire during sex is as great—or greater."

Nine (22 percent) stated that desire had decreased since menopause. Women wrote:

"No *lust* anymore and I miss it."

"Yes, level of desire lower—more 'fragile'—can be diminished quickly and easily."

Finally, eleven women (27 percent) felt that sexual desire had increased since menopause. Two wrote:

"Greater level of desire—not so cyclical (monthly). More constant—takes less time to get aroused."

"My interest in my current partner is very high—her interest in sex is very high and fun—so my sexual interest is high also. I probably do have less physiological interest but am 'willing' to continue to experience and enjoy sex a lot."

The survey asked specifically about vaginal dryness, whether this was a problem and what women do about it. Twenty-two women (54 percent) did not experience vaginal dryness. Comments included:

"I am as 'moist' as if I were twenty years old! As in all things we enjoy and love, it is a state of heart and mind—yes?"

Eighteen lesbians (44 percent) had experienced vaginal dryness. Six women stated that this was not a problem, ten indicated that they used a lubricant, others asked partners to be more gentle, took vitamin supplements, used partner's saliva and one woman found that a longer period of manual stimulation increased vaginal lubrication. One lesbian wrote:

"I feel very old and unsexy without my vaginal fluid *and* the smell of it, which I always liked. This was always a very important part of sex for me, mutual fluids."

We asked women whether they had experienced any differences in how it felt to be touched sexually or non-sexually (such as feelings of numbness or extra-sensitive skin). The majority of lesbians (27, or 66 percent) did not experience such effects. Ten women (24 percent) had noticed a difference in touch sensitivity since menopause, including dislike of skin contact during hot flashes. One woman wrote that she was both more irritated and more sexually sensitized by the vaginal dryness.

Next, we asked about changes in clitoral sensation or sensitivity since menopause and how women felt about this. Twenty-eight lesbians (68 percent) felt no difference in clitoral sensation since menopause; thirteen (32 percent) had noticed diminished sensitivity. One felt she could reach orgasm more quickly due to the enhanced sensitivity of her clitoris, another because she could enjoy "rougher" sex and yet another said the orgasms are slow but are "more powerful—rolling" when they happen.

All the lesbians indicated that they have had orgasms. All but three women (93 percent) have orgasms when they masturbate and thirty-seven (90 percent) were orgasmic with a partner. Twenty-four (56 percent) experienced no change in orgasms since menopause, eight women (twenty percent) had fewer orgasms since menopause. These women wrote that reasons for fewer orgasms included less sexual arousal:

"Less able to sustain sexual arousal long enough to climax. Can get uncomfortable physically—skin pressure—or tired."

Fewer orgasms during masturbation but the same amount with partner:

"I continue to be able to orgasm more or less instantly at one level, but deep uterine orgasms-by-vibrator can take up to 45 minutes. They used to take 5-45 minutes. I could control and prolong them. Now they just take longer. Sometime I'll masturbate and *not* come (through lack of time). That's different than before when I *never* didn't come, but it feels right, appropriate for now."

Nine women (22 percent) stated that they were experiencing increased orgasms since menopause. As one woman wrote:

"I am experiencing more multiple orgasms. I feel good about that. It makes me feel alive and robust—and sexy as hell."

We asked whether the women had seen a change, since their menopause, in how their sexual partners responded to them. Only nine women had noticed a change and these varied widely in range. Some examples are:

"My partner is still very much interested in love making and often feels rejected by my lack of desire. These differences have arisen since menopause has started."

"When I had communicated to my partner at the time that my nipples felt sore, it put her off from continuing to 'arouse' me. In talking with other women, she was told that I was using that as an 'excuse' not to have sex. (I was twice as old as my partner; those giving the advice were about the same age as she, perhaps a little older—in their late twenties, early thirties). A lot of emotional damage can be done by those who do not understand what changes a menopausal woman goes through."

But some women were puzzled as to whether the changes in their partner were really related to menopause or other factors:

"No/yes/no/who knows? Her menopause preceded mine. She has orgasmic and desire problems now—are they new since my menopausal symptoms are beginning—or since hers are advancing? How much are they related to menopause at all and how much to unresolved conflict, resolution of monogamy/non-monogamy questions, etc."

In an attempt to rectify the usual research focus on pathology during menopause, we specifically asked lesbians about positive changes in their lives since menopause, including positive sexual changes. In addition to the many women who wrote back about the enjoyed absence of menstruation, women also mentioned a variety of other changes in their lives: increased sex, increased orgasms, greater self-acceptance, coming out as a lesbian, feeling more free, positive changes in body fat distribution, viewing life more seriously and wondering about the security of the future, professional security, being less driven, relishing their maturity, wonderful sex, financial security, nothing to prove, kids leaving home. Only nine lesbians (22 percent) indicated that there had been no positive changes following menopause.

The following are some of the responses to our request for additional comments.

"I've discovered I'm *not* the run-of-the-mill senior citizen sexually!!"

"It's not so much the frequency of sexual encounters that has changed, but the amount of *time* and *energy* we pour into the encounters. My (our) bodies growing older (breasts losing elasticity, joints creaking a bit) is fascinating and a source of tenderness for both of us, engendering fantasies about growing old together, starting a sex-positive nursing home for dykes, etc. We're just beginning to think about maybe there are some other ways to make love when we're no longer able to do what we used to."

"Loss of pubic hair. It's devastating..."

"In the days when I am very down (four per month) it is difficult to live my normal life. This would include sex."

"Finding partners at ages 45-60 (is) easier as a lesbian than as a straight woman."

"I'm grateful in almost every way to have found this woman to share all aspects of my life with, including our experiencing menopause together. Going through this with a man must be a real drag for both partners!"

"When my doctor told me I was going through menopause at age 45, I thought I would die. I thought it was a sign of shriveling up and growing old—and I thought age 45 was too damned young for that. I am okay about it now but I *hate* the silence about it. (I don't even want people to know for fear they'll think of me as over the hill)."

"At first I thought you wouldn't want my participation because I have no current sex partner, nor for a few years now. But then I thought there must be lots of lesbians my age who have no partner. We are nonetheless sexual women! And I wanted your study to acknowledge that there are healthy lesbians whose sexuality is not diminished by menopause and aging."

Finally, we asked women to complete the following sentence: "Based on my experience, sex at menopause is…" Here are some the responses to this question:

"…a conundrum. Guidance, knowledge, literature are minimal and oversimple and dishonestly cheery."

"…the same as before."

"…unbelievable—wonderful—the best time of my life. Wish my sex life had been this good when I was *twenty!*

"…still great."

"…no different unless you have a negative attitude regarding it because your body goes through a change."

"…great. It helps me feel good about myself—an opportunity to celebrate life. It's fun. I love the playful times, they're terrific for little aches and pains. Releases tension, makes me feel connected to my physical being, to all of humanity and to the universe. I love it."

Clearly, there are cautions in interpreting these findings. It is a small sample; and just as clinical samples are biased toward pathology, this one—a volunteer sample—may be biased toward health. It must be noted, too, that we put together categories that, with a larger sample, should ideally be separated in the reporting of results. For instance, we did not distinguish between women who were early, middle and post-menopausal. The majority of these lesbians, however (69 percent), are post-menopausal, i.e., it has been at least one year since their last menstrual flow. We did not distinguish between women taking and not taking replacement hormones, although the majority (68 percent) are not. We did not distinguish between surgical and natural menopause. However, only three women (less than ten percent) have had their ovaries removed. And, finally, we did not distinguish between women who came out as lesbians at midlife and life-long lesbians, so that in a few cases, our respondents have compared sex with men before menopause and sex with women after menopause.

On the one hand, then, this is a "conglomerated" sample. On the other hand, the group is largely post-menopausal; not on hormone replacement; naturally, as opposed to surgically, menopausal; and consists of women who have identified as lesbians for most or all of their sexually active adult years. While we understand the results must be considered with caution, the data are nevertheless important. To the best of our knowledge, this is the first systematic survey of the sexual attitudes and behaviors of lesbian women at menopause.

Heterosexual women in previous research were concerned with sexual functioning, with arousal time, dry vaginas, loss of clitoral sensitivity. They expressed a great deal of worry about their deteriorating sexuality, performance pressure and fears of disappointing their partners. In contrast, and for the most part, the lesbian women who responded to our questionnaire talk about their sex lives as good as or better than ever. There is a celebratory quality to their responses. Furthermore, they discuss sexuality in relationship. The emphasis is firmly on the quality of their relationships as opposed to their sexual functioning. And, finally, when a change is noted, it is frequently described as a "difference" rather than a "problem."

What can we make of this group of women who run solidly counter to the stereotypes and the research on sex at menopause? Why would one group feel discouraged and the other life-affirming, positive and zestful?

It is possible that ours is indeed a biased sample. It is possible that only satisfied people would take the time to respond to an ad and then fill out a questionnaire.

Perhaps the more likely key is that lesbian women are not as intercourse or penetration focused as heterosexual women and therefore the physiological changes of menopause might not be so disruptive.

Western culture, and patriarchal culture, especially in North America, extols and glorifies youth. It is possible that lesbian women, who have had a great deal of practice living outside the mainstream, are less susceptible to the pitfalls of these values. Perhaps lesbians have an advantage when it comes to accepting the changes that the years bring.

Ours is a homophobic society, where it is not acceptable to be lesbian or gay. Perhaps lesbians learn to feel more comfortable with their sexuality over time; the women who did not come out until midlife may for the first time in their lives be able to genuinely express their authentic sexuality.

Partner expectation may not be as much of an issue for lesbians. The social patterning of males gives rise to high levels of expectation and performance pressure and women in heterosexual relationships may be prone to resultant feelings of not measuring up.

Sex at menopause for lesbian women does seem to be as good as or better than ever. It is possible that if all women, lesbian and straight, could be free of heterosexist hangups about sexual functioning and the aging process, if all women were not handicapped by fears of aging, partner expectation and the extolling of youth, there would be many more reports of unchanged or better, more rewarding sex and deeper relationships, in our fifties, sixties and beyond. It is certainly something to celebrate that many lesbians already experience menopause very positively indeed.

*Rediscovering
Our Creativity
And
Spirituality*

Time's Gifts

CARMEN DE MONTEFLORES

"Time's power, the only just power—
would you give it away?"
-Adrienne Rich, *Time's Power*

Wakefulness. Reviewing my day and my life. Life as something to be contemplated. Responsibility for one's actions, for one's environment, for one's past. A willingness to hear other opinions about myself and at the same time a clearer sense of my own viewpoint. Criticism as a gift.

Fragility. A sense of limits: of my strength, my possibilities. A knowledge that there are certain things I will not be able to do, things I will never even be aware of; that there are things that will survive me, a time when I will not be here. A sense (sometimes) that I am not the center of the universe.

An age of paradoxes. Fear of death and at the same time discounting death as an abstraction. A greater fear of illness and loss of function and yet a hopefulness that spirit will triumph over the body. But also a knowledge that the spirit deteriorates if not cared for.

A new appreciation of aloneness. A luxury, I suppose, since I don't have to be alone. And patience, since I have seen the same things happening over and over again.

Much wakefulness, as if so much seeing is hard to put to rest. Hard not to see, not know, while at the same time it is difficult to remember what prompted the seeing. A recognition that I am not in possession of myself: pieces fall off, become part of something or someone else, lose the stamp of something owned. Sometimes returned to me via another in a way that seems strange, when I didn't even know a piece of my "self" (or maybe my history) had been lost. Edges blurring, yet also an encroaching rigidity, which may be an attempt at holding onto my view of my own story, or the way I tell it. But, the defeat of my certitude in itself becoming restful, as if, finally, I don't have to be right.

A knowledge, ultimately, that all of this has already been said, more artfully, with more conviction or insight. And yet, that my "self," despite its obvious and overly examined limitations, does not readily give up the desire to have a voice, be singular, even at the cost of loneliness; to be seen, even for a moment, and to see with loving clarity the fine detail of my life.

I shouldn't ask for more, yet invariably I do. Want to go beyond what appears to be my own ending. Beyond the words I find a limitless blank space, a resonance of emptiness, a music, for lack of better words—maybe just what I construct as possibility, at the margin of everything that demands my effort, what isn't yet and maybe never will be. What I need is a matrix of dreams.

I ask for more.

And now to rewrite the beginning. Renewal. Picking up again: toys, bits of ideas. Looking out of a new window, walking on a different street after the secret pleasures of doing the same route for as-far-back-as-I-can-remember. Tracing the picture on a vase with my finger; looking for a word in the crevices of my brain and letting go; feeling the howling of a speeding silence in my ear as I hang on to what I know, in terror. Or, someone turning their head away revealing the texture of a cheek, enlivening the air. Simple things. Unaccountable. The richness: a piece of old jewelry found on my mother's bureau, a piece of ocean caught in a window. Souvenirs. Returning, moving.

Relating to adult children: caring, letting go, not being able to let go; not being let go of; worrying and recognizing (how many times?) that I cannot live their lives for them. Having to unlearn mothering as attachment and learn mothering as detachment. Another paradox.

The pain of letting go of my daughter who is becoming a mother herself; who wants to and has the right to make the same mistakes I made. Or, different ones. Adulthood as gaining the right to make your own mistakes and not account to anyone for them except your own children twenty years from now. And at midlife one gains the added right to see one's life as classical theater (and to speak that way also, in pronouncements and declamations), of seeing the end already in the beginning.

The uses of feeling useless. Of contemplating error (my own); of *having* to contemplate error. A great battle between Goodness and Guilt.

The value of being silly: of laughing in the middle of the night about something one can no longer remember in the morning; of playing (that's the joy of having small children around), of making sandboxes, rediscovering croquet, making up imaginary creatures.

At times life becomes metaphorical, does not represent itself, is full of fading lights, sunsets, withering flowers, falls and winters, harvestings, wanings. A sense of standing at a peak looking at a wide expanse of land. Perspective. Distance. Pattern becomes more important. There is more of a sense of how it all fits together. A softness to this view.

My body, on the other hand, feels more vulnerable, my bones and muscles less flexible. My mind also tolerates less change. I become more opinionated and righteous, more assured of my prejudices. At the same time I see myself adopting an attitude of this-will-also-pass.

As a lesbian, I take my identity more for granted, which is soothing. I am less stridently political. My activism consists of having both of our names on the checkbook, giving my lover power of attorney in case of serious illness, writing her name under *spouse* on official forms and acknowledging our relationship everywhere I go.

In terms of the "long run," equality in our relationship takes a different form than it might have for me at an earlier age. We don't need to both have everything we need at the same time. There will be time for each one to fulfill dreams. I think more in terms of wills, the future, some dim "time after" when I won't be there. And I try to remind myself of what is really important in my life, like kindness, and that in life as in poetry it is the texture of the detail that counts, not the grandiose intent.

Creativity not as something separable from the rest of my life but as the result of a new harmony between different parts of my life. The nature of the sacrifices which have to be made in order to be an artist: real ones in terms of time and immediate rewards, such as money and approval. At this age I know all the "monsters" that ridicule me, tempt me, threaten, seduce, on my way to my study. They are always there. I could count them as friends if they didn't betray me at the slightest opportunity—by being "nice" and giving "just a few minutes" of my time picking up, answering phone calls, by feeling ashamed of how the grass is dry, or the walls dirty, or my papers disorganized. Dirt is the sin of the middle class.

Creativity at midlife. Easier to see what I don't do than what I do: I don't beat myself; I don't doubt myself (as much as I used to); I don't make excuses for myself; I don't (always) take differing opinions as criticism; I'm not as afraid. I do know that the material is there and have trained myself to believe that it is leaving clues everywhere and I just have to pay attention to find them.

It is never too late to find a good teacher: someone you can follow. Another paradox: trusting someone else will teach you to trust yourself. Danger at midlife of feeling I-know-it-all, losing the "beginner's mind." On the other hand, there is a need to assume responsibility for being a teacher too. For knowing, even if I feel I don't know very much. I may be teaching unconsciously, without knowing what it is that I teach, but as a woman and as a middle-aged woman, I need to learn to respect what I do know and know that my experience has value for others; that I should teach consciously also and should also be consciously aware of my power as a teacher.

After a lifetime, I am back from the war with concepts. I have to relearn how to be peaceful, how to hold a smooth cup in my shaking hand,

how to hear a ticking clock in an empty room early in the morning when
the light still has a blue cast on the sill. Or, watch the seams of things: the
edge where wall meets floor, how the lamp weighs on the table, the pen on
the paper, the place where I can hear minutes rubbing against each other.
Time's gifts.

Today I walked past the house where I used to live in another life. I
was pushing a stroller with my littlest child. I don't know what drew me
there: where I once had five children, where I once used to paint, where I
stopped painting, where I began to write. I was looking, I guess, for the
woman I was, the woman who "cut off her fingers," who chose not to paint.

I found out today that the "fingers" I lost are still making signs and
that writing is what I do to get to the silence of poetry, where I can hear
my signs:

> My body memorizes old gestures
> to make a catalogue of who
> I was. On a street, silent
> with the silence of morning
> when small children nap
> and older ones are at school
> and the women can be seen
> through windows looking
> for themselves. The backyard waits
> to be discovered as art,
> after ducks, forts and swings
> have been folded neatly
> into the earth. They happen again.
> Looking out of those windows
> at myself, walking up the street
> looking for that woman who was
> looking at herself,
> looking at the light on the polished
> floors, looking in the yard
> with the lemon tree,
> with the resurrected
> earth, with the tears
> buried in mounds, burying
> a piece of hose, a children's ball
> burying color, breath,
> digging with the fingers
> I cut off, dirt mixed with color
> and tears. Up that hill again
> to find that woman
> who buried marbles,

cut her fingers,
put them in a mound
and watered them with colors
near the lemon tree where the children
had listened to stories
and the big faces
leaned against the fence
not seeing. I keep making signs,
remember my fingers
as if I had been deaf.

Creativity. At this point it comes with urgency. There is not enough time. (Time again!) Choices need to be made. A need for focus, for a finely delimited attention. Some things need to be given up.

Overflowing with lived life. Have to pour myself on the page. Like a painting. All drips and stains, forms that reach, stretch, jump off the surface, imitating dissolution, while somewhere there is an intention at work even if only an intention to discover.

Everything's here: sitting still I fly through time, imitate life, hang on the turn of a bird's wing, listen to the murmur of water as if it were a poem, lie alongside the wave tossed into unconsciousness, into dream. There I see the loose skin of my throat, eyes painted on a wall, blue bodies, transplanted palms. An imaginary land, tolerating juxtaposition. Among the polished tables possibilities emerging: words falling quietly between the delicate fruit dishes, mango, cayenne, a bit of French accent, a considered life, purposes, purposes. A gray sky I would like to fold like silk and stroke secretly in my breast pocket. A cat draws an Egyptian hieroglyph on the ridge of the roof. A leaf drifts by, reminding me of flight, winged things.

Midlife is clutter, distillation, ache and triumph. Searching for essence, yet desiring the wild specimen, the silence around it already, the wonder.

I'm a Vital Woman and There's Beauty in That

MURIEL MIGUEL
as interviewed by BARBARA SANG

I think I may have been in midlife for a very long time. Like since I was 25. So I'm not quite sure what midlife issues mean to me. But I like being older and I like being quirky. Last year I broke up from a ten-year relationship. For a year I did not even think of going out to find someone and that scared me. All those things that you don't like to talk about, like my breasts sagged, or I have a belly, I'm fat. They're going to find out that I'm not as glamorous as I look from the outside. I hadn't thought in those terms for a very long time and it threw me back into that judgmental place about myself. And so what I did was just turn off: "I don't know if she's interested in me" would turn into, "I better leave." It was scary. Now it's not quite so scary. I started to move out into the world again and people seem to be interested in me because I'm me, not because of my belly, or my breasts sag. Sometimes I wonder what happens if you stick with the mind set that no one's going to be attracted to you because you have a belly or your breasts sag, or you're not young anymore, or as agile.

I work with my two sisters in Spiderwoman, a feminist theater group. Spiderwoman is fourteen years old. My sisters are straight; I'm a *lesbian*. My sisters went through a midlife crisis before I did. A couple of years ago, I thought I had a brain tumor. I was getting dizzy at weird times, but my older sister said, "It's menopause, you'll see in a year or so that things will start changing." And she was right. It was certainly a relief to know I didn't have a brain tumor! Watching my sisters go through it made it more natural for me. I know where my feet are. It wasn't like I was thrown out there and had to figure it out for myself.

My mother is a Rappahannock Indian from Virginia and my father came from the San Blas Islands off the coast of Panama. My father's tribe is called Cuna. They met in Brooklyn. I was born and raised there in an Indian community. The Indians that live in Brooklyn all go to this one Community House, though it's not the same as it used to be when I was growing up or when my mother and my sisters were growing up. Then, most Indians lived in one section around Atlantic Avenue, but now people are all over the place.

My mother was a psychic and it seems to me that she got stronger as she got older. When I was growing up she was really into it. I ran away from it a lot of my life. My mother read tea leaves and coffee grinds and felt vibrations from people way before vibrations were popular. People would come to her. I thought it made my mother a kook: on the block people called her a witch. As I moved further into middle age, I realized I could give up a lot of the stigma behind it. My daughter and my niece accepted the way their Grandma and their Uncle Joe, a medical man, were. That's the way Grandma was. Uncle Joe was like that too. They accepted it, which took a lot of pressure off me somehow.

I have two daughters. I don't see the youngest now; she's with her father. I'm not too sure if the issue is me being gay or her loyalty to him. She lived with me until she was eight and then I saw her on and off until she was twelve. The last night she was with me she slept between me and my lover. And my feeling was that she was saying it was okay, but she was also saying goodbye to me because she had to do something else. It still gets me, though I do feel that she will show up again.

Their father had both children, but eventually my older daughter Muriel (she's named after me) started to seek me out. I tried very hard to keep in contact with her, sending presents and writing letters. I first met her again when she was eighteen. We had lunch together and I was talking to her and she said, "Are you still with your girl friend?" We never talked that I was with a woman. She just let me know—just like that—that she knew and it was okay. She came to live with me when she was nineteen and now she's 22.

Muriel studies dance and theater. I'm in awe of her: her spunkiness and her quirkiness. I see all of that and I admire it. I think I paved a way for a certain type of security for her...that failing isn't a terrible thing and if you fail you could fail big. She takes risks and that's what I admire. I feel like I took a lot of risks. Starting Spiderwoman Theater was a big risk.

Before I started doing women's theater, I was a dancer and an actress. I was in Open Theater for several years. I loved avant garde theater, but in order to make a living I had to do commercial theater and I got really tired of being an actress who was only doing mothers and prostitutes. There are not many roles that Native American actresses are given. You never get the chance to play Juliet; it has to do with an ingenue being blonde, so you always look old compared to that. And if you're big, you look older. A lot of times you play the heavy, but never the lead. That's what is wonderful about Spiderwoman. We can be skinny, we can be young, we can be anything.

Going into menopause opened up another whole area for me. I know that in my community, I'm starting to really feel like an elder. I'm not as old as the people who are usually elders, but I feel this connection. After menopause, a lot of energy doesn't have to go into things that I used to worry about. I'm not worried about reproducing. Because of that, I'm freer to pick up a those vibrations from other people that my mother talked about...and that I used to be afraid of. Sometimes I sit with someone and I know the silent question they're asking me and I'm able sometimes to answer it; it's becoming more and more that I can answer it, whatever it is. At this point in life, I am spiritually free. That's what makes me feel like an elder. I'm a functioning woman; I'm an attractive woman; I'm a Native woman; and I'm a spiritual woman.

All of these things really came into the foreground at a recent gathering of gay and lesbian Native Americans in Minnesota, where I really felt like an elder and a needed, wanted, individual. I had the feeling that I had a lot to offer in knowledge and it didn't mean I had to be like a grandmother. It didn't mean I had to be retired.

People came down from Canada, from Alaska, and it was quite exciting, absolutely wonderful. There were maybe 50 or 60 of us and we camped out for four days. It was a relief for me because it was the first time since I broke up with my lover that I really felt connected. These were all brown-skinned people and we were finding connections and we had talking circles where each person talked from their heart. A lot of us were feeling the connections between not coming out and alcoholism, and how brave so many people have been by coming out in Native communities... especially when you feel like maybe there are two Native American lesbians in all of New York City.

When midlife changes started, I realized that I began saying more and more things from the heart. I'm past manipulating. Yes, I can be kind, but there are some times when things have to be done and have to be said, and you can't waste time. Sometimes it jars younger people, but you can't say you're sorry. This is a comfortable time of my life. I mean spiritually comfortable. In my community I'm accepted. And somehow to most people, though I can't tell everyone I'm a lesbian, it just doesn't matter.

I remember once at a funeral sitting next to this little Indian boy who was having a hard time. He didn't want to sit; he didn't want to stand. He wanted to make a disturbance. In a moment of silence he started to carry on. I remember turning to him and looking at him and saying, "Are you Indian?" He said yes. I said, "Well, act like one." This kid got really silent and when we stood up I saw his eyes slide to the corner and look me up and down. I had this vision of years from now, this kid saying, "This old Indian lady said to me, 'Are you Indian? Well act like one!' " If you can say things like that to this little kid, make him stop dead in his tracks, you're an elder.

Thank God I'm not twenty. I'm not 30 either. That's good too. I remember when I was growing up, a lot of my friends among Indian people did not reach 40. Hard lives, drink, drugs. Accidents from drink and drugs. I remember reaching 40 and being ecstatic, really feeling like I made it. Forty. And I went out to say this to people and they said, "Shh, don't tell people you're 40. What's wrong with you?! You're an actress." So after a while, I started to get very uncomfortable; I couldn't say I was 40. It was how old are you—I'm fffff...I couldn't get past the f word—I'd say 35.

Living in the white world, people have very strange attitudes about menopausal women. In Indian culture midlife is wisdom. You are a vital woman and there's beauty in that. But it doesn't seem to be the same with most young white women. I've come up against that rejection and it really made me jump. I've worked with women who saw me as a fun person until I said I'm through with menopause...the look on young women's faces! All of a sudden I'm old to them. They're looking at the same person, but all of a sudden I'm old. This may sound roundabout, but there's something I want to say about younger women. They should not only be *learning* from older women, but they should also accept the fact that you're a vital person even if you're not reproducing. And that's something that has not really been addressed because people don't like to face ageism like that.

So I'm here to say that this part of my life is very vital.

Moving Toward Balance and Integration

BARBARA E. SANG

I usually like to read the psychological literature that is relevant to my own life. Naturally, at middle age, I was curious to know if other women's experience was similar to my own. As I read accounts of midlife and attended conferences on the subject, I found that some of the issues that were important to me were missing. Because middle age has been examined almost exclusively from a heterosexual and male perspective, this might explain why the findings did not always fit my own experience and those of other middle-aged lesbians I knew.

Models of adult aging and development have been based on the white nuclear family and, therefore, we have little knowledge about the development of individuals who do not marry, child-free women, lesbians, gay men and ethnic minorities.

Current research on middle-aged women suggests that for heterosexuals this is a time when women are searching for their own identity, separate from children and husbands.

Most lesbians have rejected the traditional female role, not only by relating sexually to women but by being economically independent of men. Since lesbian women have not necessarily gone through the traditional stages of female development, I wanted to know what our experiences and concerns would be at midlife. What is new to *us* at this time of life? What gives our life meaning? My main concern was to describe how lesbians between the ages of 40 and 59 deal with the existential issues of midlife. What I mean by existential is the searching for something that goes beyond everyday survival: the quest for deeper levels of life meaning and the formulation of one's life philosophy.

Based on feedback from two discussion groups and a preliminary questionnaire, I developed a ten item, open-ended, essay-type questionnaire. A few examples of some of the questions I asked are:

How do you feel about being middle-aged?

Are there any issues (thoughts, feelings, conflicts, fears, problems, aspirations, etc.) that are *new* to you as a middle-aged person?

What gives your life meaning?

I intentionally biased my results by including my proposal and rationale for the study with the questionnaire. I was inviting lesbians to collaborate with me rather than to be "subjects" in the traditional sense. Although names were optional, many gave their full name. Each woman put considerable effort into telling her story, and her own unique personality and struggle towards growth came through clearly. The degree to which the women shared intimate and personal details about themselves surprised me and further suggested that this approach to research was conducive to openness.

A total of 110 self-identified lesbians between the ages of 40-59 (average age was 47) completed the questionnaire. I recruited these women through lesbian friendship networks, newsletters, conferences, professional organizations and older women's magazines. Although considerable effort was made to include women of color, they comprise only five percent of this sample. Responses came from 24 different states and from Canada, Holland and Israel.

A little more than half (57 percent) of the lesbians had been married heterosexually at some point in their lives. Forty-four percent of the total sample have one or more children. Twenty-five percent of the women "came out" at midlife and a majority of those had children (75 percent). At the time of the study 67 percent of the women were in a lesbian relationship of varying duration and the other 33 percent were single.

The lesbians in this study were a highly educated group of women. A large number hold doctorates (24 percent) or have had training beyond the bachelor's degree (45 percent had MA's, MSW's or more than a BA). All the rest had high school degrees or beyond. Of the midlife lesbians in this sample 78 percent were professionals; the others were in business or held working-class jobs. Half had careers that can be considered nontraditional for women, e.g., psychologist, dean, professor, financial analyst and truck driver. Of that half, 34 percent are mental health professionals. Virtually all these women were self-supporting, having become so at an average age of 26.

The major themes that emerged from the questionnaire for this group of midlife lesbians are as follows.

Greater Self-Confidence, Self-Acceptance and Self-Direction

The majority of midlife lesbians reported feeling more fulfilled, more self-confident and self-accepting, and more comfortable with who they are. They were more self-directed and cared less what other people thought of them. Practically all the lesbians in this study liked themselves better at this age (93 percent) and most (76 percent) felt midlife to be the best period of their lives. They were "more mellow," "better grounded," "less defensive," "kinder, softer, wiser," "more balanced" and "had greater self-knowledge and acceptance of faults." "I no longer feel the necessity of apologizing for who I am." "I seem to have less bravado and more feeling of real stature and accomplishment."

How do lesbians feel about being middle-aged? A typical response was, "Middle age brings with it the right to generalize from one's own experience—you've got enough life under your belt by then—one hopes! I have confidence that I know what I'm talking about now. Theories don't interest me...."

Another woman says "One, if not *the* greatest, blessing about being middle-aged dykes is that while heterosexual women are frantically chasing the rainbow of 'lost youth' and are frightened by their loss of 'beauty' and 'sex appeal'—we old dykes are daily growing more comfortable and *accepting* of our aging faces and bodies and are therefore able to see beneath the superficial to the glowing beauty of a mellow soul."

Thus, middle age for lesbians is a time to be oneself; to feel more authentic as a person—less concerned with pleasing others and fitting into a prescribed mold. Many women said that because of their lesbianism, they spent a lifetime fighting to be themselves rather than conforming to societal expectations of women at the time. As a result, in middle age they find themselves quite skilled at being able to stand up for what they believe and to be who they feel they are. In other words, in fighting their oppression as lesbians they have developed a stronger sense of self.

A Time to Play and Have Fun

A major theme that emerged for this group of lesbians, who had been career- or work-oriented most of their adult lives, is a desire to have more fun and to be less achievement-oriented. Many lesbians reported not wanting to push or strive anymore the way they did in their twenties and thirties. Several had retired or have shortened their work hours to accommodate other needs, such as creativity and/or intimacy. As one lesbian put it, "A lot more play and a lot less caring—don't have to be serious and work all the time—relate more to people—not be so work-oriented."

A few women reported consciously having to make time in their busy schedules for fun and enjoyment: "I think I would try to be less compulsive, less a perfectionist and play more. I am so serious about my work that I often overdo. I still need to learn how to relax and have fun and that it is okay to do so."

For many lesbians in this study, work itself at this point in time has become easier, less stressful and consequently more enjoyable and satisfying. There is a new sense of freedom; women describe themselves as more open, playful and spontaneous. These are the qualities that are characteristic of creativity. Middle age, therefore, for this group appears to be a time of heightened creative expression. Paradoxically, as these women are "pushing" less, they are better able to be more creative, whether it be in their careers or outside interests.

A Time for Change, Refocusing and Integration

Although the term "midlife crisis" comes from a psychological model of heterosexual development, I included a question on it to see whether it had any relevance to lesbians. Approximately half (46 percent) of the midlife lesbians indicated that they had had or were going through what could be called a "midlife crisis." Such a "crisis" took the form of an illness, loss of a relationship, or an awareness of one's limitations. A 45-year-old woman says, "I passed a serious crisis at 40 to 42—had to let go of all hopes and dreams and finally accept myself as an average person regarding set values and goals." The loss of possibilities and options is felt to be part of this crisis. A "crisis" usually forces the individual to reevaluate her needs and priorities and, in the process, may facilitate growth and development. For one lesbian it was a life-threatening illness which made her more aware of what gave her pleasure and that she needed to take care of herself. Another woman who left a nineteen year relationship felt that she had lost her sense of self.

Most of those lesbians who did not experience an actual midlife crisis reported that at midlife they made a conscious decision to reshape their lives or do something different. A woman who had free-lanced for fifteen years wanted the security of a regular job; another who had worked in a constraining academic environment opted for the freedom of independent practice. Lesbians who had been exceptionally active politically became less so now, whereas those who had not been political become involved for the first time. A woman who had been a serious athlete all her life was learning to deal with lessened endurance.

A significant change reported by one-fourth of the women was the awareness for the first time of feelings toward other women. Several women who had buried their lesbian feelings at an earlier age were more accepting of them at midlife. One woman reported that "coming out" in middle age contributed to the positive way she felt about herself. She said, "I feel close to being whole—like a major piece of the puzzle of my life fell into place." A few of the women who are just coming out reported feeling sexual for the first time.

Self-discovery in middle age may also take the form of a change in inner awareness or increased knowledge about the self. One lesbian writes:

"This feels to be the most expansive and deepening time of my life. I grow daily more profoundly aware of myself—particularly lately of the 'shadow side'—and grow more loving and appreciative of *all* the ways I am inside myself and the world."

"Letting go" or knowing when you have outgrown something was another important theme for the lesbians in this sample. This can include relationships that are not working, habits, "life dreams" or a particular way of relating to the world. Having spent most of her life being "strong, independent and reasoned, following the male model of wholeness," one subject reported this change in herself:

"Middle age is a time to reclaim and reinvent the female principle—to be 'power-filled' as opposed to 'powerful'—to be in touch with one's vulnerability and to allow things to flow rather than manage them."

Middle age was also a time to reconnect with former interests and aspects of the self. A woman who has not written poetry since adolescence resumed this form of self-expression at age 49. Another who majored in English but who went into a different field had just begun to write in her current profession. She experienced a new sense of vitality and adventure in being able to combine both interests. Part of the integration process that takes place in middle age often has to do with reestablishing connections with interests and parts of the self that existed during the adolescent period. Adolescence is a time when many paths and options are open, particularly for women who have rejected traditional roles. Tapping into this period can be a source of renewal and vitality. In contrast to the women in other midlife studies whose only dream in adolescence was getting a husband, adolescence appears to be a rather complex period for lesbians. A little more than half (62 percent) of the midlife lesbians in this study reported career expectations as adolescents. Also, about half the group described themselves as nontraditional adolescents for that time period, that is, they were bookish, rebellious and athletic. Women who identified themselves as lesbians in their teens and twenties were more likely to have had career expectations (79 percent) and to have been nontraditional adolescents (60 percent) as compared to women who identified as lesbians in their thirties and midlife.

What Gives Life Meaning

Midlife lesbians derived meaning and satisfaction from their intimate relationships (47 percent), friendships (38 percent) and work (37 percent). Other sources of meaning were spirituality (twenty percent), children (thirteen percent), hobbies and interests (ten percent) and personal growth and development (nine percent). Many women also expressed their own personal sources of meaning such as "making a difference in the world" or "being your own person."

At midlife, a common perception is that many traditional women are first getting in touch with work outside the home and developing independent interests, while the midlife task for men is to get more in touch with feelings and intimacy. For lesbian women in this study, *both* work and relationships have been an important source of meaning in the past and continue to be so at midlife. Sharon Fertitta, in her sample of 68 midlife lesbians from the West Coast, also found lesbians to give career *and* love relationships high priority. Careers had greater meaning for lesbians than for her control group of midlife heterosexual women who were never married and were childless. It is interesting to note that in my study, women who came out as lesbians in midlife also appeared to be more similar to traditional women: intimate relationships were more meaningful to them (61 percent) than work (21 percent). Because these women just "came out," the excitement and novelty of relating to women may account for the importance placed on relationships as compared to work. However, women who came out at midlife are just as likely to be committed to and satisfied with their work as women who came out in their teens, twenties and thirties.

One woman responded to the question "What gives your life meaning or satisfaction," saying, "Good work—being useful—producing good things, e.g., good poems—a sense of growing, learning. A strong connection to others: conversation, working together, sex, giggling, beauty." Another wrote, "People and a significant other and a sense of doing something that is worthwhile and maybe even important. I also need nature—to be near the water with some regularity, to be outside, to appreciate the beauty of nature."

In addition to relationships and work, the lives of lesbians in this study were significantly enriched by a wide range of interests, such as artistic expression, reading, political participation, sports and the out-of-doors, gardening, gourmet cooking, meditation, yoga, travel, theater, etc.

Striving for balance and wholeness was a major theme for midlife lesbians in this study. Finding a balance between work life and home life was difficult since many women held responsible jobs with long hours.

A lesbian wrote, "My philosophy revolves around the concept of *balance* between inner and outer focus, work and play, etc. It also includes the notion of integrating aspects of self previously compartmentalized. I think positive action comes from integration and balance for myself."

Although many lesbians expressed an interest in giving even more time to others and to their community, they also reported wanting to take better care of themselves, needing more time to be alone and for exercise and proper nutrition. They place considerable emphasis on the quality of life, including personal growth and development through a process of change and self-awareness.

Life Philosophies

After 40 or more years of experience, each woman appeared to have developed her own life philosophy. What gave these lesbians' lives meaning and direction was not simply work, other interests, or relationships. Each had a philosophical framework in which these activities were embedded.

For many of the women, their life philosophy was a part of a spiritual quest. For example, one woman wrote, "My own personal and spiritual growth and unfolding brings me my greatest delight and is really at the center of all I do in the world. My life and my work are one, and both are my spiritual journey."

In response to the specific question, "What is your life philosophy? Describe it as best as you can," each lesbian had her own unique philosophy or world view. These life philosophies fall into five distinct categories and each woman expressed two or more.

LOVE, CARE AND RESPECT FOR OTHERS (63 PERCENT)

This category includes making a difference in people's lives, accepting people for who they are and developing and maintaining friendships. For example, "To respect my feelings and those of others. To be kind to others and see the wonder that connects one human being to another."

CONCERN ABOUT SOCIETY, COMMUNITY AND THE ENVIRONMENT (56 PERCENT)

Included in this category are life philosophies which express connections with the universe, respect for the planet, being political, promoting peace, justice and equality. For example: "I believe I should live easy on the earth, live harmoniously with the earth and all creatures and help when the opportunity arises in my path."

SELF-DEVELOPMENT AND LIVING LIFE TO ITS FULLEST (55 PERCENT)

Themes in this category are: making the most of each day, being in the moment, being true to oneself, living the best one can and participating in the fullness of life. For example: "I will seek to live life fully with zest and sensitivity and compassion for others. I will, now more than ever, concentrate on giving something back."

HEALTH, HAPPINESS AND THE ENJOYMENT OF LIFE (28 PERCENT)

Themes expressed in this category are the achievement of joy and pleasure, appreciation of life and what it has to offer, and a humorous approach to situations and people. For example: "Smile each day. Laugh often. Don't forget to take time to play and time to be alone. Hug a tree, stand in the rain...."

CONTROL OF ONE'S DESTINY (25 PERCENT)

We are basically in control of what happens to us. We take responsibility for our lives. For example: "My time on earth in my current form is intended to help one learn and grow on a spiritual level. That I do have a part in creating my reality and I'm not a victim."

The life philosophies of lesbians in this study clearly reflect a concern with nurturing and caring, whether that caring is for the self, others, the community or the planet. Each lesbian wants to take in, enjoy and develop herself and at the same time, give back to others and the environment. This relationship among the personal, the political, the spiritual and the environment was expressed by each woman in her own unique way. The sense of balance that many lesbians were trying to create for themselves at midlife involved giving to the self as well as giving to others and to nature. Although it is true that women have traditionally been socialized to be nurturing and caring, these women seem to have reached a level of balance and integration in their own lives that allows them to focus on larger issues of the world outside themselves.

What I found in this study is that lesbians have different developmental issues at midlife than those reported for both males and traditional females. One of the major issues was the need to *balance* the diverse aspects of their lives, i.e., work, relationships, interests, community and spirituality. Unlike traditional women and men who were first getting in touch with the part of themselves that had been excluded until midlife, career or intimacy, lesbians have been developing both these areas over a lifetime. The lives of midlife lesbians in this sample appear to be more diverse and complex than those reported for other midlife adults, with more roles and aspects of the self to integrate.

Even within this sample of 110 mostly professional, white, middle-class, lesbian women, there were considerable differences in life patterns and midlife issues. Some women "came out" later in life, others had children, some were coping with illness, while still others were concerned with retirement. Existing models of adult development need to be modified to include individuals with different life experiences. Also as societal times change, so will the nature of midlife issues for lesbians.

The middle-aged lesbians in this study are a group of self-actualized women who hope to continue growing and developing. They feel considerable optimism about the future based on the confidence that comes with having coped effectively with one's past. As one subject put it, "I have no idea what will unfold for me but I have an abiding trust based on my experience so far that my life will always delight me and bring me richness of all sorts."

ENDNOTES

I would like to express my appreciation to all the women who took the time to participate in this study. I also wish to thank my friend and colleague Robyn Posin for her theoretical/conceptual input into this paper.

For additional information about the questionnaire, please refer to my article, "Reflections of Midlife Lesbians on Their Adolescence," in *Women, Aging and Ageism,* ed E. Rosenthal (New York: Haworth Press, 1990).

Sharon Fertitta, (1987) "Never-married women in the middle years: A comparison of lesbians and heterosexuals." Paper presented at the annual convention of the American Psychological Association, New York, NY.

Meditation on the Goddess Kali

MADONNA GAUDING

I have driven here from my apartment in Chicago. I am sitting at a picnic table at a beach by Lake Michigan. The air is crisp, the sky blue, the water shades of green/blue/gray. The waves are softly washing the shore. Blades of new grass and dandelions poke through the sand. The air smells fresh. My yellow pad sits blank before me. I am going through hell trying to write this article on Kali and my midlife journey. Once I was so absorbed by this goddess and her image, when I agreed to write the piece long ago. Now I am unfocused and I feel disconnected. My old issues with work, completion, discipline, rise to the surface; a familiar pain lodges somewhere in my throat, radiates through my breast and down to my stomach. It is the fear of judgment and criticism. The cruel tyrant I create inside me demands nothing less than perfection in order that I justify my very existence. She demands that I earn the right to live when she allows other mortals to just be, to have their humanity, their own place in the world, their mistakes, their unique flawed expression. I have worked through so much, yet this perfectionistic, judgmental woman still haunts me. How long it takes to dislodge her voice from my brain, to pry her fingers from my soul…but I am slowly doing just that. How long it has taken for me to realize and make the many changes I have made. I find myself crying suddenly at the sight of a grown man eagerly running up to the water's edge, just to look, to experience it, like a child. I want this spontaneity, this simplicity, this absorption in life. I grieve for the time I have lost, but I cry with relief that finally I am beginning to live in the moment. I feel relief because my reconnection to myself, to the universe, is happening, at the age of 42. I am pleased that I have somehow weathered this journey this far, when two-and-a-half years ago the world couldn't have been blacker, my rage and pain more intense, at the beginning of this so-called midlife crisis.

I am an artist. I work on paper, with computers and with film and video. In all mediums I gravitate toward collage. I take unrelated images that have a presence or energy for me and find or create relationships between them, integrating them, making sense out of them. I have to approach this written piece in a similar way, pulling together the images and experiences of the last few years in order to make sense out of this

complex passage in my life, the issues that have emerged, the changes I am
attempting to make and how this seemingly "negative" Hindu goddess Kali
has inspired me and guided me through this passage. Kali held more energy
for me through the darker times, when I needed her extreme presence as a
mirror for my own extreme state, but she continues to provide a perspective
and inspiration that I need and want to carry with me into the future.

So who is Kali and what does she represent? The typical description
of this ancient Hindu goddess, who continues to be widely worshiped in
India today, is disturbing by anyone's standards. She is usually represented
with four arms, a garland of skulls and disheveled hair. She often holds a
freshly cut human head and a bloodied scimitar in her left hands and makes
the signs of reassurance and boons with her right. Her neck is sometimes
adorned with a garland of severed human heads dripping blood; from her
waist hangs a string of severed human hands. She is dark and naked, her
teeth are fanglike and she has prominent breasts. At times she has a smile
on her lips glistening with blood, or she has her tongue extended in a
demonic grimace. She is understood to have a terrifying laugh and live in
the cremation ground, surrounded by screaming jackals. She is sometimes
depicted standing, in intercourse with Siva, who lies corpselike beneath
her.[1]

Is this goddess merely a patriarchal nightmare, another projection of
the negative onto women? Some feminist authors would argue that the
Hindu goddess Kali is just that...the destroyer aspect of the ancient triple
goddess split off by patriarchal culture from her other balancing aspects of
creation and preservation. For instance, Monica Sjoo and Barbara Mor,
authors of *The Great Cosmic Mother,* dismiss Kali as an artifact of the
historical shift to patriarchal religions. According to Sjoo and Mor, this
denial of the Great Mother brought increasingly obsessive fears of her sexual
and death-dealing powers. Therefore everything negative and bad was split
off and projected onto Kali.[2]

However, I feel it is important to reread patriarchal writings and
images for the truths they have attempted to obscure. Kali's roots are very
ancient and her meaning goes beyond patriarchal fear and guilt. The "bad
times in the human cycle" have been blamed on women but they are integral
to life and unavoidable, as death itself is unavoidable. The negative or
destroyer aspect of the Great Mother was understood and valued by women
priestesses of prepatriarchal times who identified with the dark side of the
triple goddess, knowing that this was the truth of the universe.

Any woman traversing the rough seas of a midlife crisis knows the
dark side of life. Kali provides me with a way to reclaim a positive relationship to and acceptance of this dark side of life and the dark side of the self,
both of which are split off, denied and feared in the Judeo-Christian
tradition. Another feminist researcher and writer, Barbara Walker, locates

Kali in this broader context and notes that her powerful archetype, which has surfaced in many ancient cultures, is difficult even for modern psychologists to ignore. The angry, punishing, castrating father presents less of a threat than the destructive mother who symbolizes the inevitability of death.[3]

Ajit Mookerjee, in his book *Kali, The Feminine Force,* admits the patriarchal bias in her mythology but also the need for a feminine viewpoint on this goddess with very ancient roots. In the traditional myth of Kali, the world was in the grip of destructive male forces. Even the male gods could do nothing. They prayed and the Great Goddess Durga emerged to battle the arrogant earthly males. Kali manifested herself as the forceful aspect of the Great Goddess Durga for the annihilation of demonic male power in order to restore peace and equilibrium to the world. This account of Kali's origins is from the early history of Kali found in the *Devi-Mahatmya,* a Hindu scripture. This self-revealing patriarchal tale in which men fear the collective rage of women presents women with a profound political symbol. She is indeed the active principle that breaks the male dualistic deadlock.

However, Kali's deeper meanings go beyond this patriarchal myth, beyond the masculine based commentaries that describe her as terrible and horrific. According to Mookerjee, the challenge of sakti (feminine force) with its vast sakta literature has not been properly presented to the world from the feminine viewpoint to bring out its truth. Kali is the "Great Mother" who represents the entire cycle of life, from womb to tomb. Her "negative" or destroyer aspects may be emphasized, but the creation and preservation aspects are clearly represented and contained in her imagery and mythology. Her dynamic sakta (female) energy consumes and transforms all life in a constant, never ending cycle. Acceptance of her reality offers the promise of release from fear and ignorance, a fear and ignorance that have claimed much of my life.[4]

When I began to explore the layers of Kali's meanings, I found great inspiration and validation for myself as a woman and a lesbian engaging in midlife changes…this painful coming to terms continues to engage me and has engaged me for several years. I needed her rage to match my rage; her power in order to come to terms with myself in the world; her incessant cycle of creation and destruction to understand myself as an artist; her identity as the Terrible Mother to free myself from negative bonds to my own mother; her shameless, aggressive sexuality to validate my own repressed desires; her position as an outlaw outside the dharmic order (the ultimate Hindu law) to validate myself as a lesbian. Having been initially drawn by her image in books on Tantric art, I found beneath her frightening surface the deeper truths I needed to accept in order to face the fears that have blinded and imprisoned me. Kali has provided a form, or a container, helping me make the connection between psychology and spirituality, between my individual story and the rest of the universe. I have found in her a powerful and compelling source of inspiration and an incredible symbol of freedom and independence, especially for myself at this stage of my life.

I am a 42-year-old, white, middle-class, educated lesbian. I am not agonizing over a career change because I have never had one as such; I am not grieving over children leaving home, because I don't have any; I am not getting a divorce from a man, because I have never been married to one. So what is this midlife crisis for me? What is it that has caused so much pain? It was not "it" but everything, something more indefinable, more all encompassing. My life had ground to a halt as if something had broken once and for all and could not be fixed. I have had to find a new vehicle for the rest of the journey. The way I have gotten around in the world no longer worked. In fact, for my first twenty adult years, I was not truly in control of my life. I have often felt, as in my past dreams, that a stranger is driving my car, a menacing male cab driver, or a woman I am lovers with, or I'm on the bus not sure where I am going, or in a train station not able to find the right train. I have held jobs, had relationships, tried to be an artist, often felt ungrounded, a fraud, waiting for something in the future to change, to free me from a sense of bondage, of being underwater, pulled under. I have felt held back by some force, often projected onto my mother, or my lover, or a boss, or a job. I have had trouble with anger, rage, depression. I think my life ground to a halt because I could no longer avoid dealing with what lay behind the rage and depression, the pain of the past, most of which had to do with my childhood relationship with my family, particularly my mother, and the pain of the present, which was my failure to face this pain and free myself from bondage to patterns created in relation to her. She was the first Kali I had to deal with; Kali the changeable, unpredictable mother, the terrible mother, the indifferent mother. In my midlife crisis, I have had to come to terms finally with the reality of my mother's relationship with me and how I have recreated that relationship with my mother with other women.

One of Kali's famous devotees in the twentieth century, Ramakrishna, had a vision about Kali. He saw a beautiful, young, pregnant woman emerging from the Ganges. Soon, she lay down on the bank and gave birth to a son. She nursed him at her breasts and caressed him fondly. Suddenly she was transformed into a terrible hag. She grasped the infant, crushed him in her jaws and returned into the waters of the Ganges.[5] My mother was unpredictable, inconsistent, at times pleasant, at other times abusive. In the past I have felt great frustration and even rage at my lovers for not "being there for me," and not giving me the nurturing and mirroring my mother would have liked to have given but could not. I felt that I had to focus on them rather than myself in order to maintain the connection, the relationship.

I had to prevent them from turning on me and abandoning me. In the process, I resented them and lost myself. I looked for love from women who were needy, narcissistic, seductive and emotionally unavailable, like my mother. I repeated this original relationship over and over again, because, in its own way, it was familiar and secure. I could not yet accept my mother as she was, grieve and go on. At 40 I separated from an important woman in my life. It was then that everything ground to a halt. I have remained alone for the past two and a half years. Instead of taking my rage and pain out on another lover, I began to face my mother's inability to love me in the way I needed, to face that all my manipulations and caretaking cannot make someone be there as I needed as a child.

In the Hindu tradition Kali is a reminder of the idea of maya. Maya is what prevents us from seeing the world as it really is, without illusions.

It is grounded in "not-knowing" or avidya and is said to be the result of superimposition. In our ignorance, we superimpose various structures and images upon things as they really are, thus preventing true "seeing." In our state of not knowing, we have the illusion that the world is permanent, pleasant and worthy of our ultimate attachment. We also see it as fragmented into bits and pieces, something to which we must respond and react continually. Maya, therefore, creates a false sense of security and fragments our picture of reality.[6]

In my relationships with women, I had difficulty seeing them as individuals separate from myself. Psychologically, the idea of maya is comparable to projection. I projected onto them my childhood relationship with my mother. I projected onto them my own negative aspects, I raged at their irresponsibility when I wasn't even responsible to myself and the development of my own life. I projected onto others my own undeveloped positive aspects, the artist in me, the creative, imaginative spirit in me I saw residing "out there" in my lover. In the process I have been cut off from my own desires and needs, spiritually, sexually, creatively, economically.

It is this business of maya or "projection" that has been a key in owning myself. In the process of owning myself, I have spent a lot of time alone. As I discovered my shadow, and began to accept the negative aspects of myself, I began to discover my own power, my own repressed energy. Kali in her wild darkness gave me permission to do this. "Her disheveled hair, flying free, represents both the entanglements of maya and the loosening of bonds." As I slowly begin to develop and own my own talents and skills, I give up less power to others. Nor Hall, author of *The Moon and the Virgin,* reminds us that we have to give something to the destructive aspect of the Great Goddess, acknowledge her presence, admit our own dark side. She says of this process: "If you give a part of yourself to lunacy, she will permit you to pass to and from the realm of the moon's dark phase. Otherwise she will detain you. Stupor and blackness will possess you."[7]

The deeper I go into my own issues and owning my own self, negative and positive, and the more I feel the sadness and pain of the past, the more separate and whole I feel and the clearer I see other people and allow them to be who they are. Finally I can let my mother be who she is and love her with her faults and virtues. And I see clearly how I am like her. It is both exciting and frightening to see the world as it is, beautiful, fleeting and painful. But what has Kali to do with this? Isn't this just a therapeutic process, a journey toward individuation? I would contend that this is not just a psychological adjustment but a spiritual journey. Kali has helped me relate my personal journey to a universal journey, a journey felt as cyclical rather than linear and female rather than male. Unlike the patriarchal tradition that places god "out there," she has functioned as a model, an aspect of myself, a potential in me, the teacher and guide that is within myself. When the familiar, deadly, critical, judgmental voice enters my psyche I turn to the outrageous Kali who in her mad continuous dance of life mocks the very idea of static, airless perfection.

At 42 I have questioned everything, including my sexual identity. Having had such difficulty in my relationships with women made me question being a lesbian. However, coming to terms with my mother has allowed me to reaffirm my lesbianism and begin to truly love myself and other women. I feel a warmth and depth of feeling for women that I have never known before. Kali's sexual preference appears to be heterosexual, however, her aggressive and blatant sexuality encourages me to own and act on my own sexual desire for women. Another important aspect of Kali is her virginal aspect, virginal in the ancient sense of being actively sexual yet one-in-herself, belonging to no man. If she were a lesbian I suspect she would belong to no woman. It is her singularity and wholeness unto herself that provides a model to help me struggle with issues involving possessiveness and control, and focus on others instead of myself. It is from a perspective of freedom that I feel I can give fully and responsibly to another woman, knowing that I, not my lover and/or friend, am responsible for my own happiness.

But it is Kali's uncontrollable nature, her being clearly outside the moral order, the pure dharmic order, the patriarchal order, that validates my lesbianism. Hindu scholars speculate that Kali was originally an indigenous, non-Aryan goddess, associated with tribal groups living on the periphery of Indian society. She was later included, probably reluctantly, in the Hindu pantheon. It has been suggested that her popularity is due to her encouraging her devotees to seek a broader and more redemptive vision of their lives. As a woman, not being sexually available to men is being an outlaw in a patriarchal society, as patriarchal society ensures male access to women. Lesbianism has the potential of offering women a broader and more redemptive vision of their lives, the space to be who they want to be, outside the narrow and constricted roles of the patriarchy.

Kali is clearly a mother figure, yet she is clearly associated with the confrontation and acceptance of death. Kali is best understood both as paradox and as transformation. Knowing Kali, one can no longer live in an either/or world. She is simultaneously about birth and death. She is simultaneously an indifferent and loving mother. She is fearsome in appearance, yet one of her outstretched hands makes the sign of "fear not."

My own death has been on my mind for the past few years. Time seems to be going by so quickly now. I look in the mirror and the young face that used to stare back is gone. There is now an older woman. There is a tiredness around the eyes, a jaw line that once had more definition and gray hair that is daily more noticeable. But I am learning to love, appreciate and take care of this woman, whereas I did not love or appreciate or take care of the younger one. When I am walking down a city street and I see myself in a store window, I am sometimes a little shocked. How did I get to be this old? How much time is left? What happened to the first 42 years? I am scared for a moment, panicked. I think ahead…twenty more years and I will be a bona fide "senior citizen." How can that be when I remember so clearly being twelve years old and riding my bike during the hot St. Louis summers? Death, how will it come? Quickly or after a prolonged illness? Or will it happen in a car accident tomorrow morning on the way to work? Do I really understand that I am going to die? Do I accept this? This wasn't such an issue when my face looked younger, in my twenties and thirties. But the challenge of Kali is seeing life as it is. Life begins, grows, dies and putrefies, relentlessly and incessantly, and with indifference to the individual ego. Kali throws death in one's face. To meditate on death, on Kali, to let her reality sink in transforms my relationship to the present. My perspective on my life changes radically—life is absurdly short, but as someone once said, very wide. There are so many more options than I imagined, decisions are no longer so anguished and momentous, life is suddenly there to be relished, to be plunged into fully. The idea of clinging to a lover, a job, an idea, in this fleeting, transitory world seems ludicrous. "To accept one's mortality is to be able to act superfluously, to let go, to be able to sing, dance and shout."[8] This is Kali's boon.

ENDNOTES

1. David R. Kinsley, *The Sword and the Flute: Kali and Krishna, Dark Visions of the Terrible and the Sublime in Hindu Mythology* (Berkeley and Los Angeles: University of California Press, 1977), p. 1

2. Monica Sjoo and Barbara Mor, *The Great Cosmic Mother: Rediscovering the Religion of the Earth* (San Francisco: Harper and Row, 1987), p. 182

3. Barbara Walker, *The Women's Encyclopedia of Myths and Secrets* (San Francisco: Harper and Row, 1983), p. 488

4. Ajit Mookerjee, *Kali, The Feminine Force* (New York: Destiny Books, 1988), p. 8

5. Kinsley, p. 134

6. Ibid., p. 133

7. Nor Hall, *The Moon and the Virgin: Reflections on the Archetypal Feminine* (New York: Harper and Row, 1980), p. 65

8. Kinsley, p. 145

Blessing of
the Children

MIRIAM CARROLL

Strange, I am the Crone
            in the seven
Yet I am the Child
            to whom all blessings flew
This dichotomy causes me to think
            of the Oneness
            of how it is possible
            to be ancient and young
            in one Being.
It makes me feel playful and solemn at once
            a babe full of wisdom
            a silverhaired youth
fulfilled
            by nurturing of the clan
giving
            by nature of myself

Hecate's Whereabouts

MIRIAM CARROLL

Here am I
           Old Crone   Hag   Witch Woman of Universal
                    Knowledge!
           Survivor of life's traumas   Birth and death
I am everywhere   ageless
Do not turn from staring at old women
Find courage in withered body
It is illusion that beauty sags with belly and breasts
Look again in the mirror
I am here
           ageless crone in every direction
You find me gleefully digging for fossils and crystals
           for I have become durable as stone
You find me in geodes filled with water
           created when Time began
You find me in pockmarks on the face of Lady Moon
           old scars from my childhood
You find me in vapors belched from Mother Earth
           flowing from nation to nation
           across vast seas
           as deep as the mysteries of my life
Crone   Hag   Witchwoman is you
You are Zodiac   Quaballa   Tarot   crystal ball
           future present and past
           fulfilled with wisdom of what you have
                accomplished
Seek me not in the physical mirrored image
           for that is merely my cloak
           in flux from the moment of my birth
Seek me not in miasmic corruption of matter
           for I am Pure Spirit within thee
               within thee
You are Old Crone   Hag and Witch Woman!

A Joyous Passage: Becoming a Crone

JACQYELYN H. GENTRY
& FAYE M. SEIFERT

It's easy to determine how people in the United States feel about aging—
just read some examples in the birthday greeting section of a local card shop:

> You're having a birthday and I'm not.
>> This is good.

> Growing old...
>> Is a pisser!

> Blame your parents!
>> It's not your fault you're so old!

> You have just turned 30.
>> You will never have fun again for the rest of
>> your life.

> Wrinkles are God's little way of saying,
>> "I'm stepping on your face!"

Cards and banners even encourage "Over the Hill" parties for
individuals who reach the remarkable age of 40! Taken together, all these
items send a powerful message: getting old is a miserable experience and
old people are a legitimate target for sarcastic jokes and degrading comments.

Such attitudes and messages are part of the general phenomenon
called *ageism*. Like racism or anti-Semitism, ageism refers to systematic
discrimination and negative attitudes—but the targets are older people.
Unfortunately, ageism is a pervasive characteristic of American society.

A former director of the National Institute on Aging, Robert Butler,
has noted three distinguishable but interrelated aspects to ageism: (1)
prejudicial attitudes toward aged persons and the aging process; (2) dis-
criminatory practices against the elderly, especially in employment; and (3)
institutional norms, practices and policies that perpetuate negative stereotypes, limit opportunities and undermine the dignity of older persons.
These three mutually reinforcing factors have transformed aging from a
natural process into a social problem and the elderly bear the consequences.

In everyday life ageism takes various forms. Some are blatant—like threatening and abusing older people, refusing to hire qualified persons who are older, or ignoring an older person's opinions and needs. Some are so subtle and familiar that we accept them as "the way things are"—like people who will never tell their age, considering "how young you look" to be the ultimate compliment, considering sexuality among elders to be a joke and not looking directly at older people or recognizing their presence.

Both men and women are subject to prejudice and to societal messages to be passive, docile and controlled as they grow older. Those who don't comply with social expectations are quickly given labels such as "stubborn old codger" or "crazy old lady." Sexuality among older people is especially misunderstood, with some common misconceptions being that older people don't have sexual desires; that they are sexually undesirable; that they can't make love because they are too fragile; or that the whole notion is perverse and shameful. Sadly, many older persons themselves have adopted these attitudes.

Why does ageism exist? *The New Our Bodies, Ourselves* (Boston Women's Health Collective, 1984) cites three sources of ageism: (1) our society denies the reality of infirmity and death, clinging to notions of rugged independence; this subtly encourages distancing ourselves from aged and infirm persons who remind us of our mortality and mutual dependence; (2) times of rapid social and technological change call for the quick adoption of new ideas and concepts, thus setting a climate for discounting elders' skills and wisdom learned through life experience; (3) our profit oriented economic system tends to devalue all those who don't "produce"—in other words, the young, the old and their caregivers.

For women, the effects of ageism are intensified by sexism, an equally pervasive characteristic in this society. Sexism has the effect of devaluing women from infancy through adulthood. Then, as they become old enough to feel the influence of ageism, women may feel that society is ready to discard them altogether. A gray haired, mature look can be "distinguished" for a man, "over the hill" for a woman. While an opinionated older man may be "assertive," the same characteristic in a woman is more likely to be labeled "batty." The older man who spends time with younger women or men is "sowing his oats," while the older woman who spends time with younger men or women is weird.

Certainly society's ideals for physical attractiveness and youthfulness are difficult to maintain as one ages, and those ideals are more rigid for women than for men. As they age, many women try relentlessly to maintain a youthful appearance; aging women are particularly susceptible to quackery, fraud and consumer exploitation in cosmetic and beauty aids marketed to maintain youth.

Nonetheless, the problems (and the pleasures) of aging belong primarily to women, for they outlive men. While contemporary aging is accompanied by problems for the older woman, there was a time when the aged woman was held in highest esteem as one of the most treasured members of her community.

In *The Crone: Woman of Age, Wisdom and Power,* Barbara G. Walker describes a time when older women, Crones, held an honored status; this was the era of the Goddess. Back then the word *hag* meant *a holy one*; *sage* meant *she-who-speaks; crone* meant *wise one*. Family and tribal systems were established on mother-right and inheritance was matrilineal. Priestesses kept a library of papyrus scrolls the Greeks called "bibles." The cauldron, a central religious symbol, signified the cosmic womb, the source of regeneration and rebirth.

The Crone was "mother's mother, the ultimate authority for the children of earth." Old women were not perceived as useless; wrinkles were honorable. Older women, the Crones, were revered—they were seen as healers and teachers; they commanded respect and their advice was sought.

The Crone concept was found in the images of the Goddess that were prominent in matriarchal cultures scattered across the Eurasian continent. The Goddess was the first Holy Trinity; her three personae were the Virgin, or birth giver; Mother, or nurturer; and the death dealing Crone.

The Goddess figure was not a monolithic concept, but a worldwide presence underpinning all natural cycles—everything was considered to be interrelated, so that hierarchies of better/worse or we/they did not exist. Known as the Great Mother, she was conceived as actually *being,* among many things: the earth, sea, moon, Milky Way, mountains, fate, birth and death. This was in stark contrast to the later religion of the "Heavenly Father," a spirit whose realm was remote from the earth. Early scriptures credited the Great Mother with the creation of the universe, the temporary preservation of each living creature and the transformation of nonliving things into continuing creations of new life.

In the early matriarchal communities, menstrual blood was a source of wonder. A pregnant woman did not menstruate while the "magic blood" created new life inside her body. When the "blood of life" no longer flowed regularly from the body of an aging woman, it was assumed to be held inside her for a grand purpose. This was perceived as wise blood; therefore, old women were the wisest of mortals and the retained blood was believed to be the source of their wisdom. The Crone, therefore, was a post-menopausal woman. The magnitude of her wisdom gave her a mystique—a magic quality that empowered her. She was considered to have qualities similar to those of a "good witch."

The Crone's title was related to the word *crown*; she represented the power of the ancient tribal matriarch, the embodiment of wisdom. She created systems of law and made decisions for her subjects and descendants. The cyclical, transformational character of nature was central to people's understanding of the world. Existence was not described as being, but as becoming. In this thought system, where the only constant is change, "growing up" was viewed as a continuing process, moving through maturity into growing old—as a seed becomes a fruit and then withers away. In nature everything that was alive was gradually dying and everything that seemed lifeless eventually would become part of something alive. Individually, a woman's life was seen as a state of transition in which the Virgin became the Mother, who in turn became the Crone. The birth giving Virgin and the death dealing Crone were one, so reflections of the young goddess were intertwined with the old one.

The Crone image was associated with death and the power to destroy. Characterized in myth after myth as an old woman, she was the strongest of the Goddess's three personae. Under one of her Teutonic names, *Elli*, or "old age," she was said to have beaten Thor, the god of strength, in a wrestling match.

In Tantric Buddhism, the Crones were known as *dakinis*, elder priestesses who comforted and prepared the fatally ill for death, counseled their families, established the customs for the funerary rituals and, in spirit form, "took the soul through the dark spaces of nonbeing" to its final resting place. The Crone image offers us a way to deal with the realities of aging by conquering our fear, by accepting the object of our fear and finally by facing death.

Recognizing our ancient history, we invite you to join us in reclaiming the power of the Crone—the wise one—through the Croning celebration!

The Celebration

A Croning is a celebration—a special birthday party, typically for a woman who is 50 or older or who is post-menopausal. As such, it is a "rite of passage" through which we make our transition into the next stage of our lives. It is a ritual to use in reclaiming the revered status of Crone and it is a public pronouncement to counteract our internalized oppressions of ageism and sexism. It resurrects the archetypal Crone image in order to "bring our old woman out of the closet of suppression, social invisibility and pejorative labeling." Unlike the cultures that worshipped the Goddess, our society does not have traditions to develop our Crone persona—that is, to prepare us for aging with pride. Our Croning celebration begins a new tradition—for taking constructive action to reverse ageism and sexism, individually and collectively.

The Croning celebration is a symbol for all women—not just for lesbians. Yet, as in so many other women's activities and issues, lesbians are in the forefront of searching for the ancient Crone image and stories and of trying to reclaim her status for contemporary older women.

Honor the importance of this passage. The only universal transition into aging for all women is menopause—a private, biological phenomenon. The Croning celebration is a public rite of passage that recognizes for women the wisdom that comes from life experience and reclaims respect and honor for older women in American society.

It is a time to celebrate with our friends, honor older women, accept affirmations and extol the historical significance of the Crone. It is a celebration of a woman's development as an individual and a recognition of her connectedness to other people and to the universe. Women we know are choosing age 50 as the marker for Croning, but a woman can choose for herself the age at which she wishes to be recognized as a Crone. Becoming a Crone is your celebration! The following suggestions may be helpful as you plan your Croning:

—Make sure your friends and family know what kind of celebration you want. You can organize it for yourself or let others organize it for you. Whatever you choose, participate in it fully.

—Weave into your celebration the elements that you enjoy. Some women embellish the croning ritual with singing, dancing, enjoying food, wearing special clothing or jewelry, sharing stories and pictures, creating works of art and giving or receiving flowers, crystals, gifts, or small tokens of appreciation.

—Your celebration can involve scores of friends or can be as small and intimate as you like. What you want is most important.

—Allow yourself to be affirmed by your friends, freely accepting their love for you, their positive statements, compliments, praises, congratulations, or any honors they bestow.

—Recognize and honor other Crones—older women—who attend your celebration. Invite them to participate in your Croning.

—Claim your age—tell people how old you are!

—Openly share with others the lessons you have learned in your life experience.

—Tell your friends about your vision for the next part of your life.

The amethyst, a stone that is associated with spirituality and wisdom, was a symbolic element in our Croning rituals. As part of the celebration ritual, we have created a tradition in our community that a woman who has been Croned gives an amethyst to the new Crone.

The amethyst, however, is only one symbol for Croning. Throughout history women have used other symbolic elements in their rituals—for example, crystals, flowers, plants, other items from nature and special music or other artistic works. This is your opportunity to choose and include the symbols that are important to you.

We suggest that a Croning celebration include the *Crone's Commitment* as a public statement for older women who have chosen to reclaim their Crone status. The Crone (or, if appropriate, several Crones) leading the ritual recites these words:

"As a Crone I invite you (name) to join me in spreading the joyous tradition of Croning. I lovingly pass to you this amethyst—a symbol of spirituality, wisdom, personal growth and connection with the universe. It is a marker of your rite of passage into the next stage of your life. I ask that you in turn pass an amethyst to other women in your community who claim the status of Crone.

"As part of accepting your identity as a Crone, I ask that you commit yourself to these important tasks:

"Love yourself completely and unconditionally;

"Honor the historical significance of the Crone, wisest of women;

"Proudly claim your own status as a Crone;

"Tell others of the Crone's power and wisdom;

"With your historical and personal Crone's strength, work to reverse ageism worldwide;

"Claim and take full responsibility for your passage into the next stage of your life.

"Welcome to the Sisterhood of Crones!"

The following vignettes describe a few of the Croning celebrations that have been held in the Washington, DC area:

Having attended a Croning celebration for the first time just a few months before she turned 50, Sarah described the Croning concept to a close friend. That friend then set plans in motion to have a special celebration for Sarah's birthday—the first surprise party Sarah had ever had! The party, held in the evening in Sarah's office, included a large group of women friends, festive decorations and special food. Sarah was honored by her companions and she was given a large amethyst geode as well as delicate amethyst jewelry and a copy of Barbara Walker's book *The Crone*. It was only after reading the Walker book that Sarah began to fully understand the significance of reclaiming the status of Crone for women.

When Peg turned 50 she planned an event to underscore for herself the significance of the Crone and to share her feelings with others. First her friend Jackie explained what a Croning celebration means, then Peg read the Desiderata, one of her favorite meditative statements. A friend read a poem written especially for Peg, then Peg read from her own journal:

"Turning 50 is like looking down the barrel of a gun (from the wrong end).

"Turning 50 is...like looking down a long, beautiful tunnel with pictures, emotions, smells, touches, elation, sadness, joy, pain, confusion, bedazzlement, befuddlement, wonder, curiosity, fear, anticipation, and on and on. It really is a kaleidoscope and the years make up the colors. If you've been lucky, a rainbow lives inside your kaleidoscope.

"People make such a big deal out of it. I made such a big deal out of it, but now that it's here, I don't feel any different. I feel privileged. I feel cheated. I feel as if I should have something wise, sage, or at least not dumb, to say....

"I guess this rambling stream of consciousness has been/is about choices—the ones I've made and the ones I have ahead of me. I feel a sense of urgency that's new to me. I feel that I must be wise and even judicious in my choices from now on because the clock...really is ticking. But how it ticks, to whose rhythms and reasons it ticks are my decisions."

On Toni's 60th birthday her friends gave a Croning celebration for her; it included readings, music, affirmations from friends and the gift of an amethyst. Symbols representing the elements were an integral part of the ceremony as Toni read "From a Distance," a Navajo prayer of blessing.

Winnie already had been celebrating her 50th birthday for an entire month before she created a social occasion for celebration. She began by issuing a letter to friends at work announcing that she was 50 years old. To each person who responded positively to her announcement, she gave a "50—Let's Celebrate!" button.

Winnie did the planning and cooking for her Croning celebration, a brunch for sixteen women friends. Each person was asked to bring a small token rather than a traditional birthday gift. Winnie laid out a red cloth (representing female energy) upon which each person laid her gift.

The Croning celebration began as each guest on arrival was invited to write her age on a paper on the wall in the entry. On a smaller paper, each person was asked to write the name of at least one woman who was influential in her life. Using the figures on the entry wall, the years were added up to determine a collective age for the group. Later each person was asked to share with the group the name(s) of the influential woman in her life and explain what her influence was like.

The guests were asked one by one to present their tokens (shells, rocks, etc.) to Winnie. At the end each woman cut a piece of the red cloth to take home with her.

A friend who had read about a Croning celebration proposed the idea of a Croning for my (Faye's) 50th birthday. As we planned the event, it seemed important and symbolic that I take charge of my celebration as I must now take charge of my transition into a new phase of life. I invited all my women friends. The Croning ritual included symbols of earth, wind, fire and water—representing my connectedness to the universe and spiritual development. I chose an amethyst as a symbol of my Croning and asked a woman friend to knit a pouch for its safekeeping. I also wanted to pass one on to the next Crone.

At my celebration I read passages from *The Crone* to reawaken the positive images of the Crone in our herstory. I received beautiful affirmations from my friends. The Crones among us were asked to share lessons they had learned and each Crone was given an amethyst to accompany her through her rite of passage.

The celebration began with dancing and eating good food; the evening progressed with feelings of fullness and pride in my 50 years and in being among my friends. On my (Jackie's) 50th birthday my friends and I had a dinner party for about 75 people. I rented a building in a state park for the occasion and an artist friend designed the invitation. Some friends purchased and prepared the food, others helped decorate and set up the party site. Guests included women and men friends, neighbors and professional colleagues.

After dinner I described the Crone's role and place in history. Faye, who had been Croned a few months before, had a key role in my Croning ritual. She commented on her own experience of Croning and on some of the elements of nature that are especially precious symbols for her. She presented to me an amethyst held in a protective pouch that had been made by a Crone. Accepting my new status, I related some of the valuable lessons I had learned in my 50 years. Then I recognized other Crones—women over 50—in the audience and asked them to reflect on their own lives and the lessons they had learned. A number of them spoke and shared their wisdom with all of us. Throughout the evening I felt warmth, joy, good humor and a precious connection to friends from many parts of my life.

ENDNOTES

Gentry, Jacquelyn and Faye Seifert. *The Croning Celebration.* (Bethesda, MD: The Feminist Institute Clearinghouse, 1988)

Walker, Barbara G. *The Crone: Woman of Age, Wisdom, and Power.* (San Francisco: Harper & Row, 1985)

Note to readers:
We are collecting stories of Croning to chronicle this grass roots movement. We know many of our readers have had similar celebrations—perhaps not calling them Cronings—to mark special birthdays. If you have had a Croning celebration,

or another special celebration for an older woman, please send a written or tape-recorded description of it to the authors at this address:

Women and Aging Project
The Feminist Institute
Box 30563
Bethesda, MD 20814

Preparing
For
Our
Future

Not for Jocks Only: Fitness and Fun After Forty

MARY LORENZ

Forty-year-old women aren't supposed to get sweaty and dirty doing anything, particularly not groveling in the dust behind home plate. But they do. Fifty-year-old women aren't supposed to venture into the wilderness alone hefting heavy backpacks. But they do. Sixty-year-old women aren't supposed to stand on the pitcher's mound risking line drives. But some do just that every summer.

If you want to maintain the level of health and fitness that makes softball (or any other sport) possible at 50, listen to the advice of Dr. Linda Zwerin, an exercise physiologist. She emphasizes that it is especially important for women in midlife to develop a regular program of fitness and that this means more than a weekly softball game or a few sets of tennis. There are real benefits to be derived from a program which includes aerobic exercise, stretching for flexibility and building muscle strength.

The most valuable result of exercise for older women may be the prevention of osteoporosis. This disease is caused by a loss of bone marrow, especially at menopause when our bodies stop producing estrogen. Regular activity, such as walking or swimming (three to five times a week for 30 to 40 minutes), can reduce the incidence of osteoporosis. Combined with proper nutrition, such a program can minimize the chances of contracting this disfiguring disease. While it is never too late to begin, women should start being concerned about preventing osteoporosis in their early thirties.

Other advantages of regular fitness activity include proven benefits in lowering cholesterol, high blood pressure, blood clotting time and stress. Inactive people lose muscle mass faster than active people. Aging itself has certain effects, such as the tendency to acquire more fat, and the reduction of maximal lung capacity. According to the authors of *Ourselves Growing Older,* cardiovascular endurance can be increased with any exercise using the major muscle groups that raises the heartbeat to 60-85 percent of capacity for twelve minutes or longer. (Maximum capacity heart rate is derived by subtracting your age from 220. Take your pulse for ten seconds during exercise and multiply by six to compare your rate to the desired rate.) Aside from swimming and vigorous walking, other aerobic sports could include cycling, running, racquetball, or cross-country skiing. Flexibility can be achieved by regular, gentle stretches to keep joints limber. Finally, strength can be improved by doing some work with weights to tone muscles in the abdomen, chest, back, arms and legs. Exercise will not stop the aging process or eliminate any disease, but it will delay or minimize their effects. It's a question of the quality of life you want to maintain as you grow older.

The major risk in undertaking an exercise regime in middle age or anytime, is the danger of overdoing it. Too much exercise is as bad as too little. Working out at too high an intensity, too often, can lead to overuse injuries such as stress fractures, tendonitis, or bursitis. To lessen these risks, women should begin gradually. If you are just starting out, take three or four months to build up to your goals. Don't exercise only on weekends, as this irregular activity can overstress the body.

Many women who do participate in regular sports emphasize the importance of choosing activities which are fun. Motivation is a crucial factor. If you don't enjoy it, you won't make it part of your routine. For some lesbians the social life is an inducement, so they may join an outdoor club or go to a gym. Others find buddies with whom they jog or bike regularly. Still others need to make sure the equipment they bought doesn't go to waste. Maybe a dog will be the key to get someone fast-walking daily.

Betsy, a 53-year-old lesbian athlete advises, "Do what you enjoy doing the most. You'll have to push yourself a little to get the benefits, but in the long run you'll feel so good." For her, exercise improves her general physical and psychological well-being. She finds it generates energy rather than reduces it, especially as she grows older. She may feel tired after a day at work, but realizes it is more a matter of stress than fatigue. When she runs or rides her bike, she feels terrific.

It is vital for beginners and experienced athletes alike to pay attention to the body's messages. If you feel pain, stop rather than working through it. Try to detect the difference between normal exertion and serious aches. The notion of "no pain—no gain" is a fallacy.

What about the other side of the coin? Some women who have been active all their lives reach midlife and find themselves in less than perfect condition. They may grieve the loss of their health or mobility which prevents them from pursuing the activities they love.

Lesbians in this position need to be gentle with their reduced capacities, learning patience, flexibility and new ways to take care of themselves and be active. These lessons don't come easily but are faced by each of us at some point in our lives.

Since we all recognize the value of keeping physically fit, what options do we have? What follows are the thoughts of some older lesbians who participate in a variety of sports and fitness activities. None by itself is a complete regimen, but if you find one that turns you on, you will discover that it is more enjoyable if you are in fairly good shape.

Tennis

If you don't break your ankle climbing a fence to retrieve a ball, as did one ambitious lesbian, tennis can be a risk free sport. Some warm-up and stretching will help prevent the muscle strains and sprains that any hard exercise can cause. It's a game requiring minimal equipment that can be played more or less strenuously depending on your style and more or less competitively depending on your attitude. Carol, a 51-year-old book-keeper, finds it to be excellent mental and emotional therapy. "I think about very little else; I'm totally focused while playing. It's good for clearing the cobwebs at the beginning or end of the day." She recommends it to anyone in reasonably good health, but advises taking lessons if you're just starting. Since it is a popular sport among all ages, it is not difficult to find others who play. A notice at the local Y, health club, or women's center should produce some willing players. In the summer, public courts make tennis available for everyone. During the winter, the sport reverts to its elite roots since affordable clubs are not plentiful. It is, however, a lifetime sport. Katherine Hepburn, still playing in her eighties, can be our role model. She just lets the ball bounce twice before returning it.

Swimming

Kathleen, a therapist, finds swimming to be the ultimate in relaxation. "Sometimes it feels so effortless, I imagine I'm flying. I think I go into a trance and my skin feels no boundaries with the water." She also appreciates swimming for the good aerobic workout she gets at least three times a week. Another benefit is that it helps her process things. Although she doesn't think about problems while swimming, she often discovers, as she climbs out of the pool, that she has come to a decision. "It's like dreaming a solution." Most doctors and exercise advisors recommend swimming as one of the easiest sports on the body. The main disadvantage is locating a place in which to swim year-round.

Mountain Biking

Mountain biking doesn't seem like the type of activity anyone would take up in middle age. The sport conjures up images of grinding up a steep trail on two wheels, fording streams astride a small, fat tired bike, or risking life and limb zooming downhill through the trees. "You have to look below the surface," advises Bobbi, a 41-year-old educator. "Speed is not what it's all about. The sport has gotten a bad reputation because of the wild young boys who first popularized it." Bobbi was intrigued by the idea of combining two activities she loved: cycling and hiking in the back country. When she tried it, she was hooked immediately. She finds it challenging to ride a trail leaving only a tire mark—no skidding, no tearing up the environment. The sport is a test of technique and an aerobic workout. It requires full attention or "you land on your head." The risks can be minimized because each person can set her own risk level. Begin by riding on dirt roads. When you take to the trails you can always stop and walk down a steep hill. Wearing a helmet is a must, as is having a sturdy bike. For Bobbi, there is exhilaration in a thrilling downhill run and satisfaction in facing the challenge of staying balanced on rugged terrain. Her advice to anyone contemplating the sport: "Go for it."

Running

Although she began jogging in the '70s when the sport became popular, Jane, 51, had been involved in track since high school. She's running again for physical conditioning, relaxation and emotional rewards. "It smooths out the rough edges." She loves getting into the woods on a crisp fall day and running on trails or logging roads. "It's an enabling feeling. I feel healthy, strong and happy to be alive. I feel like I can run forever." According to Jane, anyone can do it if they begin slowly, gradually increasing their time and distance. "I'm not a macho runner," she says. "If I have a hip or knee acting up, I just lay off rather than risk a permanent injury."

Martial Arts

At 45, Sue was looking for something to do. She wasn't particularly interested in self-defense or searching for a strenuous activity, but she ended up trying aikido. This judo-like sport was frightening at first. Weekly, she confronted large men in a one-on-one exercise. There was the risk of personal injury from a bad fall and fear of appearing foolish in front of a group. She persisted and for a year this self-employed craftsperson has been enjoying it. "It's a good workout. Not only do I feel better physically from the stretching, tumbling and aerobics, but I feel better about myself." She derives personal satisfaction from dealing with new people, learning complicated physical techniques and confronting her fear of injury. She appreciates the Eastern philosophy which meets some of her spiritual needs and feels aikido is a process-oriented sport rather than a strictly competitive one.

Backpacking

"I see myself doing it at 80, certainly for as long as I can walk." Hedy, a 51-year-old grandmother, takes an annual two-week backpack trip with her partner to the High Sierras of California. Carrying everything they need on their backs, these two women often surprise troops of Boy Scouts with their endurance. "It's the best way to be outdoors, living close to nature day and night." Besides keeping her physically fit, hiking becomes a spiritual experience. Viewing a panorama from the top of a hard won peak, she feels moved in a way that no other activity duplicates. To anyone who is considering hiking and backpacking, Hedy says, "Do it now." Begin with day hikes, then try an overnight. There are many good resources in the form of books, outing clubs and professionally led trips. Women-only groups exist and these provide a way to enjoy nature and the outdoors without the typical male attitude of conquering the wilds.

Weight Training

On the recommendation of her chiropractor, Sue took up Nautilus training at age 42. Using the machines at the club where she works out, Sue feels she exercises her whole body. "It really opens things up. I work hard for 30 to 35 minutes and then reward myself with a sauna. It's very relaxing and it makes me strong." She can tone her muscles while enjoying some solitary time to free her mind and just breathe. The only risks involved are injuries resulting from not warming up or from using the weights improperly, i.e., using them too fast or taking on too much weight. Though she wouldn't call it fun, this type of workout is a disciplined activity that satisfies her with results she can feel.

You can also begin a simple toning program at home using soup cans in socks or milk cartons filled with sand. There are books of instruction about which muscles to work, how much weight to lift and the number of repetitions to do. Try it. It's an important part of any fitness program.

Cross-Country Skiing

Laura, a 41-year-old career counselor, loves the freedom of sliding through woodsy trails and over spectacular mountainous terrain in Colorado on skinny skis. She took to this total body workout immediately. It exercises the arms and legs to a heart pounding degree. For her, though, it is mainly a way to be outdoors in the winter. Cross-country skiing can be pursued alone or with friends and it can be enjoyed at any skill level. It's generally a safe sport but Laura did manage to strain a knee ligament by taking on a steep hill in icy conditions. "I should have slid down on my butt," she states with clear hindsight. For anyone wanting to try skiing, she suggests lessons and a book to learn about dressing for the cold and trail etiquette. A special highlight for her was a week spent in Yellowstone one February skiing past geysers, bison, deer and other wildlife.

Cycling

"Bicycling is an excellent fitness sport without the pounding on the joints that accompanies jogging," says a 40-year-old teacher. Of course there are disadvantages, such as insensitive drivers, bumpy streets, flat tires and loose dogs, but she finds these are easily outweighed by the invigorating feeling of coasting over country roads or pedaling through city parks. Biking is also a wonderful way to explore new places. On a bike, you can travel fast enough to cover some territory and still "stop to smell the flowers." Mary advises women of any age to try cycling. "You could rent a ten speed and familiarize yourself with it before making a big investment." A drawback to the sport is that the equipment is expensive and security can be a problem. However, if you can deal with these factors, cycling can be a satisfying and fun form of exercise. Mary and some friends began getting together for weekend rides. Soon, through word of mouth, there were fifteen lesbians meeting regularly for Sunday breakfast and a bike tour.

Racewalking

Sharon is a paralegal who used to run for exercise, but in her late thirties her knees began to bother her, especially on hills. "I also liked racing but could never be competitive (in running) and wanted at least the chance to do well in races." She took a class to learn the specific technique of racewalking and found she was practically a natural. She recovers fast after a hard workout and won third prize for her age group in the first competition she entered. "It's a wonderful aerobic sport and if you do it regularly you can eat whatever you want," she says enthusiastically. "An additional advantage is that it puts half the pressure on the knees as compared to running." She joined a club in which most of the participants are 50 or older and Sharon expects to be racewalking for the rest of her life.

You can also fast-walk without the special hip-swinging toe to heel motion peculiar to racewalking. However, it is this special movement that allows for the most efficient stride and the best cardiovascular workout. If you enjoy it, get out and walk at any pace at first. You can gradually increase your speed and distance to get your heartbeat into the acceptable conditioning range.

Racquetball

"I play like a fool," says Jane, a computer programmer. Having been a jock all her life, she was finding it hard to know what to do as she got older to replace the team sports she had played in school and in the Army. At 46, her knees and back give her a great deal of pain, but she wanted an activity that was vigorous, competitive and exciting. While you play hard whether you win or lose, racquetball provides more than exercise. Jane appreciates the social interaction in the league she joined. In addition, it's an easy sport to learn, you can play at any ability level and Jane notes that women with any body type and some with disabilities can enjoy this sport. Some of the risks involve the possibility of eye injuries, muscle strains and sprains. "It felt dangerous to play against men," Jane says, "but I love to get on the court with a woman near my skill level and concentrate totally on the match. I feel rejuvenated."

Snowshoeing

"On snowshoes you can appreciate the winter woods in a slow and silent way. I first tried it last year at 39 and hope to be doing it forever. There is a woman in my town who is 92 and still straps on the shoes and goes out regularly with her friends." Maureen thought snowshoeing would be an awkward, difficult exercise but instead she found it easy to maneuver her modified bear paw shoes in woodsy terrain. "There's no special technique to it. Just put one foot in front of the other. It's so peaceful." Trekking through the trees or over fields with her partner, Maureen enjoys watching for animal tracks and observing the wilderness clothed in white. Sometimes she gets together with friends from a women's outdoor club to make it a more social activity. Besides being easy to learn, snowshoeing is relatively risk free. Dealing with the cold is a problem but you learn to dress in layers. This sport is also a very good workout, especially on an uphill climb, but it is not as exhausting as one might think; you set your own pace. Maureen remembers snowshoeing across a field under a full moon on a quiet February night. "The snow shimmered. It was exquisite."

Volleyball

For this 53-year-old Girl Scout administrator, volleyball provides a social connection and an opportunity to have fun with her co-workers. When Bev learned the game in school the rules were quite different, but she has adapted. The weekly games provide a winter replacement for softball. They are played "in a reasonably serious way, but mostly we enjoy doing things together." She has found that her attitude about competition in this and other sports has changed as she has gotten older. "After 50 you really begin to prioritize and take care of yourself. For me, that means putting less emphasis on winning and more on the enjoyment of the activity itself." Bev tries to prevent problems by taking the time to stretch and warm up properly. She wasn't always so concerned about this when she was younger, but notices now that the sore muscles occur more easily and take longer to heal. To Bev, the risks of sore muscles are worth the rewards.

Yoga

"I was doing anti-nuclear work and also working in the battered women's movement. I was spending time in jail and feeling utter despair with the world." It was at this time, in her early fifties, that Jean began doing yoga. She felt it helped give her the inner peace she needed to continue her political work. Now yoga is only part of a fitness regime that at 59 keeps

Jean centered. Her rowing machine and weight training supplement the flexibility she strives to maintain with yoga exercises. She advises women who may be interested in increasing their activity to start with yoga. "Do it for a year and your body will be a whole different instrument. Then you can begin adding other activities to your program." For Jean, the aging process and the natural changes that come with it present challenges in learning new ways to integrate the changes into her life. She is learning to slow down when she gets tired, to dress in layers for hot flashes and to make adjustments in gauging the flight of a softball as it appears through bifocals.

There are even more sports to consider when choosing ways to stay fit: aerobics, basketball, canoeing, kayaking, golf, rock climbing, skating, soccer and squash among others. In all of these activities you can find women of all ages and sexual orientations participating. However, look for lesbians out there, especially among the older players. As Jean says, "We are leading the way as we always do."

Financial Planning for Retirement

S. LISA HAYES

From the day you know you are a lesbian you know that you, and you alone, are responsible for your life—there is no false sense of security that marriage to a man, who will "take care of you for life" will solve all your financial problems.

In the National Lesbian Health Survey, the number one concern for lesbians was money problems. According to this national survey of 2000 lesbians throughout the country, 69 percent had been to college and/or had college or advanced degrees. Most worked full time in professional or managerial positions and yet among the midlife lesbians they surveyed all but twelve percent earned less than $30,000. Sixty-four percent earned less than $20,000. These realities make it particularly important that we learn to use what money we have in the most effective way possible to achieve financial independence.

This chapter will address both general and specific concerns of lesbians to help us enhance our financial power and gain a greater understanding of the "money game." I hope to educate and motivate you—educate you as to what financial tools are available to achieve your monetary goals and motivate you to take action toward financial independence. *You* will need to provide the self-discipline to save.

The key elements of a financial plan are: to earn money, retain your earnings (keep as much as you can out of Uncle Sam's coffers), protect your assets, save your assets for emergencies and allow a portion to grow to outpace inflation.

The realities of sexism are that women are paid less than men for many jobs. The shocking statistics I mentioned earlier of low income levels in relation to the high education level of lesbians make this reality very clear.

However, the goal of a comfortable retirement is do-able, especially during midlife. Midlife is a time of traditionally peak earning years, and by making prudent decisions to save a small portion of your earnings today, you will be surprised at the impact compound interest and time make on modest investments. As I will explain later, it is possible at even low income levels to make small monthly investments that will compound and grow tremendously.

Earn

The first step toward financial self-respect and independence is the ability to earn money. Today, lesbians are in all areas of the work world—corporate leaders, managers, business owners, artists and service providers.

Do not be afraid to charge for your time if you have a service or talent that others might need. By networking with other women in your community or city, you will find that many women are truly interested in and supportive of your success. Ask for help if you need it. Take action and seek out support groups such as national organizations like the American Women's Economic Development Organization and local organizations that are listed in the phone book. Midlife years provide the time you need to make your assets grow for the golden years which may be enjoyed in health, prosperity and wisdom.

Retain

After you earn your money, you must keep as much in your own pocket as possible and not Uncle Sam's. Because taxes are progressive in nature, the more you earn, the more important tax planning becomes. There are plenty of tax-saving tools available—IRA's, municipal bonds, annuities and home ownership. It is important to work out a plan using these tools so you keep more of what you earn.

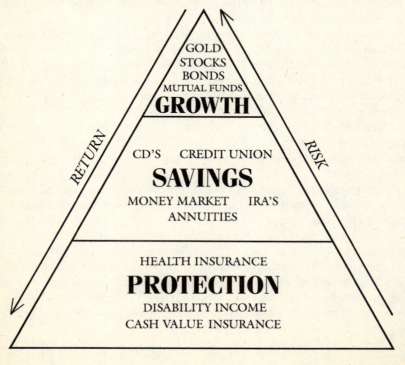

GOLD
STOCKS
BONDS
MUTUAL FUNDS
GROWTH

RETURN — RISK

CD'S   CREDIT UNION
SAVINGS
MONEY MARKET   IRA'S
ANNUITIES

HEALTH INSURANCE
PROTECTION
DISABILITY INCOME
CASH VALUE INSURANCE

Protect

Protection is the foundation of your financial planning structure. Here you evaluate how your hard-earned assets will be protected in the event of any emergency.

Insurance is used to minimize your risk of financial ruin if a crisis occurs. Do you have adequate health insurance? If you are unable to work because of an accident or illness will your income be replaced? Briefly, health insurance is comprised of three components—hospital room and board, physician bills in the hospital and major medical. If you work for a large-to-medium-size company, you are probably covered for medical insurance. Read the terms of your policy to know to what extent you are covered. If you are self-employed, you can select individual or group coverage; there are certain companies that do insure groups as small as one person. The cost of health insurance is ever-increasing. To keep the cost down, you can select a high deductible and/or a high co-insurance limit. Co-insurance is that part of your doctor bills which you are expected to pay. For example, many insurance companies will pay 80 percent of the first $5,000 in bills; thereafter, they will pay 100 percent. The twenty percent is co-insurance.

The self-employed have another concern regarding risk and that is continuation of income if they cannot work because of a sickness or accident. A sole proprietor is often the "goose that lays the golden egg" for her income, and if she can't bring in money because of a disability, there are usually no other sources of compensation. Disability insurance, also known as income replacement protection, is designed to provide you with a monthly income, after a certain pre-selected waiting period, for an extended time (usually to age 65) if you cannot perform the substantial and material duties of your occupation. Speak to a financial planner or insurance agent to learn more about this vital coverage.

Life insurance is a way to protect the assets you and your life partner have built together. Life insurance can be used strictly as a death benefit, which upon your death will enable your spouse to pay off the mortgage, continue a joint business or eliminate accumulated debts. Life insurance can also be used as a method to accumulate cash that you can use while living. The cash-value type life insurance policies grow at a specified interest rate on a tax-deferred basis (you do not pay tax on the growth of cash).

Savings

The savings component is designed with an eye toward liquidity, safety of principal and tax deferral. Within this area, you will find money market funds, Certificates of Deposit, annuities and savings accounts. In any of these, your principal cannot fluctuate—you just earn interest. Standard advice is that you need three to six months of your earnings to be liquid (immediately available) in case of any emergency. The best place to invest for your emergency fund is in a money market fund or a treasury fund. Money markets earn slightly higher interest than traditional savings accounts and treasury funds have a slightly higher yield than a money market. However, treasury funds can and do fluctuate ever so slightly. If you haven't started saving yet, these liquid savings are a good place to begin.

Annuities are tax-deferred vehicles that provide safety and growth by compounding interest without the negative effect of taxation on the interest. Only when you begin to withdraw money from an annuity is the interest taxed. The benefit of an annuity is in the tax-deferred growth for the years during which the interest is accumulating. Annuities have penalties for withdrawals prior to age 59.

IRA-type vehicles such as pensions, 401(k)s, Keoghs and Simplified Employee Pension plans (SEPs) can be within the savings component if they are held as annuities or money markets. We will discuss retirement vehicles later. Please note the difference between money that is tax-deferred and money that is tax-deductible. Non-IRA annuities are only tax-deferred; that is, the growth from interest is not taxed until you begin to withdraw and use the money, then you will pay tax on the part that is deemed to have been interest. Tax-deductible vehicles are "qualified" monies such as IRAs, Keoghs and other pension-type plans. Tax-deductible dollars are those which you can deduct dollar for dollar from your tax return. For example, if you earn $16,000 per year, you pay tax on the $16,000; but if you contribute $1,000 into a tax-deductible IRA, you pay tax only on $15,000. Qualified money is a term that means the Internal Revenue Service (IRS) gives special tax treatment to those monies. If you earn more than a specified amount of money or have a pension plan offered at work, the extent to which you can deduct your IRA contribution from your taxes may be limited.

Growth

The growth component of financial planning is the area in which you will increase the velocity of your dollars. This term, "velocity of dollars," means the time period it takes to multiply one dollar into three dollars. Growth component investments include stocks, bonds, mutual funds and tangibles, such as real estate and coins.

Let's look at mutual funds, since they are an inexpensive vehicle for women to accumulate wealth and a good place for beginning investors. A mutual fund is a compilation of various stocks or bonds with a particular theme, i.e. conservative growth, aggressive growth, utilities, bonds or socially responsible companies. Mutuals are professionally managed and require a low initial investment. Whatever your risk tolerance and goals, you can find the investment that is just right for you using mutual funds.

Any investment other than IRA's and annuities can be jointly owned. By registering a mutual fund in both your and your lover's name, you are guaranteeing that upon either of your deaths, the money reverts directly to the other without having to go through probate (see the chapter on legal issues in this book).

Because the goal of growth investments is to increase your money, it is important to be able to evaluate your investment's performance. A good general method for determining how quickly your invested money will double is the "Rule of 72" which states that money doubles in the number of years your rate of return on your investment is divided into 72. For example, an investment in an annuity earning eight percent will double in nine years and a mutual fund whose historical average annual return has been twelve percent will double in six years.

Because inflation is a very real factor in planning for financial independence, your money must not only be safe, it must also work as hard for you as you have worked for it. Inflation has averaged more than five percent per year over the past fifteen years. This five percent inflation can easily erode your retirement account as seen in the following example: Janet invests $1,000 in a CD that is earning eight percent. Janet's tax bracket (federal and state combined) is 34 percent. That brings her CD return down to an effective rate of 5.6 percent, after she pays taxes on the interest. After inflation, her money has really earned only 0.6 percent—not much of an inflation beater. Wherever possible you want an investment (that is in agreement with your risk tolerance) that will give you the greatest after-tax return above the inflation rate.

The secret to accumulating wealth is simply compounding money over time. The simplicity and effectiveness of this secret can be seen by the following example: Betty and Sally are both 45. Sally can manage to put away $200 a month after expenses and taxes. She begins a savings plan into a mutual fund that has averaged a sixteen percent total rate of return over the past ten years. By age 65, Sally will have accumulated over $285,000. Betty, on the other hand, has $25,000 in the bank already and plans on keeping it there because she was told banks are "safe." Betty's money, after twenty years in a bank at an average rate of seven percent will grow to only $90,000.

Which amount would you prefer to have? Of course, all of us would want to have $285,000 instead of $90,000. While the difference is tremendous in the end, the difference in the beginning is not.

First, select the appropriate age bracket, 35, 45 or 55 years of
age. In the "Savings Required" column choose the amount
closest to your goal. Now, read across. These charts show
how much you would have to invest, either in a lump sum or
in regular monthly investments at various asumed rates of
return.

LUMP SUM CONTRIBUTION				

PRESENT AGE 35 (30 Years Until Retirement)

SAVINGS REQUIRED	Lump Sum Contribution Invested At:			
	8%	10%	12%	16%
$100,000	$9,144	$5,041	$2,782	$849
250,000	22,861	12,602	6,954	2,124
500,000	45,722	25,205	13,908	4,247
750,000	68,583	37,807	20,863	6,371
1,000,000	91,443	50,410	27,817	8,495

PRESENT AGE 45 (20 Years Until Retirement)

SAVINGS REQUIRED	Lump Sum Contribution Invested At:			
	8%	10%	12%	16%
$100,000	$20,297	$13,646	$9,181	$4,163
250,000	50,743	34,115	22,951	10,408
500,000	101,486	68,231	45,903	20,817
750,000	152,229	102,346	68,854	31,225
1,000,000	202,971	136,462	91,806	41,633

PRESENT AGE 55 (10 Years Until Retirement)

SAVINGS REQUIRED	Lump Sum Contribution Invested At:			
	8%	10%	12%	16%
$100,000	$45,052	$36,941	$30,299	$20,404
250,000	112,631	92,352	75,749	51,011
500,000	225,262	184,703	151,497	102,021
750,000	337,893	277,055	227,246	153,032
1,000,000	450,523	369,407	302,995	204,042

These illustrations were prepared using a fixed rate of return
and assume no fluctuation in the value of principal. They do
not reflect the impact of income taxes.

MONTHLY CONTRIBUTIONS

PRESENT AGE 35 (30 Years Until Retirement)

SAVINGS REQUIRED	Monthly Contribution Invested At:			
	8%	10%	12%	16%
$100,000	$67	$44	$29	$11
250,000	168	111	72	29
500,000	335	221	143	57
750,000	503	332	215	86
1,000,000	671	442	286	114

PRESENT AGE 45 (20 Years Until Retirement)

SAVINGS REQUIRED	Monthly Contribution Invested At:			
	8%	10%	12%	16%
$100,000	$170	$132	$101	$58
250,000	424	329	253	145
500,000	849	658	505	290
750,000	1,273	988	758	434
1,000,000	1,698	1,317	1,011	579

PRESENT AGE 55 (10 Years Until Retirement)

SAVINGS REQUIRED	Monthly Contribution Invested At:			
	8%	10%	12%	16%
$100,000	$547	$488	$435	$342
250,000	1,367	1,220	1,087	854
500,000	2,733	2,441	2,174	1,709
750,000	4,100	3,661	3,260	2,563
1,000,000	5,466	4,882	4,347	3,418

These illustrations were prepared using a fixed rate of return and assume no fluctuation in the value of principal. They do not reflect the impact of income taxes.

Sally's method of savings is called "dollar cost averaging" and is the secret to successful wealth accumulation. Dollar cost averaging (DCA) is the most important aspect of investing. It's a generic term that describes reducing the risk of investing in growth vehicles such as mutual funds, by investing small amounts consistently every month. By investing a small amount each month, over time your price per share will be less than the overall average of the fund. DCA removes the emotion from investing which is exactly what you want to do. People lose money in the market because of two emotions—fear and greed. Remove these two killers and you will be a successful investor.

Dollar cost averaging is especially useful in retirement planning. The magic of compound interest, time and consistency is on your side when you use this technique in retirement saving. The second most important aspect of investing is to diversify your assets as they grow (placing a percentage in stocks, a percentage in bonds and a percentage in cash). Be careful to build up your cash position first, keeping approximately fifteen percent of your assets in this area and the balance of your assets divided into roughly equal parts between bonds and stocks, depending upon market conditions.

Retirement Planning

As you might have guessed, retirement planning is the number one concern of all Americans today. Americans are living longer and with longevity comes a need to plan so that your assets will live as long as you do.

In the 21st century, a greater emphasis on self-reliance will be placed on all Americans with respect to retirement because there will not be enough money in the government coffers. Today, Social Security benefits average less than $10,000 per year and private pensions average $8,300. For a comfortable retirement, we cannot rely exclusively on social security or a private pension—we need to contribute to our own retirement needs. It's never too soon or too late to start retirement planning.

Retirement planning is especially important to lesbians, many of whom are employed in the types of jobs that have no stated retirement policy, no retirement planning programs and no continuation of health insurance into retirement. For a middle-aged lesbian, retirement planning is crucial because she must rely upon herself for her future comfort and income. Since self-reliance and personal responsibility are nothing new for us, these character traits will help in reaching your retirement goals.

A common retirement strategy is to keep your IRA contributions going. Seventy-five percent of single women are still entitled to a deductible IRA contribution. IRA contributions are fully deductible if your income is under $25,000 per year (as of publication date). Even if the amounts you contribute are only partially deductible, do it, because all IRA's are still tax-deferred.

If you are self-employed, a great tax-deductible retirement vehicle is a Simplified Employee Pension plan (SEP). A SEP is available to the sole proprietor, partnership or sub (S) corporation. The plan allows you to contribute a bit over thirteen percent of your earnings up to a maximum of $30,000. You do not need to contribute to the plan every year and the administrative paper work is very inexpensive. Consult a financial planner to learn about this simple but effective tax savings tool.

If your IRA is totally not deductible, there are several alternative investments that will also give you tax-deferral and growth.

A variable annuity is a great product for tax-deferred growth if you can keep the money invested until age 59. A variable annuity is similar to a regular annuity in that both are tax-deferred. A variable has a bit more opportunity for growth because you can divide your money between a fixed account with guaranteed interest and the variable side which is a series of mutual funds that will also grow tax-deferred.

Lastly, within the concept of tax savings there are municipal bonds, which are completely tax free, and government bonds, which are state-tax free. With government bonds, such as treasuries, your principal is not at risk and your dividends will be state tax free.

How Much Do I Need To Save For Retirement?

To determine how much money you need to save to have your ideal retirement nest egg, ask yourself first:

STEP ONE

How much would I need today if I were to retire?

Let's say you are 45 years old and you decide that you need $25,000 per year to live on when you retire, using today's dollars. You may decide you want to work to age 67 or so, to make your retirement plan work better for you and to receive greater Social Security benefits. In that case, you would retire in the year 2012.

STEP TWO

Next, determine the effect inflation will have on your present dollars by using the inflation table below. If your retirement year is 2012, then the inflation factor is approximately 4.25.

Age Now	Year of Retirement at age 65	Inflation Factor
64	1989	1.06
63	1990	1.12
62	1991	1.19
61	1992	1.26
60	1993	1.34
55	1998	1.79
50	2003	2.40
45	2008	3.21
40	2013	4.29
35	2018	5.74
30	2023	7.69
25	2028	10.29

*based on long-term inflation rate of 6%

WHERE WILL IT COME FROM?

How much money do you anticipate receiving each month from:

Your Retirement Plans $_____

Social Security (call Social Security Administration at 1-800-937-2000 for information on how to determine your estimated benefit) $_____

Investments $_____

Insurance & Annuities $_____

Other $_____

Total Monthly Income Estimated $_____

STEP THREE

Multiply the inflation factor by $25,000. The result is $106,250. This new amount is how much you will need in 2012 to equal what your $25,000 buys today, based upon an average inflation rate of six percent.

STEP FOUR

Determine how much income you can reasonably expect from social security, employer-sponsored savings or retirement plans.

If you write to the Social Security Administration in Washington, DC and tell them your name, date of birth, Social Security number and your last year's earnings, they will send you a printout of your expected benefits at your retirement age. Please remember that the minimum age for Social Security benefits beginning in 1992 will be 67. To continue the example, let's suppose your Social Security benefits amount to $14,000 per year in today's dollars and your employer pension plan is $6,000 per year in today's dollars. Using the inflation factor of 4.25, this means that in 2012 you'll have $85,000 per year from Social Security and a pension plan. You'll need an additional $21,250 to meet your goal of $106,250 ($25,000 in today's dollars).

To generate that $21,250 per year, you'll need a lump sum of $265,625, earning an average of eight percent per year. This will generate $21,250 in interest while leaving your principal intact.

If these big numbers seem scary, remember they reflect twenty years of inflation.

Still with me? Good.

STEP FIVE

Use the "Retirement Timer" chart below and look at the columns for $100,000 and $150,000. Add those together to get $250,000 (closest amount to $265,000). You will see that if you are 45 years old today, you need to save $424.42 per month to accumulate $250,000 in twenty years. If you can earn better than eight percent interest, you'll need to save less per month. Also, if you have savings now, real estate you plan to sell, or other tangible assets, you will need to save less per month. What's important to know is that at age 45, you can still achieve significant retirement income through savings.

Retirement Timer

	AGE NOW							
	25	30	35	40	45	50	55	60
To accumulate these amounts* at age 65	SET ASIDE THESE MONTHLY PAYMENTS							
$ 20,000	$6	$9	$14	$22	$34	$58	$110	$273
40,000	$12	18	27	43	68	116	219	545
60,000	$18	27	41	64	102	174	328	817
80,000	$23	35	54	85	136	232	438	1089
100,000	$29	44	68	106	170	289	547	1361
150,000	$43	66	101	158	255	434	820	2042
200,000	$58	88	135	211	340	578	1094	2722

*Based on a fixed 8% interest rate, compounded monthly, and assuming no fluctuation in value of principal. The figures are not intended to be a projection of any investment results. Mutual fund shares will rise or fall in value and the dividends will vary in amount. No adjustment has been made for income taxes.

The point to this step-by-step process is to show you how saving toward a goal is possible and achievable if done in small steps at a time. Even a $100 per month investment now will make a tremendous difference.

I leave you with this thought—there is always more than one solution to any problem and the way to begin solving any money problem you may have is to simplify each area and do a little saving each day. The rewards will be yours in the not too distant future.

Legal Protections for Lesbians

PAULA L. ETTELBRICK

As lesbians, we are legally vulnerable at all stages of our lives. The vast majority of the country does not recognize basic civil rights protections against job, housing or public services discrimination which occurs on the basis of sexual orientation. Lesbian couples are not allowed to marry in any state, nor are our relationships legally recognized in any other way. In fact, in half of the states we are still criminals under archaic laws which criminalize sexual conduct between two consenting adult women. As women, we encounter certain inequities in the system which keep us from the top-notch jobs and from aspiring to the same level of security granted to men. Lesbians of color face the additional burdens of racial tensions, discrimination and inequities. As we grow older, these factors work against us even more.

Though the acquisition of full civil rights and reform of the criminal laws, which affect us directly and indirectly, is some ways off, there are many things we can do to protect ourselves in the most intimate aspects of our lives and to ensure for ourselves some level of autonomy and freedom. Though we do not necessarily grow any needier of the law's protections as we grow older, we do become more aware of our own mortality and the need to put our personal affairs in order. The suggestions made in this article certainly do not affect only lesbians; however, since our relationships to friends, family and lovers are not generally recognized in the law, it is more important that we know how to protect our families from the negative effects that the heterosexually based law can have on us. Though there are many issues to address for the benefit of lesbians who are reaching their middle years, I will focus only on those basic legal documents and considerations which we can all attend to tomorrow, and not on those political or legal movement issues which we all hope will be successfully resolved sometime in our lifetimes.

All of us have seen our worst fears realized when reading of the difficult legal battles of Karen Thompson, and women like her, who fought for basic recognition of their relationships with lovers and children. Though lesbian relationships are not legally recognized, there are some steps each of us can take to feel somewhat less vulnerable in a time of crisis. Though it is best to seek the advice and skills of a lawyer sensitive to the needs of lesbians, many lesbians cannot afford to retain a lawyer. In that case, consulting one of the many self-help manuals or watching out for free or low-cost legal seminars offered by lesbians in your community might provide enough information about those legal documents you need to draft and how to do so.

Perhaps the best way to illustrate the workings of the law and the steps lesbians can take to protect themselves is to start with a mythical, though not out of the ordinary, lesbian couple: Clare and Susan have been together for a number of years. Both are in their late forties. Clare has worked for 25 years as a middle school teacher, while Susan has consistently owned and run her own small business. They live together with Clare's two children from a prior marriage in a house that they own. The children are twelve and fifteen; their father plays a minimal role in their lives, seeing them on holidays, birthdays and occasional weekends. Their family includes two large, lovable dogs. Their two cars and most of their household belongings were purchased jointly, though Susan has several family heirlooms which were passed down through the generations. Though their blood families have been basically supportive of their relationship, Clare and Susan are concerned about the legal clout their families and Clare's ex-husband would have if something happened to one of them. Also, they want to know what would happen with their belongings in the unlikely event that they should break up. What steps can they take?

Last Will and Testament

Since Clare and Susan's relationship cannot be legally recognized through marriage, they have none of the rights and preferences which the law affords to a legally recognized spouse. If either of them wants someone other than their parents, siblings or children to inherit their property, it is essential that they make their wishes known by executing a will. Wills are not only necessary for those who have money or tangible property, since wills also allow individuals to express their wishes on other matters. Following are some of the ways in which a will can make a difference:

A WILL CAN DISTRIBUTE PROPERTY.

In Clare's and Susan's case, they can each state that they want all of their property to go to each other or to anyone else they choose. Clare may want to make special provision for her children since they are still minors. She may do so by setting up a trust and indicating in her will that a certain portion of her assets go into a trust which will be used exclusively for the children's well-being. If Susan wants to be sure that her family heirlooms go to siblings or others, she may say so in her will. They may also leave money or other property to their favorite charity.

A WILL CAN APPOINT A GUARDIAN.

In her will, Clare may nominate a guardian to care for her children in the event of her death. Though she may nominate Susan as the guardian, most states do not view her nomination as mandatory, particularly when another biological parent or family member is present. If the father does not challenge Susan's nomination, the court would probably appoint her the guardian and maintain visitation rights for the father. Much depends on the circumstances of each case, and Clare should talk to both Susan and the children's father beforehand to prevent an unnecessary custody battle after her death. In any event, it is important to nominate an alternative guardian in the event that Susan is unable or unwilling to fulfill that role.

A WILL CAN PROVIDE FOR PETS.

If Clare and Susan were to die at the same time, they can make provision for their pets in their will. They can name the person to whom the pets should be given and can allocate a certain amount of money for the care and feeding of the dogs. Of course, fair warning to the recipients of two large dogs would be a good idea.

A WILL CAN PROVIDE FOR FUNERAL AND BURIAL.

This is particularly important for individuals whose personal wishes may run contrary to those of blood family. For instance, if Clare does not want the Catholic funeral which she knows her parents would arrange, but would prefer cremation and a memorial service, she must make her wishes known. She should set forth her wishes, any arrangements she has already made and paid for, and disposition, if any, of anatomical parts.

A WILL MAY APPOINT AN EXECUTOR.

The executor of the will is the person who oversees the distribution of property and execution of the provisions of the will. Clare and Susan may appoint each other as executor, or another trusted and reliable friend.

Lesbians typically fear that blood family members will be able to successfully challenge their wills, particularly if they leave all or most of their property to their lover, to lesbian friends or to organizations. If the will is properly drafted and executed, the person is of sound mind and there was no fraud or undue influence by one of the beneficiaries of the will, it is highly unlikely that a family member will succeed in overturning the will. The sexual orientation of either the person drafting the will or the beneficiary is not a basis for challenging the will. Of course, you cannot prevent a family member from challenging the will, but you can take special precautions to ensure that the challenge will not be successful. The best policy may be to let all interested parties know of the contents of your will ahead of time so that you can explain your reasons and they can get used to any provisions that might otherwise trouble them. Legal advice is strongly suggested if you think your family might cause problems.

Joint Property

Since probating a will takes time and costs money, and resources may be needed by a surviving partner in order to pay expenses or debts, it may be wise to own property jointly with that person. The largest item in this respect is usually a home. If Clare and Susan purchased their home as "joint tenants with a right of survivorship," it would allow Clare, for example, to assume full ownership of the home immediately upon Susan's death and not have to wait until Susan's will is probated. That way, if she cannot afford to pay the mortgage on her own, she can sell it, rent it, or do whatever is necessary to survive. Furthermore, joint ownership with a right of survivorship puts the property out of the reach of any of Susan's blood family who may be inclined to challenge her will.

If, on the other hand, Clare and Susan bought the home as "tenants in common" they would each own a divisible one-half share of the home. In that case, they would have to make provision for the distribution of their half of the home in their wills, leaving their share either to each other or anyone else to whom they would wish to leave it.

Bank accounts and many other financial funds may also be owned jointly with rights of survivorship, so that upon Susan's death, the money in the account would automatically belong to Clare. Clare could have immediate access to the funds to continue making car or house payments and to provide for her children. This course is advisable because it ensures that a surviving partner has enough money to hold her over until life insurance proceeds are paid and/or the will is probated. One should always be aware of a potential pitfall of joint accounts: either party to a joint account may withdraw all of the funds at any time.

Cohabitation contracts

Naturally, when we are madly in love, we are certain that nothing could ever happen to our relationship or that if it does end, we will be totally reasonable and rational in dividing everything from the silverware to the stereo. Negotiating a relationship contract in the midst of passionate bliss seems anti-romantic. Well, perhaps it is. Nonetheless, those who talk about these things beforehand, and put them in writing, seem to have an easier time dividing up their property and making other important decisions at a time of heightened emotional tensions. Therefore, when you reach a point where you and your partner are sharing most expenses, buying more household items together, or there one is giving more financial support to the relationship than the other, it is wise to consider putting your agreements and expectations in writing.

From a legal perspective, one big concern is whether such contracts are enforceable in court. To be enforceable, the parties must have the capacity to enter a contract (be of majority age and mentally competent); the purpose for the contract must be legal (an agreement dividing up your respective shares of an illegal drug running operation would not be legally enforceable); and there must be indicated a bargained-for exchange (a contract which gives everything to one partner in exchange for nothing from the other partner may raise questions). Most contracts deal with each party's rights and responsibilities regarding property distribution, income and expenses. In Clare and Susan's case, they might also want to discuss each of their responsibilities towards caring for and paying the expenses of Clare's children. Susan has no obligation by law to provide for Clare's children, but she may wish to help support them in return for some assurance that she will be entitled to maintain a parental role with them should she and Clare ever separate. (The question of whether a lesbian who is fulfilling a parental role with her lover's children assumes any legal rights is, at present, unresolved.)

There are many details which can, and should, be addressed in a cohabitation contract. Should one partner provide financial support to the other if they break up (if so, for how long: for life, until the house is sold?); who will stay in the home if they break up and for how long; who gets the two large dogs (in Susan and Clare's situation); and if they cannot resolve these things despite the contract, should they submit their dispute to a mediator (a third party who will help them come to an agreement) or an arbitrator (a third party who will render a binding decision)?

There are dozens more questions to be asked and decided. Generally, any agreement dealing with property and finances will be upheld unless circumstances indicate that fraud or extreme overreaching by one party exists. However, agreements regarding sexual relations may not be included as part of the bargained-for exchange and would most likely render the entire contract void. That is, requiring each other to provide companionship or to be monogamous is most likely unenforceable and could destroy the enforceability of the other provisions of the contract.

Conservatorship

A conservatorship is a legal mechanism by which someone is appointed to make decisions for another who has been incapacitated, rendering her unable to manage her assets or personal care. In some states, the term guardian is used even if the incapacitated person is an adult. A conservatorship might be particularly important for someone in Susan's position who owns and runs her own business. If she were to undergo major surgery, become disabled or become legally incompetent to tend to her business, a conservator could be appointed by the court to assure that routine matters, such as issuing paychecks to employees, paying the business bills and entering into business contracts, are taken care of. A conservator may also handle extraordinary matters such as liquidating the business. Susan may nominate a conservator, using the basic formalities of a will. The conservator would then petition the court at the point in time when Susan became incapacitated. If she does not nominate someone herself, most states presume that a blood or legal family member is best suited to handle such matters, not her lesbian lover.

The benefits of nominating and appointing a conservator lie primarily in having the court's backing to make decisions, making it less likely that a family member could successfully challenge any single decision. The drawback is that no decisions can be made until the court appoints a conservator, which could result in dangerous delay. Conservators may also be appointed to handle personal care, such as medical treatment and institutionalization; however, the simpler mechanism of a durable power of attorney may be better for more routine matters.

Durable Power of Attorney

A durable power of attorney is a written authorization that another person may perform certain acts on your behalf. Unlike a traditional power of attorney, a durable power of attorney can be used in the event that you become physically or mentally incapacitated. The durable power of attorney may take effect immediately or at the time of incapacity without a court order. For instance, if Susan is out of the country for any length of time, plans to undergo major surgery or becomes physically or mentally incapacitated, she may want Clare to have the power to do anything from handling certain business matters to selling the car. She may specifically state that Clare may take any action that she (Susan) could take if she were able, or she can limit Clare's authority to only certain areas.

In some states, "Durable Power of Attorney for Health Care" statutes have been enacted specifically allowing you to appoint another person to make health care decisions on your behalf. These may include the power to change physicians, move to another hospital, have access to medical records and to be allowed to visit a partner in the hospital, relieving many lesbians of the fear that they will not be allowed into the intensive care unit of a hospital to see their lover because they are not "immediate family members." Since patients have a right to give their informed consent, a health care appointment is an important tool to allow someone other than a blood or legal family member to make important health care decisions. For this reason, all lesbians should consider executing such a document, whether you have a lover or not, if you do not want a parent, sibling or adult child to make your medical decisions.

Samples of forms for both the durable power of attorney and the durable power of attorney for health care are available in the book *Why Can't Sharon Kowalski Come Home.*

Living Wills

With the advent of medical technology that can mechanically prolong a patient's life, most states have passed laws allowing someone to direct her physician in advance to not apply or to remove artificial life-support systems if her condition is terminal and irreversible. These documents are called living wills. To be valid, the living will must conform precisely to the procedure outlined in the state law. The patient's intent must be expressed very explicitly. For those who have a family physician, it is always advisable to tell her of your intent not to have life-support systems and to provide her with a copy of your living will. If you have no particular physician, be sure someone you trust has an original copy of the document which can be provided to the physician if necessary. Since living wills are directives to a physician and do not involve anyone other than the person who executed it, there are few special precautions directly related to one's sexual orientation.

Conclusion

All of these documents are available through self-help books, legal workshops and feminist (and other) lawyers. I recommend them to any lesbian who has concerns about decision-making powers, transfer of property or the like. By no means do I suggest them only for women who are in couples or who have children and extended family members. Many of these devices represent the few chances we, as lesbians, may have to get courts and others to respond to and respect our decisions and choices. All of us should take advantage of them.

These steps are not difficult or time-consuming. Do them now before you need them. By the time you need these documents it will be too late to get them.

Two Excerpts from *A Burst of Light: Living With Cancer*

AUDRE LORDE

December 15, 1986
New York City

To acknowledge privilege is the first step in making it available for wider use. Each of us is blessed in some particular way, whether we recognize our blessings or not. And each one of us, somewhere in our lives, must clear a space within that blessing where she can call upon whatever resources are available to her in the name of something that must be done.

I have been very blessed in my life. I have been blessed to believe passionately, to love deeply, and to be able to work out of those loves and beliefs. Accidents of privilege allowed me to gain information about holistic/biological medicine and their approach to cancers, and that information has helped keep me alive, along with my original gut feeling that said, *Stay out of my Body.* For me, living and the use of that living are inseparable, and I have a responsibility to put that privilege and that life to use.

For me, living fully means living with maximum access to my experience and power, loving and doing work in which I believe. It means writing my poems, telling my stories, and speaking out of my most urgent concerns and against the many forms of anti-life surrounding us.

I wish to live whatever life I have as fully and as sweetly as possible, rather than refocus that life solely upon extending it for some unspecified time. I consider this a political decision as well as a life-saving one, and it is a decision that I am fortunate to be able to make.

If one Black woman I do not know gains hope and strength from my story, then it has been worth the difficulty of telling.

Epilogue

Sometimes I feel like I am living on a different star from the one I am used to calling home. It has not been a steady progression. I had to examine, in my dreams as well as in my immune-function tests, the devastating effects of overextension. Overextending myself is not stretching myself. I had to accept how difficult it is to monitor the difference. Necessary for me as cutting down sugar. Crucial. Physically. Psychically. Caring for myself is not self-indulgence, it is self-preservation, and that is an act of political warfare.

Time in this place is speedy, rich, and stark. My days are a thirsty atonal combination of the mundane and the apocalyptic. Mingling without much warming. Moving without missing a beat from the report of peritubal metastases (Does that mean escape into the abdominal cavity?) to estimates for constructing my workspace in St. Croix. Drastic life-changes laced together with the eternal ordinary.

My aim is to move more easily between the two, make transitions the least costly, approach a student's completed manuscript and the medical reports and the house estimates in some open-hearted way, with a sense of proportion. I order a perfume from Grenada called "Jump Up and Kiss Me."

I try to weave my life-prolonging treatments into a living context—to resist giving myself over like a sacrificial offering to the furious single-minded concentration upon cure that leaves no room to examine what living and fighting on a physical front can mean. What living with cancer can teach me. I go to Germany this fall for further mistletoe treatment. I look forward to working again with the Afro-German Women's Group.

I believe that one of the ways in which cancer cells insure their own life and depress the immune system is by creating a physiologically engendered despair. Learning to fight that despair in all its manifestations is not only therapeutic. It is vital. Underlining what is joyful and life-affirming becomes crucial.

What have I had to leave behind? Old life habits, outgrown defenses put aside lest they siphon off energies to no useful purposes?

One of the hardest things to accept is learning to live within uncertainty and neither deny it nor hide behind it. Most of all, to listen to the messages of uncertainty without allowing them to immobilize me, nor keep me from the certainties of those truths in which I believe. I turn away from any need to justify the future—to live in what has not yet been. Believing, working for what has not yet been while living fully in the present now.

This is my life. Each hour is a possibility not to be banked. These days are not a preparation for living, some necessary but essentially extraneous divergence from the main course of my living. They are my life. The feeling of the bedsheet against my heels as I wake to the sound of crickets and bananaquits in Judith's Fancy. I am living my life every particular day no matter where I am, nor in what pursuit. It is the consciousness of this that gives a marvelous breadth to everything I do consciously. My most deeply held convictions and beliefs can be equally expressed in how I deal with chemotherapy as well as in how I scrutinize a poem. It's about trying to know who I am wherever I am. It's not as if I'm in struggle here while someplace else, over there, real life is waiting for me to begin living it again.

I visualize daily winning the battles going on inside my body, and this is an important part of fighting for my life. In those visualizations, the cancer at times takes on the face and shape of my most implacable enemies, those I fight and resist most fiercely. Sometimes the wanton cells in my liver become Bull Connor and his police dogs completely smothered, rendered impotent in Birmingham, Alabama by a mighty avalanche of young, determined Black marchers moving across him toward their future. P.W. Botha's bloated face of apartheid squashed into the earth beneath an onslaught of the slow rythmic advance of furious Blackness. Black South African women moving through my blood destroying passbooks. Fireburn Mary[1] sweeping over the Cruzan countryside, axe and torch in hand. Images from a Calypso singer:

> *The big black boot of freedom*
> *Is smashing down your doorstep.*

I train myself for triumph by knowing it is mine, no matter what. In fact, I am surrounded within my external living by ample examples of the struggle for life going on inside me. Visualizing the disease process inside my body in political images is not a quixotic dream. When I speak out against the cynical U.S. intervention in Central America, I am working to save my life in every sense. Government research grants to the National Cancer Institute were cut in 1986 by the exact amount illegally turned over to the contras in Nicaragua. One hundred and five million dollars. It gives yet another meaning to the personal as the political.

Cancer itself has an anonymous face. When we are visibly dying of cancer, it is sometimes easier to turn away from the particular experience into the sadness of loss, and when we are surviving, it is somehow easier to deny that experience. But those of us who live our battles in the flesh must know ourselves as our strongest weapon in the most gallant struggle of our lives.

Living with cancer has forced me to consciously jettison the myth of omnipotence, of believing—or loosely asserting—that I can do anything, along with any dangerous illusion of immortality. Neither of these un-scrutinized defenses is a solid base for either political activism or personal struggle. But in their place, another kind of power is growing, tempered and enduring, grounded within the realities of what I am in fact doing. An open-eyed assessment and appreciation of what I can and do accomplish, using who I am and who I most wish myself to be. To stretch as far as I can go and relish what is satisfying rather than what is sad. Building a strong and elegant pathway toward transition.

I work, I love, I rest, I see and learn. And I report. These are my givens. Not sureties, but a firm belief that whether or not living them with joy prolongs my life, it certainly enables me to pursue the objectives of that life with a deeper and more effective clarity.

August 1987
Carriacou, Grenada
Anguilla, British West Indies
St. Croix, Virgin Islands

ENDNOTES

1. ex-slave who led a workers' revolt in St. Croix in 1848

With Such Wonder

ANGELA VAN PATTEN

With such wonder the children look to us
while aspiring to a sort of earthy sainthood.
We are role models, gentle love, remember?
They would have our poise and inveterate wisdom;
your clear eyed gaze, my firmset jaw
at last their own. Could they be privileged
to see us digging our nails in our palms,
choking on intimacies, battling childhood demons
half forgotten, they would thereby gain access
to all the secrets of love we have to give them:
Use caution, people are learning to trust here.
And there should be a neon sign somewhere about that.

Contributors

Angela Bowen, 54, is a black lesbian feminist writer, mother and organizer who often speaks on a variety of issues aimed at radical change. Her work has appeared in *Conditions, Sojourner, The Village Voice, Gay Community News* and *Woman of Power.* Her book of short stories, *Aleta in the Forties and Fifties,* was the 1989 recipient of the Fannie Lou Hammer award from the Barbara Deming Foundation, and will be published in 1991 by Kitchen Table: Women of Color Press.

Judith Bradford is Associate Director of the Survey Research Laboratory of Virginia Commonwealth University. She is active in community HIV programs and is a board member of the Richmond Lesbian and Gay Pride Coalition.

Miriam Carroll is an ageful Atlanta transplant thriving on a multitude of community experiences. She does massage and healing work, and one hobby is writing. She visualizes an optimistic future.

Claudette Charbonneau has been a lesbian for as long as she can remember. Along with writing and filmmaking, she teaches English to international students.

Ellen Cole, Ph.D., has been practicing psychology and sex therapy for several decades and conducting menopause research since 1985. She is on the faculty of Prescott College, in Arizona, and co-edits the journal *Women and Therapy.*

Clare Coss is a psychotherapist and playwright. She also works at The Retreat, a shelter for victims of domestic violence in East Hampton, New York. Her book, *Lillian Wald: Progressive Activist* is published by The Feminist Press.

Margaret Cruikshank teaches writing and lesbian/gay literature at the City College of San Francisco. She is the editor of *The Lesbian Path, Lesbian Studies, New Lesbian Writing* and *Fierce with Reality*, an anthology of literature about aging. Her partner, Barbara Giles, appeared too late to be included in this story of midlife improvement.

Lauren Crux, as an aspiring bon vivant, weird, wicked and wild woman, has decided to grow old as disgracefully as possible (to borrow from a friend) and to relish being part of the problem, not the solution.

Carmen de Monteflores, at 57, is learning the grace of acceptance while at the same time beginning to know how to fight. The paradox of each age is also its creative essence. She is the author of *Cantando Bajito/Singing Softly,* which is published by Aunt Lute Books.

Paula L. Ettelbrick is the Legal Director for Lambda Legal Defense and Education Fund, a national lesbian and gay organization. Since joining Lambda in 1986, Paula has litigated cases, spoken nationally and written primarily on topics related to lesbian and gay relationship and family issues.

Ayofemi Stowe Folayan says "Writing is the umbilical cord which attaches me to the universe and energizes me to continue my work as a poet, playwright, journalist and activist to end oppression on this planet."

Madonna Gauding is a middle-aged lesbian woman awakening and healing through the daily practice of a spiritual path, a deepening relationship with her lover, blessed relationships with her friends, the opening up of her creative expression and tentative explorations in the world of self-employment.

Jacquelyn H. Gentry is a longstanding feminist activist with special expertise in women's mental health. She is a psychologist and directs the Women and Aging Project for the Feminist Institute.

Shirley Glubka is currently working on a series of poems which evolved in response to personal/professional challenges posed by doing therapy with women who have Multiple Personality Disorder. Her work has been previously published in *Conditions, Sinister Wisdom* and *Feminist Studies.*

Jewelle Gomez has lived in New York City for twenty years, yet she says that most of her writing is informed by her childhood in Boston, where she was raised by her great-grandmother. Her most recent work, *The Gilda Stories* (Firebrand Books, spring 1991), uses vampire lore to explore the relative nature of time and maturity.

Jean Lois Greggs, of African-American and American Indian heritage, was born in Monroe, Louisiana. She graduated from Grambling University with a degree in Fine Arts and from Adelphi University with an MSW. Jean is a full-time Gestalt psychotherapist in private practice.

Ann Gregory is a professor of business at Memorial University of Newfoundland who for a long time has wanted to do research in an area of deep personal meaning. She decided to ignore warnings of the dire consequences of addressing this "taboo" subject, and took the plunge. The water feels quite good and Ann intends to continue this line of research.

Marny Hall spends most of her time asking bewitching women about the intimate details of their lives. Whether this activity is love or work is impossible to say. A psychotherapist in the San Francisco Bay Area for twenty years, Marny is the author of *The Lavender Couch: A Consumer's Guide to Psychotherapy for Lesbians and Gay Men.*

S. Lisa Hayes began her career seven years ago with the aim of helping women gain confidence and empowerment in the financial arena. With knowledge comes strength and Hayes emphasizes education with her clients—not just investing blindly. Today Hayes has a practice comprised mostly of success-minded women.

Dolores Klaich, author of *Woman Plus Woman: Attitudes Toward Lesbianism* and the novel *Heavy Gilt,* is a writer, editor, lesbian/gay, feminist activist and HIV/AIDS educator. She lives on Long Island with her partner Pat Maravel and Pat's two children.

Patricia Lander is a social anthropologist who teaches at Brooklyn College-CUNY and never considered the possibility that she could be a lesbian until she went on sabbatical at age 38.

Ronnie Lesser, Ph.D., does psychotherapy and research in the New York City area. She is a student at New York University's Postdoctoral Program in Psychotherapy and Psychoanalysis. She is currently writing a book on psychoanalytic theory about lesbians.

Leota Lone Dog, Lakota, Mohawk and Delaware, is a board member of the American Indian Community House. She is a promising stage manager for Spiderwoman Theater and several other Native American theater groups in New York City, as well as a founding member of We Wah and Bar Chee Ampe, a Lesbian and Gay Native American organization in New York City. She's also the mother of a wonderful daughter now attending the University of Massachusetts.

Audre Lorde, Black, Lesbian, mother and cancer survivor, was born in New York City in 1934. She is the author of more than twelve books, both non-fiction and poetry. For many years she has taught English at Hunter College in New York.

Mary Lorenz is a 41-year-old teacher and free-lance writer who enjoys most of the activities mentioned in her article. She lives, works and plays near Northampton, Massachussetts.

JoAnn Loulan is a mother, psychotherapist, author and public speaker. She co-authored *Period* (Volcano Press, 1979), and is the author of *Lesbian Sex* (1984), *Lesbian Passion: Loving Ourselves and Each Other* (1987), and *The Lesbian Erotic Dance: Butch, Femme, Androgyny and Other Rhythms* (1990), all published by Spinsters Book Company.

Muriel Miguel, Cuna-Rappahannock, is a director/performer, was a member of the Open Theater and performed with them for five years. She is also a founding member of Spiderwoman Theater and the Thunderbird American Indian Dancers.

Susanne Morgan is a medical sociologist with a long interest in women's health and sexuality, which has included writing *Coping With a Hysterectomy* (New American Library, 1985). She teaches at Ithaca College in New York State, where she is currently involved in HIV/AIDS prevention work.

Adalaide Morris lives in Iowa City, Iowa, where she teaches feminist criticism and theory and writes on modern and contemporary poetry. "Cuttings" is her first personal essay.

Elfrieda Munz is a Holocaust survivor who has an undergraduate degree in music from City College of New York and an Ed.M. from Harvard University. She is working full time as a counselor and part time as a massage therapist.

Joan Nestle, co-founder of the Lesbian Herstory Archives, says, "I have lived all my 50 Jewish fem years in New York City. In this struggling city, I found my work, my loves, my community."

Robyn Posin is a seeker, therapist, artist and writer, and has an uncompromising commitment to openly naming, honoring, taking responsibility for and being fiercely compassionate with, her fears, flaws, incompleteness, vulnerabilities and confusions.

Esther D. Rothblum is an associate professor of psychology at the University of Vermont. She has written on lesbian relationships and lesbians and depression. She is co-editor of the journal *Women and Therapy*.

Matile Rothschild, Ph.D., MSW, (also published under the name Matile Poor) is a psychotherapist in San Francisco. She has facilitated a group for lesbian parents of teenage and older children and has taught a course, "Life as Improvisation: Making the Most of the Second Half of Life."

Caitlin Ryan is a clinical social worker and policy researcher who has helped develop lesbian and gay networks since 1977. She coordinated the National Lesbian Health Care Survey and organized several groups including the National Lesbian and Gay Health Foundation.

Faye M. Seifert has a social work background and is on a spiritual path. Using her reevaluation counseling and outdoor skills, she works for the reemergence of all people and empowerment of children and women.

Susan Turner is a feminist community organizer, psychotherapist and consultant, AIDS volunteer, poet, mother and an activist in the disabled women's rights movement as a consumer and a professional.

Angela Van Patten is a midlife lesbian who is using her own growing older as a test case. She is a co-founder, with Adrienne Smith and others, of Gray Pride Chicago, and is devoted to building our lesbian and gay family.

Barbara E. Sang

Barbara Sang is a psychologist in private practice. She specializes in working with lesbians, artists and dyslexic individuals. She also runs support groups for midlife women. For the past 23 years she has been active in the lesbian feminist movement. Recently she received a Community Service Award from the National Lesbian and Gay Health Foundation. She is a co-founder of the Homosexual Community Counseling Center (1971) and the Artist Therapy Service (1978).

PHOTO: MORGAN GWENWALD

About her leisure time, Sang says, "When not writing articles and speaking on panels, I can be found riding my bicycle, hiking or swimming. I am a serious nature photographer and painter and have had several shows of my work. My other interests include listening to experimental music, dancing, yoga, flower arranging and gourmet cooking."

About midlife, Sang says, "For most of my forties I was busy 'letting go' on many levels. It was a painful time for me but one that was equally exciting and growth enhancing. During this period I developed serious allergies which lead me to making 'take care of myself' a top priority. I work out every day and as a result, have become physically stronger and healthier."

"While many changes in what was important to me were taking place, I also felt a need to simplify my life—less physical clutter—fewer professional demands. I needed to leave more spaces for another kind of 'being' in the world. I felt more in touch with my spiritual nature, especially when I was out doors expressing myself artistically. What is most important to me is that I feel in harmony with myself."

Joyce Warshow

Joyce Warshow is a psychologist in private practice. She is a member of the American Psychological Association and its divisions on Adult Development and Aging, The Psychology of Women and The Society for the Psychological Study of Lesbian and Gay Issues. She is also a member of the Feminist Therapy Institute and the Association of Women in Psychology. She has served on the Board of Directors of the Women's Psychotherapy Referral Service in New York for several years. Her current interests are in the mother/daughter relationship, eldercare and lesbian identity and its cultural context.

About *Lesbians At Midlife* Warshow says, "I met Adrienne and Barbara for the first time in 1975 at the lesbian caucus of what was then the Association of Gay Psychologists, a grass roots group within the American Psychological Association (APA). I found these women to be proud and articulate about their lesbian identities. Adrienne was conducting workshops for non-gay therapists and Barbara was presenting data from a survey on the status of lesbian nad gay psychologists which appeared in the APA publication *The Monitor*.

"This fateful meeting was for me the beginning of my own midlife passage because it influenced me to explore, with a depth not possible at an earlier age, who I was and how the different parts of my self-identification could be integrated. I thought about the many stories which have to do symbolically with coming into the fullness of our being at midlife (Moses wandered 40 days and nights in the dessert before he reached the promised land and Ahab was 40 days at sea before he encountered Moby Dick). I thought about how we, as women, need to take our own journeys more seriously and record them so that they too can reverberate in the consciousness of humankind.

"Now as a fledgling crone, I am delighted to help provide a forum for midlife and older lesbians to document our lives with all our diversity as we experience them rather than leaving our reality to be interpreted by others only. I've enjoyed making contact with many of the women who contributed to the book.

I would also like to express my appreciation to my partner Dorothy, who shares my values and my politics. Most importantly, we agree on how to have fun. We enjoy our home, our friends and our participation in the lesbian and gay community. I would also like to thank Jocelyne for being a dear friend, as well as Fern and Rosemary for their support.

PHOTO: SANDRA GOLDIN

Adrienne J. Smith

Adrienne Smith has been a psychologist longer than she has been a feminist and a lesbian longer than that. She discovered feminism in the early seventies and became an early advocate of feminist therapy, helping to found the Feminist Therapy Institute. After coming out publically as a lesbian she was president of Division 44 of the American Psychological Association, the Society for the Psychological Study of Lesbian and Gay Issues, from March 1989 to August 1990. At the time of editing this book, in her mid-fifties, she has been coming out increasingly as a Jew and reclaiming that part of her heritage and identity. During the final stages of this book she entered a new phase of her life with a diagnosis of colon cancer. After surgery she has embarked on several alternative therapies and is looking forward to a total change in her life's work from a therapist in private practice to a peripatetic writer. She is currently working on a book about women living with cancer.

Adrienne would like to thank several people who have accompanied her in her life's journey during the past decades. Angela Van Patten, poet and friend, frequently challenged and energized. Most especially she would like to acknowledge with deep gratitude her "two mothers." First, Lynn Koral, her biological mother, who gave her life, chutzpah and a belief that she would always land on her feet. Second, Ruth F. Siegel, her feminist mother, who cared, nurtured, shared, argued, supported and in general provided the nourishment of a dear friend and professional collegue.

■ spinsters book company

Spinsters Book Company was founded in 1978 to produce vital books for diverse women's communities. In 1986 we merged with Aunt Lute Books to become Spinsters/Aunt Lute. In 1990, the Aunt Lute Foundation became an independant non-profit publishing program.

Spinsters is committed to publishing works outside the scope of mainstream commercial publishers: books that not only name crucial issues in women's lives, but more importantly encourage change and growth; books that help to make the best in our lives more possible. We sponsor an annual Lesbian Fiction Contest for the best lesbian novel each year. And we are particularly interested in creative works by lesbians.

If you would like to know about other books we produce, or our Fiction Contest, write or phone us for a free catalogue. You can buy books directly from us. We can also supply you with the name of a bookstore closest to you that stocks our books. We accept phone orders with Visa or Mastercard.

Spinsters Book Company
P.O. Box 410687
San Francisco, CA 94141
415-558-9586

Other Books Available from Spinsters Book Company

Bittersweet, by Nevada Barr $9.95

Cancer in Two Voices, by Sandra Butler and Barbara Rosenblum $12.95

Child of Her People, by Anne Cameron $8.95

The Journey, by Anne Cameron $9.95

Prisons That Could Not Hold, by Barbara Deming $7.95

High and Outside, by Linnea A. Due $8.95

Elise, by Claire Kensington $7.95

Modern Daughters and the Outlaw West, by Melissa Kwasny $9.95

The Lesbian Erotic Dance: Butch, Femme, Androgyny and Other Rhythms,
by JoAnn Loulan $12.95

Lesbian Passion: Loving Ourselves and Each Other, by JoAnn Loulan $11.95

Lesbian Sex, by JoAnn Loulan $12.95

Look Me in the Eye: Old Women, Aging and Ageism,
by Barbara Macdonald with Cynthia Rich $6.50

Being Someone, by Ann MacLeod $9.95

Final Session, by Mary Morell $9.95

All the Muscle You Need, by Diana McRae $8.95

Love & Memory, by Amy Oleson $9.95

Considering Parenthood, by Cheri Pies $9.50

Coz, by Mary Pjerrou $9.95

We Say We Love Each Other, by Minnie Bruce Pratt $5.95

Desert Years: Undreaming the American Dream, by Cynthia Rich $7.95

Thirteen Steps: An Empowerment Process for Women,
by Bonita L. Swan $8.95

Why Can't Sharon Kowalski Come Home? by Karen Thompson and Julie
Andrzejewski $10.95

Spinsters titles are available at your local booksellers, or by mail order
through Spinsters Book Company (415) 558-9586. A free catalogue is available
upon request.

Please include $1.50 for the first title ordered, and $ .50 for every
title thereafter. California residents, please add 8.25% sales tax. Visa and
Mastercard accepted.